M000116342

World Monetary Equilibrium

World Monetary Equilibrium

International Monetary Theory
in an Historical–Institutional Context

JOHN E FLOYD

Professor of Economics
University of Toronto

Philip Allan
University of Pennsylvania Press

First published in Great Britain 1985 by
Philip Allan Publishers Limited
Market Place
Deddington
Oxford OX5 4SE

and in the United States of America 1985 by the
University of Pennsylvania Press
Blockley Hall
418 Service Drive
Philadelphia, Pa. 19104

© John E Floyd 1985

British Library Cataloguing in Publication Data

Floyd, John E.
  World monetary equilibrium.
  1. International finance.
  I. Title
  332.4′5   HG3881

  ISBN 0-86003-058-X
  ISBN 0-86003-164-0 Pbk

U.S. ISBN 0-8122-7983-2

Typeset by Sunrise Setting, Torquay
Printed and bound in Great Britain by
The Pitman Press, Bath

To Laurie and Ian

Contents

Foreword

This book is both a monograph and a supplementary text. It is a monograph in that it presents an interpretive analysis of international monetary history within a single unified theoretical framework. It is a text in that it develops in a simple and systematic way the basic tools of international monetary economics and applies them to real problems of international monetary organisation and policy prescription. The approach incorporates international capital movements as an integral part of the theoretical structure and not as an appendage to a zero capital flow model. While this differentiates the product from almost all standard textbook treatments, it involves no tools or techniques of analysis that are not widely used in standard upper-level under-graduate courses. The originality of approach lies in the perspective it brings to the subject and in the questions it poses rather than in the formal theoretical development.

The work is more theoretical than institutional in focus. The basic model is first tailored to address the operation of the gold standard, then modified slightly to deal with the Bretton Woods key currency system, and finally adjusted to handle flexible exchange rates and managed floating. All issues are viewed within a single unified theoretical framework which, once properly formulated, is not very complex. This avoids the practice common to most standard textbooks of posing different models and approaches for different problems, making it difficult for students to acquire a coherent understanding of the workings of the whole system.

A considerable amount of empirical evidence is presented at various points to establish the importance of questions asked and issues examined, and to test some hypotheses suggested by the theoretical development. One such hypothesis concerns why the traditional gold standard could not be permanently re-established in the inter-war period and why the Bretton Woods system broke down

after 1971. Another relates to the continued role of the US dollar as a
key currency in the recent era of managed floating. The evidence in
favour of these hypotheses should be viewed as suggestive rather than
conclusive. The purpose is to pose the right questions and stimulate
thought rather than establish definitive conclusions. No attempt has
been made to present all sides of every issue. The book is short and it is
expected that in a classroom situation other additional material that
develops alternative points of view in an equally clear, unified way will
be presented.

The material is organised in full understanding that not everyone
will wish to read directly from cover to cover. The two introductory
chapters are followed by a chapter dealing with the process of money
creation. Readers who understand the basics of the money supply
process can skip this chapter, perhaps returning to it later. The
remaining chapters, except for the concluding one, divide into three
groups, each of which can be approached independently. Chapters 4
and 5 deal with the theory of equilibrium under the gold standard, an
evaluation of the system prior to World War I, and the reasons why it
could not be permanently and successfully re-established after the
War. Chapters 6 and 7 develop the theory of international equilibrium
under the Bretton Woods key currency system and examine the
problems with that system and reasons for its demise. Chapters 8 and 9
concern the principles of world equilibrium under flexible exchange
rates and managed floating and the problems and issues that have
arisen during the last decade.

A person only interested in more recent international monetary
problems can jump directly from either Chapter 2 or Chapter 3 to
Chapters 8 and 9, returning to Chapters 6 and 7 or 4 and 5 at a later time
as circumstances require. Appendices to Chapters 4 and 8 provide a
more elementary treatment of important concepts for readers with
insufficient background. Mathematical notes are included at the ends
of these same chapters for readers who want a more rigorous
treatment. The concluding chapter summarises briefly those
conclusions that are more or less original.

This book constitutes about one-third of my upper-level
undergraduate course in international money (the other two-thirds
consists of small open economy analysis with emphasis on Canadian
problems) and is required beginning reading in my graduate course. It
presents a good part of the basics which every well-trained
undergraduate should learn. And it provides a foundation on which a
graduate seminar can be built.

The book should provide institutional depth to a theoretical course
on international money and theoretical depth to an institutional

policy-oriented course. It also presents useful supplementary reading material for a variety of courses in macroeconomics as well as international money and finance.

The content and exposition has benefited from detailed comments by Edward Tower of Duke University and Jeremy Greenwood and David Laidler of the University of Western Ontario. My colleagues Allan Hynes, Harry Eastman and Jack Carr also commented on parts of the manuscript and provided intellectual stimulation and discourse that has left a mark on the final product. Finally, I would like to thank June Wood, Brenda Samuels, Mary Pacy, and Gail Brady who suffered through numerous drafts with a balky word processor.

1

Introduction

World monetary affairs are currently the subject of much concern and debate. A long period of stability ended in 1971 and the past decade has seen major movements of exchange rates along with continued unsuccessful efforts to re-establish the kind of order in international financial affairs we had after the Second World War. This book presents a straightforward development of international monetary theory from a world rather than individual country perspective, and applies it to the whole range of institutional arrangements that have governed international monetary relations over the past 100 years. The application of the theory in an historical context provides insights necessary for constructive thinking about current international monetary problems.

The past 100 years have witnessed a wide variety of international currency arrangements. In the last two decades of the nineteenth century the international gold standard was in its heyday. This came to an end with the onset of the First World War. A period of inconvertible paper standards with flexible exchange rates ensued, followed by a largely unsuccessful attempt to resurrect the gold standard in the late 1920s. The economic troubles of the 1930s ended any hope of re-establishing a gold standard of the traditional sort. Few countries managed to stay on gold past the middle of the decade and, though the USA fixed the price of gold at $35 per oz after 1934, there was no relationship between the US money supply and the country's gold stock. The thirties were marked by highly variable exchange rates accompanied by a severe international depression of income, employment and prices. It was widely thought that flexible exchange rates and competitive devaluations were responsible for many of the difficulties experienced during these years. This provided the intellectual and political rationale for the Bretton Woods Conference of 1944, which established a world-wide regime of fixed exchange rates based on what came to be called the gold exchange standard.

The USA was at the centre of this system. The other countries pegged their currencies to the dollar, and the USA, with international support, pegged the dollar to gold at $35 per oz. This system purported to provide the benefits of currency convertibility within a framework of exchange rate stability. It appeared to work well for a while, but problems began to develop in the 1960s. The central problems were the inability of the system to provide enough liquidity, the persistence of US balance of payments deficits, and the failure to provide an adjustment mechanism to accommodate differential changes in price levels.

A very significant expansion of both the real and nominal volume of trade occurred after the Second World War. Since the price of gold remained at $35 per oz and the prices of other goods rose substantially, the real value of the gold stock fell in relation to the volume of trade. To provide the reserves necessary to finance trade, countries began to accumulate US dollar denominated short-term liabilities in lieu of gold. These could be converted into gold at any time and were accumulated by selling more goods, services, and securities to the USA than were being purchased from that country—hence, the persistent US balance of payments deficits. As time passed, the stock of US dollar short-term liabilities outstanding began to exceed the gold stock and it became clear that there was inadequate gold to redeem all these liabilities. This lead to the speculation that the price of gold would eventually have to be allowed to rise. Resulting conversions of dollar liabilities depleted the gold stock in US hands and increased the likelihood that the gold exchange standard could not ultimately be maintained. In 1968 it was necessary to suspend support of the private gold market. Henceforth, gold was exchanged among central banks at $35 per oz but not between central banks and private individuals. Gold prices in the private market were allowed to rise above the official price.

About this time a number of European countries, especially Germany, were experiencing inflation which was attributed to increasing inflation in the USA and to the persistent deficits in the US balance of payments. The issue of whether the US dollar was overvalued then became confounded with the problem of insufficient world liquidity.

Problems persisted until, in August of 1971, the US Government announced that it would no longer buy or sell gold at $35 per oz. This ended the gold exchange standard. Some exchange rates floated briefly after the announcement but new fixed parities and a wider band of permissible fluctuations around them were introduced by an international agreement at the Smithsonian Institution in Washington in December 1971. The European countries adopted a narrower band of permissible fluctuations within the framework of the Smithsonian Agreement. The new parities soon also became unworkable and by 1973 all the major exchange rates were floating.

The Jamaica Conference in 1976 modified the International Monetary Fund rules initially established at Bretton Woods to permit countries to adopt essentially whatever international currency arrangements they wished. At present, the major continental European currencies, which are tied together in a European currency unit, float jointly against the US dollar, the pound, the Japanese yen, and the other major currencies. The smaller countries either let their currencies float or peg to one of the major currencies or to a weighted average of several major currencies. In most cases where exchange rates are flexible the authorities intervene actively to influence the external value of their currency. For this reason, the past decade has been termed the era of managed floating.

An understanding of the economic effects and significance of these changes in international monetary organisations requires an appropriate grounding in international monetary theory. This theory must be viewed not as a set of mechanical relationships but as general principles with which to examine contemporary and historical problems. The purpose of this book is to develop and apply such a body of theory.

The theoretical focus takes a world perspective rather than the vantage point of individual countries embedded in the system. The world economy is viewed as consisting of one large country like the USA and a number of small ones. Two-country aggregations, consisting of the large country and the rest of the world, or a small country and the rest of the world, are convenient at a number of points in the analysis. The emphasis for the most part is on situations where capital is internationally mobile though some discussion is devoted to the case where capital movements are not allowed to respond to market forces. As the theory is developed, it is applied to the major international monetary developments of the past century. Though the analysis is not entirely chronological, the pages that follow contain a rather complete summary of world monetary developments since the middle of the nineteenth century.[1]

The international monetary system is the entire set of existing intercountry monetary arrangements. Since the arrangements are often not the same for different pairs and groups of countries, the world system has usually been some mixture of different types of regimes. Three types have been important historically—flexible exchange rates, common currency arrangements, and key currency systems.

None of these has ever exclusively existed worldwide in purest form—
the usual pattern is a mixed arrangement containing derivatives of
more than one of the pure types.

Our task here is to outline the different kinds of international
currency system and to analyse the functioning of the international
economy under each, making specific reference, of course, to the
problems that arose at each stage in our monetary history. Chapter 2
introduces the discussion with a brief description of alternative
international monetary arrangements and a short outline of some of
the problems and implications of each. The problem of money supply
determination is analysed in Chapter 3 with reference first to the
international gold standard and then to key currency and flexible
exchange rate systems. This sets the stage for the construction of a
basic model of world monetary equilibrium in Chapter 4. An
evaluation of the problems and benefits of the gold standard and
commodity standards in general is undertaken in Chapter 5. This is
combined with a discussion of the operation of the gold standard in the
years prior to 1914 and in the inter-war period. Chapter 6 focuses on
the conditions of world monetary equilibrium under a key currency
system such as existed between the end of the Second World War and
1971. The liquidity and other problems of the Bretton Woods system
along with some of the proposed solutions are examined in Chapter 7.
Chapter 8 develops the theory of world monetary equilibrium under a
regime of flexible exchange rates such as existed during the early 1920s
and after 1971. This theory is used in Chapter 9 to analyse the
functioning of the system of managed floating that existed between the
early seventies and the present time. This chapter also re-examines the
old question of whether an individual country is better off to opt for a
flexible rate or to peg to the US dollar or some other reserve currency.
The final chapter summarises the lessons about international
monetary organisation that follow from our analysis.

Notes

1 For a well done and perceptive analysis of current and past international
monetary institutions, see Meier, Gerald M. (1982) *Problems of a World
Monetary Order*, Oxford University Press. The historical development of
the world monetary system is also surveyed in Tew, Brian, (1970)
International Monetary Cooperation 1945–70, Hutchinson's University
Library, and in Yeager, Leland B. (1975) *International Monetary
Relations*, 2nd edn, Harper and Row. See also McKinnon, Ronald I.
(1979) *Money in International Exchange: The Convertible Currency
System*, Oxford University Press.

2

Alternative International Monetary Arrangements

All observed international monetary arrangements are some modification or combination of three pure forms of system—flexible exchange rate, common currency, and key currency. Consider them in turn.

Flexible Exchange Rates

In a world system of flexible exchange rates, all national currencies exchange for each other on markets unfettered by official intervention. Each country's monetary and fiscal authorities effectively determine the domestic inflation and unemployment rates. These are obviously influenced by developments in the rest of the world, the effects of which can be offset by the domestic authorities. The 'world' inflation and unemployment rates are weighted averages of the individual countries' rates, and are determined by the interacting monetary and fiscal policies and other exogenous forces in all countries, with each country being the prime determinant of its own domestic economic conditions.

The only international co-operation required in a system of flexible exchange rates is an agreement among countries to refrain from foreign exchange market intervention.[1] However, no such agreement is possible and the system tends to degenerate as countries intervene to manipulate the international values of their currencies, creating either a 'dirty' float or a fixed rate with respect to other 'key' currencies.[2] Even when there is no official intervention, the external value of a country's currency can be managed by adjusting domestic monetary and fiscal policy. Countries often set monetary policy on the basis of a desired level of the exchange rate rather than desired output, employment, and price level conditions. Only in the latter case are exchange rate movements a truly endogenous response to market forces operating within the framework of fully autonomous policy settings.

Common Currencies

The simplest and purest common-currency system is a single currency for all countries. Such a system has never existed although at various times a significant part of the world has been on a common standard in the sense that all individual currencies were pegged to gold and/or silver which could be used in place of individual currencies in international exchange. In most every case the money supplies in the individual countries exceeded their stocks of precious metals as a result of fractional reserve banking combined with government-issued bank reserves backed by gold and/or silver. Though individual currency units were often pegged to gold and silver at the same time, the inevitable disparity between the mint exchange ratio of gold for silver and the market exchange ratio tended to drive from circulation the metal worth more in non-monetary uses.[3]

There are two types of common currency systems not based on precious metals—'paper gold' and commodity reserve currencies. The former is simply a gold-type standard using paper in place of gold. A world monetary authority would issue money which individual countries would then use as a base for issuing reserves to their domestic banking systems. Alternatively, this international money could be used directly as bank reserves in the individual countries, bypassing national monetary authorities. It is important to note that the supply of 'paper gold' is limited by the discretion of the world monetary authority or the rules under which it operates and not by the cost of production of the monetary commodity relative to other goods, as is the case with a true gold or silver standard.

A commodity reserve currency system is similar to a gold or silver standard except that the monetary unit is defined as a weighted sum of a group of commodities. If gold and silver happen to be the only commodities in the group, the system is a symmetallic rather than bimetallic one—that is the currency unit is defined as so many ounces of gold *plus* so many ounces of silver, rather than so much gold *or* so much silver. If it were possible to define the currency unit as a weighted average of all commodities produced in the economy with the weights being the shares of the individual goods in total output, one unit of currency would exchange for one unit of output and the price level would always equal unity and therefore be constant through time. In a commodity reserve system, money is created by the presentation of units of the commodity bundle to the authorities by the private sector. The authorities issue warehouse receipts which are used either as reserves by the banking system to back deposit and bank note creation or as the circulating medium itself.[4]

The central purpose of a common currency system is to put money creation beyond the control of national governments. This prevents politicians from raising tax revenue by debasing the currency—that is, from printing money to finance government activity. The problem with such systems is finding a suitable procedure for determining the money supply.

For many years the gold standard provided some control over national (and international) currency issue, but it floundered for a number of reasons. First, the supply of gold, which was determined by market conditions, did not expand as smoothly as would have been desired. Second, these fluctuations in the gold supply had multiplier effects on the supply of money as a result of fractional reserve banking. The latter, in turn, arose on account of the enormous benefits from using paper money backed by gold to economise on the use of gold itself. Finally, the growth of interventionist philosophy since the 1930s, according to which government became responsible for everything that happened in the economy, made the concept of money supply determination by impersonal forces outside the country unsupportable. Countries simply will not allow domestic output and employment to be determined, or appear to be determined, by international conditions without domestic intervention.

Fiduciary common-currency systems—'paper gold'—flounder on the difficulty of finding an appropriate procedure for creating international reserve currency. Some international agency must be charged with the responsibility for money creation and it must be made accountable to world opinion through some political process. It is difficult to get international agreement on anything, especially reserve creation. The essential bone of contention is the division among the various countries of the revenue from money creation, as well as the loss of independence in domestic policy formulation.

Commodity-reserve currencies also require international agreement, especially on the specific commodities to be included in the reserve bundle. Each country naturally wants important domestically produced goods to be included in the bundle—it views the scheme as a way to obtain an international subsidy for local production. Inability to obtain international agreement on these issues makes commodity-reserve schemes impractical.

Key Currencies

Like common currency systems, key currency arrangements involve fixed exchange rates. Various peripheral countries peg their currencies to that of some central or key currency country of their choice. The key currency country operates its domestic economic policy without regard to its balance of payments situation. Each peripheral country's authorities declare themselves ready to buy and sell the key currency in exchange for local currency to maintain the exchange rate between the two currencies at a pre-announced level.

Key currency systems have the obvious advantage that the peripheral countries can free-ride off the (presumably stable) monetary policy of the key currency country. Since the peripheral countries must maintain their money supplies at levels which will 'finance' existing exchange rates, monetary expansion and contraction in the key currency country will be mimicked by the authorities in the peripheral countries. Inflation in the key currency country will lead to inflation all over the world. The key currency country is assigned responsibility for world monetary policy not by formal international agreement but by the individual decisions of peripheral countries which *choose*, without its permission, to use its currency as a reserve currency. These countries chosen as key currency countries (there may be more than one at any time)[5] are selected on the basis of the demonstrated stability of their internal policies and external values of their currencies in the recent past.[6] Poor policy performance on the part of a key currency country will cause it to lose that status to other countries with better internal monetary control.[7]

Recently we have been observing what might be called a key currency dirty float—a combination of key currency and flexible exchange rate systems. National authorities allow their exchange rates to move around in response to market forces, but constantly adjust domestic monetary policy and intervene in the foreign exchange market to manage the rate. The objective would be to keep the value of currency at some appropriate level in terms of one or more key currencies. For example, a devaluation of the Canadian dollar with respect to the US dollar may be 'resisted' by the Canadian authorities through purchases of Canadian dollars on the foreign exchange market and through a tightening of domestic monetary policy. Or the Canadian authorities might adjust domestic credit conditions to prevent exchange rate changes resulting from differences in domestic and foreign monetary policy.

Key currency systems have substantial vitality under present conditions because they do not require international agreement for their implementation. Each country can choose to adjust its currency with respect to any key currency it chooses either on a rigid or a floating basis. The result is the loosely organised set of international monetary arrangements we now observe.

Notes

1 An elementary discussion of foreign exchange market intervention is contained in the Appendix to Chapter 6.

2 A dirty float is a situation where the exchange rate fluctuates in the market under the influence of both market forces and the intervention of the authorities. The float can also be dirty in the sense that the authorities gear their domestic monetary and fiscal policy to maintain particular exchange rate levels. In this case the authorities operate on market forces determining the rate rather than on the rate directly.

3 This phenomenon is known as Gresham's Law, the main principle of which was understood as early as the late fourteenth century. The notion arose as a description of the fact that coins that were worn, clipped or debased, but nevertheless exchanged at par for good coins, tended to drive the good coinage out of circulation. It was in each person's interest to use the debased coinage to discharge obligations and to hoard and/or melt down the good coins, indirectly acquiring debased coinage at face value in the process. A variant of the law is the tendency in a bimetallic system for the metal which is overvalued in the market, as compared to the mint, to be melted down and replaced by coins of the metal which is undervalued in the market, as compared to the mint. See Munro, John H. (1972) 'An aspect of mediaeval public finance: The profits of counterfeiting in the fifteenth-century low countries' *Revue Belge de Numismatique et de Sigillographie*, Vol. 118, pp. 127–48.

4 For a full discussion and evaluation of commodity reserve currency systems see Friedman, Milton (1953) 'Commodity reserve currencies' in *Essays in Positive Economies*, University of Chicago Press.

5 The US dollar and the British pound were key currencies in the fifties and sixties, with the dollar also acting as a key currency for the pound. The sterling area countries pegged to the pound and the British pegged the pound to the dollar. The dollar was, in turn, pegged to gold, although the supply of gold in no way determined the US money supply. Although officially on a gold standard, the world was in fact on a key currency system.

6 Availability of a financial centre (e.g. London, New York) providing low-cost banking, credit, and discount facilities is also an important factor determining which currencies become key currencies.

7 For example, the British pound has lost its key currency status almost completely and the loss of monetary control in the US starting in the late sixties has caused countries to look elsewhere for stable currency arrangements.

3

Money Supply Determination

The organisation of material in the chapters that follow is in outline chronological, beginning with the first well-organised international monetary system, the gold standard, and then turning to an analysis of the Bretton Woods system and, finally, managed floating. Before proceeding, however, it is necessary to establish the principles of money supply creation. It is natural to start with the gold standard, in which the money supply process is quite complex. The determination of the money supply under key currency and flexible exchange rate systems is then a simple by-product of the gold standard analyses.[1]

Money and Banking under a Gold Standard

Under the simplest gold standard system the money supply consists entirely of gold coin. The gold stock is divided between monetary and non-monetary uses on the basis of relative demands. An increase in the demand for money causes the price of gold to rise relative to the prices of commodities and makes it more expensive to use gold for non-monetary purposes. Ear-rings, watches, gold chains, etc. are then melted down and minted into coin. Similarly, a fall in the demand for money causes the price of gold in terms of goods to fall, making it desirable to melt down some of the existing stock of gold coin for non-monetary uses. In addition, of course, the money supply is affected by the ongoing production of gold. A high price of gold in terms of goods leads to greater gold mining activity and an increased growth rate of the stock of money, while a lower price of gold leads to a contraction of gold mining and monetary growth. The existing world stock of gold equals, of course, the sum total of all past gold production.

This simple system is not viable under real-world conditions. First of all, it is risky to hold one's gold stock in unsecured conditions. This makes it profitable to deposit it with intermediaries who will guarantee its safety. Payments for goods can be made through some form of cheque, or by withdrawal of coin as payment is required. Once such 'banking' facilities are established, it is extremely profitable for the intermediary holding gold to issue notes redeemable in it to permit transactors to avoid carrying around large quantities of heavy metal. And once they have done this, it is profitable to issue more notes than there are gold reserves to back them, relying on the fact that not all outstanding note issues will be presented for redemption at any one time.

The note issue function of banks can also arise independently of their role as depositories. Banks can be formed simply to profit from issuing notes, as was often the case in early nineteenth-century USA.[2] The founders of the bank make an investment in the form of specie and this 'net worth' is used as a reserve for notes, put in circulation by purchasing securities or making loans. The profits on note issue are the interest received on these loans and securities. The notes are willingly held by the public because of their redeemability in gold.

The motive for establishing banks may also be their function as credit intermediaries—a common basis for establishing 'merchant' banks.[3] Merchants with surplus funds deposit them in the bank, which then loans them out to other merchants in need of cash. Such intermediation is profitable because funds can be utilised more efficiently than through a complicated system of bilateral exchange of bills drawn on various parties. These deposits are part of the money supply and are willingly held because they are redeemable in gold. But the fact that the specie reserves are held is a somewhat incidental adjunct to the bank's services as an intermediary in the capital market.

Whatever the reasons for the establishment of banks, it is always profitable for them to have note and deposit liabilities in excess of their gold reserves. Suppose, for example, that a bank makes a $10 000 loan to a businessman who is willing to take the entire loan in notes redeemable in gold. If the interest rate is 5 per cent, the bank's profit is $500 minus the cost of printing, say, 200 fifty-dollar notes. The businessman passes these notes along to suppliers who are willing to hold them because they are 'as good as gold'. This assumption of redeemability is based on the reputation of the bank.[4]

Of course, loans are usually taken out in the form of deposits, which have the advantage of transferability by cheque. They are not as profitable for the issuing bank, however, because interest must be paid on deposits due to competition among banks and the feasibility of doing so.[5] The bank's profit will then be only the difference between interest received on loans and other assets, and interest paid on deposit liabilities.

More generally, in a competitive banking system profits will be driven to zero so total revenue from making loans and holding other assets must equal the total cost of acquiring the funds to loan out plus the cost of doing business. Thus

$$i_L L = i_D D + C \qquad (3.1)$$

where i_L and i_D are the interest on loans and deposits, L is the value of outstanding loans and other assets, D is the value of the bank's deposit liabilities, and C is the cost of doing business. The latter will include the normal rate of return on shareholders' capital invested in the bank. Competition will drive the interest rate on deposits up relative to the interest rate on loans until (3.1) holds for the marginal entrant into the banking business. Since all deposits and notes issued by banks must be issued in return for either gold or loans and securities

$$D + N = L + G_R \qquad (3.2)$$

where N is the bank's outstanding note issue and G_R is the gold reserves it holds. The ratio $f = G_R/(D + N)$ is the bank's gold reserve ratio—that is, the fraction of its deposit and note liabilities 'covered' by reserves of gold. Manipulating (3.2) to put L on the left-hand side, substituting the result into (3.1), and dividing both sides of the resulting equation by $D + N$, we obtain

$$i_D = \frac{(1-f)}{(1 - S_N)} i_L - \frac{\Psi}{(1 - S_N)} \qquad (3.3)$$

where $S_N = N/(D+N)$ is the fraction of the bank's note and deposit liabilities held in the form of notes, and Ψ is the cost of doing business as a fraction of total note and deposit liabilities. Equation (3.3) can be viewed as specifying the maximum interest rate the bank can afford to pay on its deposits given the values of f, S_N, and Ψ. If this is above the interest rate it has to pay to get its deposits the bank is making a better than normal profit. If it is below, the bank is making losses. It might superficially appear that the bank could increase its profits by lowering f, its gold-reserve ratio. But this would not necessarily be true for the long run because a smaller gold backing would increase the risk that the bank might some day not be able to redeem its note and deposit liabilities in gold and thereby increase the interest rate the bank would have to pay to get people to hold its deposits. Obviously, there will be a level of f that maximises the bank's long-run profits.

The bank has an incentive to keep S_N as large as possible since it pays interest on deposits but not on notes. But the public will make the decision as to how large S_N will be—it acquires the desired ratio of notes to deposits by simply depositing surplus note holdings or withdrawing deposits in the form of notes. The profitability of the bank will thus depend on its ability to keep its notes circulating, which will in turn depend in part on its 'reputation'.

One can visualise a banking industry containing a large number of banks, each with an equation (3.3) and each with a reputation for redeemability of its liabilities in gold. These banks will compete for deposits and loans, with the result that there will be some equilibrium deposit rate (i_j) that the jth bank will have to pay to acquire its deposits, some equilibrium reserve ratio (f_j) and some resulting ratio of note circulation to total liquid liabilities, (S_N^j). The interest rates on loans and other assets will depend on the credit worthiness of the individual borrowers and not on the particular bank making the loan or holding the asset. In equilibrium, the rate of interest the jth bank can afford to pay (as given by (3.3)) must equal or exceed i_j or the bank cannot stay in business. Apparent above normal profits can be viewed as a return on the bank's reputation, which can be regarded as a capital stock accumulated by indirect or direct investment in 'good performance', promotion, etc.

Liquidity and Solvency of Banks

The balance sheet of an individual bank can be presented in simplified form as shown by Table 3.1.

The example has been constructed so that the plant and equipment of the bank happens to be equal to its net worth—this need not be so in an actual case.[6] The bank is solvent in the sense that the loans and other assets could be liquidated for $1000 worth of gold and all note holders and depositors could be paid off in full. The fact that the bank cannot 'cover' all of its note and deposit liabilities with gold presents

TABLE 3.1

Assets ($)		Liabilities and net worth ($)	
Gold reserves	100	Notes in circulation	300
Loans	800	Deposits	800
Other financial assets	200	Net worth	50
Fixed assets (buildings and equipment, etc.)	50		
Total	1150	Total	1150

no problem, since loans and other assets can be sold in the market to obtain any gold necessary to satisfy note and deposit holders.

Solvency could be a serious problem, however, if the bank makes bad loans. Such loans cannot be sold for their book value because they are uncollectable. The left side of the balance sheet then overstates the value of assets. Suppose, for example, that the true value of loans is only $400. Then if the bank went into receivership not all of the deposit and note holders could be satisfied. If the latter came to anticipate that the bank has been making bad loans, they will try to redeem their notes and deposits in gold and the bank will find that it cannot obtain enough gold by liquidating its loans and assets to pay them off. The 'run' on the bank will lead to its collapse.

Various measures were tried over the years to shield the public against bank insolvency. Such measures include limitation of note issue to some fraction of net worth or paid-in capital and a requirement that some portion of paid-in capital be specie and the rest government bonds. The purpose was to ensure that there would be sufficient assets to cover note (and deposit) liabilities.[7] As the laws governing banking became fully developed, and drew on earlier experience, they began prohibiting banks from making loans to owners, directors, and other 'insiders'. Despite such regulations, banks not infrequently became insolvent. Depositors and note holders depended to a large degree on an individual bank's reputation for competent, conservative management. They were often disappointed.

A complicating factor in bank solvency was the implications of fractional reserve banking for solvency of the system as a whole. The supply of money in the economy as a whole (M) consists of the public's holdings of gold (G_P), bank notes (N), and deposits (D).

$$M = G_P + N + D \tag{3.4}$$

This is backed by a stock of monetary gold that is held either by the public as cash (G_P) or the banking system as reserves (G_R).

$$G = G_P + G_R \tag{3.5}$$

The money multiplier, or ratio of money to gold, can thus be expressed

$$\frac{M}{G} = \frac{G_P + N + D}{G_P + G_R} = \frac{g+1}{g+f} \tag{3.6}$$

where $g = G_P/(N + D)$ is the public's ratio of gold to note and deposit holdings and f is now the gold reserve ratio of the banking system as a whole. If, for example, the public holds $1 of gold for every $10 of notes and deposits and the banking system's reserve ratio is 0.05, $1 billion of gold will produce a money supply in excess of $7.3 billion.

The public choose g on the basis of wealth maximisation and the reserve ratio f is chosen by the banking system on the basis of profit maximisation, sometimes subject to legal reserve constraints set by the authorities.

Changes in g and f as a result of private decisions have important implications for solvency of the banking system. Suppose, for example, that world (and hence domestic) interest rates rise temporarily as a result of ordinary market forces. This reduces the market value of the assets held by banks. As a result, the solvency of some of the marginal banks in the system comes into question, and holders of notes and deposit liabilities of those banks try to redeem them in gold. When significant numbers of banks try to liquidate assets simultaneously to obtain gold to redeem their notes and deposits, they bid asset prices down further, jeopardising the solvency of stronger banks.

A spreading demand for liquidity thus means a higher desired ratio of gold in relation to note and deposit holdings on the part of the public. This increase in g reduces the supply of money, creating further downward pressure on asset prices and upward pressure on interest rates as wealth holders attempt to replenish money holdings by selling assets. This in turn puts more pressure on bank balance sheets. The situation is compounded by attempts on the part of individual banks to increase their reserve ratios—the resulting increase in f further reduces the money supply relative to the stock of monetary gold.

The usual result of a liquidity crisis of this sort was the suspension of convertibility of notes and deposits into gold by some or all banks. These notes and deposits circulate as before, but now trade at a discount in relation to convertible notes and deposits. The suspension of convertibility is actually a safety valve that prevents further destruction of the money stock in the rush to convert notes and deposits into gold.

Under suspension it is as if there were many different monies in circulation, with flexible exchange rates between them. Each bank's notes and deposits are a separate money, as is gold. Since each money has a different value in terms of goods, there are many different price levels, one for each money.

A Digression on Private Fiduciary Money

What is wrong with a system in which money, except for gold and/or token coins,[8] is provided by the banks who issue deposit and note liabilities in competition with each other?

It is often thought that competition will lead to the issue of so much money that it will become worthless and prices will go to infinity.[9] That is not generally true, however, because the various monies are not identical—that is, perfect substitutes for each other. There is thus no single price level but many different ones, each associated with a different money.[10] For prices to become infinite all monies would have to become worthless. Any money that was not over-issued would have a finite price level of goods in terms of it and would not be worthless.

Imagine a situation where each money-issuing bank is able to specify in advance the quantities of its money it will make available at each future point in time and guarantee that only these quantities of money will be printed. Then there will be a finite price level in terms of this money and an inflation rate, known in advance, at each future point in time. Competition between banks will force the profit from issuing money to zero—interest will have to be paid at a rate equal to the expected inflation rate of the price level for the money in question, plus the real rate of interest on alternative assets, minus the cost of issuing the money. It would appear that in such a world money will be provided at essentially zero cost—bond and debt instruments that facilitate the movement of savings into investment will merely be issued in many different denominations and circulate as money. Each issuer's instruments will have a value in terms of all commodities in the economy and a general price level can be constructed for that particular monetary unit. Practically every asset in the economy would perform the 'medium of exchange' function of money.

The problem with such a competitive fiduciary monetary system is the difficulty of ensuring that no more than the specified quantity will be put into circulation at each point in time. It pays to cheat. An issuer of bonds who stamps them as money by guaranteeing limited future issue has a strong incentive, once the bonds are circulating, to issue more than the contracted amount and use them to purchase goods and services. This can be done until the public becomes aware that the issuer is not honouring his commitments. The expectation that further over-issue is likely will make it unwilling to hold the paper. The money will become worthless unless a new and binding commitment as to the quantity of future issue can be made. The issuer, by breaking his commitment, has redistributed wealth from the rest of the community to himself.

It would seem impossible to guarantee private money against over-issue except by government authority and control—and this would fundamentally abrogate the notion of competitive private-money creation. The only way a private bank could establish confidence that over-issue would not occur is by performance leading to the establishment of a brand name. A highly reputable firm, whose debt obligations are well received, might induce wider circulation of them by calling them money and paying very high interest rates. With a long period of performance, as evidenced by a stable value of the asset in terms of goods and other assets, the interest rate required to get people to hold it will become lower and lower. This lower interest rate reflects the firm's developing brand name. As the brand name develops, its present value can be maximised by refraining from over-issuing the paper.[11] In such a system, money is backed not by gold but by a reserve of arduously accumulated brand-name capital.[12]

As far as is known, a competitive fiduciary monetary system of this sort has never existed anywhere for a significant length of time.[13] The main reason would appear to be that making the currency convertible into gold or into some other currency that is convertible is a much cheaper way of guaranteeing against over-issue than investing in a brand name. Thus, except in wartime and other special circumstances, the suspension of convertibility was always followed shortly by its re-establishment.

Government Control over Note Issue

As the gold standard developed, control over note issue gradually became centralised in the hands of either government or a private central bank such as the Bank of England. Either non-interest-bearing government debt was used directly, or selected private banks were permitted to issue notes secured by government debt. In this latter case, certain classes of bonds bearing the privilege of note issue are deposited with the authorities and notes issued up to some fraction of the value of bonds deposited.[14] The quantity of notes issued was thus strictly regulated by the government.

When notes are issued by the government and redeemable in gold for both the banks and the public, the banks need not hold significant gold reserves any more and can use notes as a reserve against deposits. Notes are thus as good as gold and assume the role of an asset for the commercial banks rather than a liability. These notes along with deposits of the commercial banks in the central bank (or with the government if there is no central bank) now form the monetary base on which the money supply is created by the banking system. The stock of base or high-powered money can thus be written

$$H = G_P + N_P + N_R + D_R \qquad (3.7)$$

where N_R and D_R are the note and deposit (with the central bank) reserves of the banking system (we assume that the commercial banks do not bother to hold gold). Gold and notes held by the public are part of base money because they can be deposited in the commercial banks (who would then redeposit them in the central bank), and used ultimately as a reserve on which the banking system can create deposits. The money supply still consists of the gold, note and deposit holdings of the public.

The money multiplier now becomes

$$\frac{M}{H} = \frac{G_P + N_P + D}{G_P + N_P + N_R + D_R} = \frac{g' + c' + 1}{g' + c' + f'} \tag{3.8}$$

where $g' = G_P/D$ is the public's desired ratio of gold to deposit holdings, $c' = N_P/D$ is its ratio of notes to deposits, and $f' = (N_R + D_R)/D$ is the banking system's reserve ratio of notes and deposits with the central bank or government to its deposit liabilities.

Money Supply Determination under Key Currency and Flexible Exchange Rate Systems

If the public chooses not to hold gold, or is prohibited from doing so as was the case in the USA after 1934, the money multiplier reduces to

$$\frac{M}{H} = \frac{c' + 1}{c' + f'} \tag{3.8'}$$

which is the standard multiplier for a modern economy not on the gold standard. The process of money creation under a flexible exchange rate or key currency system is thus summarised by (3.8'). The central bank or government creates high-powered money either by purchasing securities from the public or by, in effect, printing money and spending it. This high-powered or base money is either held by the public as currency or deposited in the commercial banks where it becomes a reserve on which the banking system can create deposits. The lower the public's holdings of currency relative to deposits (c') and the lower the commercial banks' ratio of reserves to deposits (f'), the higher is the money multiplier, and the greater is the stock of money the banking system creates for any given quantity of high-powered money.

Requirements for a True Gold Standard

Two conditions must be met for a gold standard to be maintained. The currency unit must be defined in terms of gold and there must be a direct relationship between the gold stock and the money supply. A commitment of the government to buy and sell gold at a fixed price is neither necessary or sufficient for a gold standard to exist. Even if the public is not permitted to hold gold, and the money multiplier reduces to (3.8'), a gold standard could still be maintained if the authorities performing the central banking function are required to back their monetary liabilities—N_P, N_R, and D_R—with gold. If b' is the required ratio of gold to monetary liabilities that the authorities must hold, then the total stock of outstanding high-powered money will equal

$$H' = N_P + N_R + D_R = \frac{1}{b'}G_T \tag{3.9}$$

where G_T is the stock of gold held by the authorities. This will equal the national gold stock, G, as long as the public and the banks cannot hold gold. When the public holds gold and the nation's gold reserves are held entirely by the central authorities,

$$G_T + G_P = G \tag{3.10}$$

The stock of high-powered money then becomes

$$H = N_P + N_R + D_R + G_P = \frac{1}{b'}G_T + G_P = \frac{1}{b'}G + \left(1 - \frac{1}{b'}\right)G_P \tag{3.11}$$

and the ratio of base money to gold becomes

$$\frac{H}{G} = \frac{1}{b'} - \frac{(1-b')}{b'}X' \tag{3.12}$$

where $X' = G_P/G$ is the fraction of the national gold stock held by the public. The ratio of the money supply to the gold stock is then

$$\frac{M}{G} = \left(\frac{g' + c' + 1}{g' + c' + f'}\right)\left(\frac{1}{b'} - \frac{(1-b')}{b'}X'\right) \tag{3.13}$$

When the public is not allowed to hold gold, this reduces to

$$\frac{M}{G} = \left(\frac{c'+1}{c'+f'}\right)\frac{1}{b'} \tag{3.13'}$$

Effective abolition of the gold standard simply involves the elimination of any relationship between G and H. The monetary authorities then control the money supply solely by direct adjustment of H through the normal open or closed market purchase, or sale of bonds from the public or treasury as the case may be.[15] Normally, also, abolition of the gold standard implies that the authorities abrogate their commitment to exchange gold for money at an official price. However, such a commitment, by itself, is insufficient to establish a gold standard. Governments typically support the prices of numerous commodities, such as wheat, sugar, etc., without putting the monetary system on a wheat or sugar standard. The key thing is that there must be a relationship between the government's holdings of the monetary commodity—gold in this case—and the quantity of base money.

Three kinds of liquidity crises can arise in a gold-standard system with centralised, government-controlled, note issue. First, the public can, all of a sudden, demand to hold its money in notes rather than deposits. This appears as an increase in c', which causes the banks to try to liquidate assets to raise the cash required by depositors. Interest rates rise and asset prices fall, eroding the banks' asset positions. Second, the public can decide that it wants to hold gold instead of notes. As the banking system redeems notes in gold, the stock of gold in the treasury declines and the central bank has to reduce its liabilities to the banking system and, as a result, the stock of base money in the economy.[16] This reduction in bank reserves forces the banking system to liquidate loans and assets to maintain desired reserve ratios, resulting again in a liquidity crunch. Third, foreign residents and/or banks may decide to hold more gold. This will result in a rise in world interest rates and a reduction of the domestic gold base. The domestic banking system will then have to liquidate loans to reduce the nominal money supply to a level consistent with this lower base.

The authorities can take the pressure off the system in these latter two cases by simply reducing b', the ratio of gold held in the treasury to central-bank liabilities. The original money supply can then be supported by a smaller gold stock and the liquidity crunch disappears. When the authorities do this, they are abolishing the gold standard as rigidly conceived because the relationship between the stock of gold and the stock of money is being severed. However, a wise central bank like the Bank of England allegedly was in the nineteenth century, might adjust b' temporarily to moderate liquidity crises and gluts.[17] In the extreme case, where no attempt is made to achieve some average level of b' over time, gold becomes a price-supported commodity like sugar or wheat and can be supported as long as the authorities have gold to sell. The only difference between gold and other supported commodities then lies in the traditional role of gold as money and the psychological significance attached to it as a result.

A good example of this occurred in the fifties and sixties when the US Government stood ready to buy and sell gold at $35 per oz, but the US money supply bore no relationship whatsoever to the stock of gold held by the Treasury. United States residents were not allowed to hold gold. Most other countries stood ready to exchange their currencies for US dollars at fixed exchange rates and were therefore indirectly committed to pay the equivalent in their own currencies of $35 per oz of gold. But their money supplies were also entirely independent of their gold holdings. The system was a key currency dollar system combined with an international price support for gold, rather than a gold standard proper. The same thing could have been accomplished by pegging the price of sugar and using it to settle international accounts among central banks. Gold had no more effect on the money supply than any other commodity, whether price supported or not.

Notes

1 Readers who are familiar with the theory of the supply of money can skip directly to Chapter 4, Chapter 6, or Chapter 8, as interest dictates.
2 See Hammond, Bray (1977) *Banks and Politics in America From the Revolution to the Civil War*, Princeton University Press.
3 This was true of the early Canadian banks. See Hammond, *op. cit.* Chapter 20.
4 Of course, some of the notes would find their way back to the issuing bank and would have to be redeemed. However, a significant fraction of the issue will remain in circulation if the bank's reputation is good.
5 Cases where interest was paid on bank notes are rare.
6 In fact in the early US banks, net worth was contributed in gold which was used as a reserve for note issue.
7 The idea was that note holders could be reimbursed with the gold reserve and the proceeds of the sale of the bonds if the bank failed. See Hammond *op. cit.* for a discussion of these measures in the context of early US banking. See also Friedman, Milton and Schwartz, Anna (1963) *A Monetary History of the United States, 1867–1960*, National Bureau of Economic Research (NBER), Princeton University Press.
8 Token coins are coins whose value as money exceeds the value of the metal they contain. If this were not true they would be melted down and disappear.
9 For example, see Friedman, Milton (1959) *A Program for Monetary Stability*, Fordham University Press, p. 7.
10 See Klein, Benjamin (1974) 'The competitive supply of money', *Journal of Money, Credit and Banking*, Vol. 6, No. 4, Nov., pp. 423–53.
11 Once the fact of overissue (in relation to past commitments or the established perceptions of note holders) becomes known, the notes will become worthless and the brand name destroyed.
12 See Klein, *op. cit.*, pp. 432–8.
13 See Klein, *op. cit.* and also (1974) 'Competitive interest payments on bank deposits and the long-run demand for money', *American Economic Review*, Vol. 64, No. 6, Dec. pp. 931–49.

14 This type of arrangement was characteristic of the development of the National Banking System in post-Civil War United States. See Friedman and Schwartz, *op. cit.* Chapter 2.

15 A closed market sale of securities is a sale by the treasury to the central bank (or, more exactly, a sale by the government to itself) in return for funds that can be used to finance expenditures.

16 In many cases there may also be legal requirements as to the maximum amount of notes the authorities may issue per unit of gold reserves.

17 See Bagehot, Walter (1873) *Lombard Street*, H. S. King and Co.

4

World Equilibrium under a Gold Standard

We now develop a model of world monetary equilibrium under an international gold standard.[1] Suppose there are two countries, neither of which is necessarily small in relation to the other, and both of which have their monetary units tied to gold. Let both have money stocks consisting of deposits and notes as well as token coins. These money stocks are backed by gold reserve holdings of the commercial banks and/or the central monetary authority.

The money stocks in the two countries are some multiples, γ and γ^*, of their respective gold stocks, GS and GS^* (an asterisk designates that the parameter or variable refers to the foreign economy). These money multipliers are determined in accordance with equations (3.8), (3.8'), (3.13) or (3.13') in the previous chapter, depending upon the relevant institutional circumstances.

Equilibrium in the world markets for money and other assets requires that the residents of each country be holding their desired quantities of each asset including money. This condition is not as complicated as it might at first seem because it turns out that if each country's residents hold the quantity of money they desire they will necessarily be holding their desired quantity of non-monetary assets. This is true because each person can only hold wealth in two forms—in the form of money or in the form of non-monetary assets.[2] If he has an excess supply of money he must necessarily have an excess demand for other assets and vice versa.[3] World asset equilibrium can thus be expressed in terms of two equations that equate the demand for money in each country with the supply,

$$GS = \frac{P \cdot L(r, Y)}{\gamma} \tag{4.1}$$

and

$$GS^* = \frac{P^*L^*(r^*,Y^*)}{\gamma^*} \tag{4.2}$$

where P refers to the price level of goods produced in the economy, r the real interest rate, Y real income, and $L(.)$ the demand function for real money balances.[4]

These equations could alternatively and equivalently be written as equalities of the real money supplies with the demands for real-money balances. The real money supplies are the nominal supplies, given by γGS and $\gamma^* GS^*$, deflated by the respective price levels, P and P^*.[5] Thus, (4.1) and (4.2) could be expressed

$$\frac{\gamma GS}{P} = L(r,Y) \tag{4.1a}$$

$$\frac{\gamma^* GS^*}{P^*} = L^*(r^*,Y^*) \tag{4.2a}$$

The demand functions for real money balances, $L(.)$ and $L^*(.)$, postulate that the desired real quantities of money in each country (that is, desired money holdings measured in terms of the bundle of goods making up the price index) depends on the levels of that country's income and interest rates. A higher level of income normally causes the public to want to hold more money at each level of prices because more transactions have to be made; an increase in the interest rate causes people to want to hold less money because the income that could be earned by holding other assets instead (the opportunity cost of holding money) is higher. Thus, $\partial L/\partial r$ and $\partial L^*/\partial r$ are negative and $\partial L/\partial Y$ and $\partial L^*/\partial Y^*$ are positive. The interest rates r and r^*, being real interest rates, do not contain a premium to compensate for expected inflation—we assume that the expected rate of inflation is zero.[6]

Full equilibrium of the world economy also requires that the market for the current flows of goods and services is in equilibrium. Real goods market equilibrium can be expressed in terms of the standard income–expenditure equations,

$$Y = C(r,Y) + I(r,Y) + GX + B_T(Y,Y^*,P/P^*) \tag{4.3}$$

and

$$Y^* = C^*(r^*,Y^*) + I^*(r^*,Y^*) + GX^* - \frac{P}{P^*}B_T(Y,Y^*,P/P^*) \tag{4.4}$$

where $C(.)$ and $I(.)$ are the real consumption and investment functions, $B_T(.)$ is the function determining the real balance of trade, and GX is the level of real government expenditure. GX can also be viewed as a shift variable accounting for a wide range of exogenous factors affecting aggregate demand. These equations state that the quantity of output produced in a country, represented by Y on the left side of the equality, must equal the aggregate demand for output, represented by the collection of terms on the right side of the equality. Aggregate demand consists of the absorption of domestic output for consumption, investment and government purposes together with the *net* absorption of domestic goods abroad. The latter equals the balance of trade—the absorption of domestic export goods by foreigners minus the domestic absorption of foreign goods through imports. Imports are deducted because not all domestic consumption, investment and government expenditure falls on domestic production—some leaks abroad to the purchase of foreign goods. The income-expenditure equation for the foreign country is formally the same as the domestic one except the foreign balance of trade is equal to minus the domestic balance of trade multiplied by the ratio of the domestic to the foreign price levels. Multiplication by P/P^* converts B_T, measured in units of domestic output in (4.3), into units of foreign output as required in (4.4).[7]

The consumption, investment, and balance-of-trade functions have the standard interpretations. Consumption responds positively to changes in real income and negatively (by assumption) to the interest rate.[8] Investment also responds positively to income and negatively to the interest rate. Thus $\partial C/\partial Y$, $\partial I/\partial Y$, $\partial C^*/\partial Y^*$ and $\partial I^*/\partial Y^*$ are positive and $\partial C/\partial r$, $\partial I/\partial r$, $\partial C^*/\partial r^*$ and $\partial I^*/\partial r^*$ are negative. Since imports increase with domestic income and exports increase with foreign income, the domestic balance of trade responds negatively to Y and positively to Y^*—hence, $(\partial B_T/\partial Y) < 0$ and $(\partial B_T/\partial Y^*) > 0$. A rise in the domestic relative to the foreign price level makes domestic goods less competitive, reducing exports relative to imports and deteriorating the balance of trade—$\partial B_T/\partial (P/P^*)$ is thus negative.

The above model could be refined by adding expectations-augmented aggregate supply curves but they contribute nothing to our subsequent analysis. Instead we impose either the simple-minded Keynesian less-than-full-employment assumptions, $P = P_f$ and $P^* = P^*_f$, or the strict classical full-employment assumptions, $Y = Y_f$ and $Y^* = Y^*_f$.[9] Thus, either prices or outputs are regarded as exogenous.

The four equations do not provide a complete model of world equilibrium because they specify nothing about the international mobility of capital. Three alternative assumptions are possible, (a) complete immobility, (b) perfect mobility, and (c) imperfect mobility. Consider the three cases in turn.

Complete International Immobility of Capital

Complete immobility of capital means that private residents of the two parts of the world cannot buy or sell securities or loan funds across the international boundary. Gold can, of course, be exported or imported, but only in exchange for goods and not in exchange for other capital assets. It can flow into a country only if that country has a balance-of-trade surplus and out only if it has a balance-of-trade deficit. Thus, assuming zero production of gold, we can express the rates of change of the gold stocks of the two countries as

$$\frac{dGS}{dt} = -\frac{dGS^*}{dt} \tag{4.5}$$

$$= P \cdot B_T(Y, Y^*, P/P^*) \tag{4.6}$$

where gold is valued in domestic currency.[10]

Equations (4.1) to (4.6) form a complete model of world equilibrium which solves for the endogenous variables r, r^*, dGS/dt, dGS^*/dt and either Y and Y^* or P and P^*, given the existing stocks of gold in the two countries (GS and GS^*), the money multipliers (γ and γ^*) and the levels of government expenditure (GX and GX^*). Actually, the system is recursive, with the first four equations solving for interest rates and outputs or prices. These solutions then plug into (4.5) and (4.6) to determine the flow of gold at each point in time. As the system evolves through time the levels of GS and GS^* change in response to (4.5) and (4.6) until gold movements cease and

$$B_T(Y, Y^*, P/P^*) = 0 \tag{4.7}$$

Equation (4.7) in conjunction with (4.1) to (4.4) thus gives the long-run equilibrium of the system.

This model presents the traditional international gold standard adjustment mechanism. That mechanism, due originally to Hume,[11] operates through transfers of gold brought about by imbalances of trade. Excess gold in a country leads to a rise in that country's price level. This makes its goods more expensive relative to foreign goods, leading to a trade deficit which must be covered by the export of gold. As gold flows out the domestic price level falls and the foreign price level rises. When relative domestic and foreign prices have adjusted so that trade is balanced, the export of gold ceases and the distribution of the world gold stock between the two countries is again in equilibrium.

To examine this mechanism in more detail, take the pure classical case where wages and prices are perfectly flexible and Y and Y^* are therefore exogenous.[12] Suppose the system is initially in long-run equilibrium and this equilibrium is disturbed by a miraculous transfer of gold stock from the foreign to the domestic economy. The resulting excess money holdings of domestic residents lead them to try to purchase assets. Asset prices are bid up and the domestic interest rate is bid down—this is necessary to satisfy equation (4.1) in the face of an increase in GS at the initial levels of Y and P. Similarly, the excess demand for money on the part of foreigners causes foreign asset prices to fall and the foreign interest rate to rise. This satisfies equation (4.2) at the initial levels of Y^* and P^* and the lower level of GS^*.

When the domestic interest rate falls, investment and consumption increase in the domestic economy. Foreign consumption and investment fall as the foreign interest rate rises. This creates excess aggregate demand in the domestic economy—the right side of equation (4.3) gets larger while the left stays unchanged. And excess aggregate supply is created in the foreign economy as the right-hand side terms $C^*(r^*,Y^*)$ and $I^*(r^*,Y^*)$ in equation (4.4) fall. The domestic price level is bid up and the foreign price level is bid down causing $B_T(.)$ to decline. A deficit in the domestic balance of payments is thus created with, as its counterpart, a balance-of-payments surplus abroad. The fall in $B_T(.)$ counterbalances the increase in $C(.)$ and $I(.)$ in the domestic economy restoring commodity-market equilibrium in equation (4.3). And it counterbalances the falls in $C^*(.)$ and $I^*(.)$ and restores commodity-market equilibrium abroad, maintaining the equality in equation (4.4).

The balance of payments disequilibrium is matched by a flow of gold from the domestic to the foreign economy to settle international accounts. This gradually reduces the domestic money supply and increases the money supply abroad until the initial equilibrium distribution of the gold stock between the two parts of the world has been restored. As this happens the above described process winds down, with interest rates, price levels, and the balance of trade gradually returning to their initial levels.[13]

A somewhat similar process arises from a shift in the demand for gold. Suppose, for example, that the domestic monetary system begins holding a smaller reserve ratio of gold to deposit and note liabilities. The money multiplier γ rises and with it the domestic money supply. Domestic asset equilibrium requires that r falls in order to satisfy equation (4.1) in the face of a higher γ at the initial levels of GS, P and Y. This increases $C(.)$ and $I(.)$ in equation (4.3) creating excess aggregate demand. The domestic price level is bid up, reducing the competitiveness of domestic goods in world markets and deteriorating the balance of trade. The fall in $B_T(.)$ is just sufficient to offset the increases in $C(.)$ and $I(.)$, thereby preserving the equality in equation

(4.3) and maintaining aggregate demand equal to aggregate supply. The deterioration of the domestic trade balance is equivalent to an improvement of the trade balance abroad. This creates excess demand in the foreign economy since it raises the right-hand side of equation (4.4). The foreign price level is bid up as a result, moderating but not eliminating the foreign trade balance surplus. The rise in the price level also reduces the foreign real money supply and thereby causes the foreign interest rate to be bid up in equation (4.2). This chokes off sufficient consumption and investment in the foreign economy to make room for the improvement in the balance of trade so that the equality in equation (4.4) can be preserved.

The deficit in the domestic balance of trade, and surplus in the balance of trade abroad, results in a flow of gold from the domestic to the foreign economy. As time passes this reduces the domestic stock of money and increases the stock of money abroad. Ultimately, this reduces domestic and raises foreign prices, choking off the domestic trade-balance deficit and eliminating the gold flow.

It is easy to show that the long-run effect of the increase in γ must be to raise the price levels in the two economies proportionally. Ultimately, when gold stops flowing, $B_T(.)$ must equal zero. Since Y and Y^* are at their initial (and full employment) levels, P/P^* must also be at its initial level—otherwise B_T could not be zero. Hence P and P^* must increase in the same proportion. When we substitute $B_T(.) = 0$ into equations (4.3) and (4.4) and note that Y and Y^* are at their initial levels, it is evident that r and r^* must also return to their initial levels in the long run.

The rise in the ratio of money to gold in the domestic economy effectively reduces the domestic, and hence world, demand for gold. World prices rise and the world stock of gold is redistributed between the two economies in accordance with their relative demands for it. An important implication is that the banking structure in one country (in particular, its ability to economise on gold) has an effect on economic conditions all over the world, depending of course on the size of the country.[14]

The effects of real aggregate demand shifts in one country, as represented in the model by shifts in the government expenditure variable GX, are also worthy of brief mention. Suppose, for example, that GX increases. The result is upward pressure on aggregate demand as the right-hand side of equation (4.3) expands. The domestic price level is thus bid up, increasing the demand for money and gold reserves backing it. The public tries to re-establish asset equilibrium by selling assets, which causes the domestic interest rate to rise. The resulting deterioration of the trade balance and decline in consumption and investment 'make room' for the increase in government absorption of goods in the face of constant output. The surplus in the trade balance abroad puts upward pressure on aggregate demand there, raising the foreign interest rate and price level. Gold flows from the domestic to the foreign economy, driving the foreign price up further. In the long run, prices must rise in the same proportion in both countries to keep $B_T(.)$ equal to zero. The domestic interest rate must be higher than it was initially to retard investment sufficiently to free the resources absorbed by the increase in government expenditure. The foreign interest rate must ultimately return to its initial level, as can be seen from equation (4.4), because $B_T(.) = 0$ in the long run, GX^* has not increased, and Y^* must remain at its initial full employment level.

The essential things to notice about the complete capital immobility case are, (a) that the equilibrium allocation of the world gold stock between the two countries is brought about gradually by flows of gold 'financed' by differences between exports and imports, and (b) the process by which a trade imbalance is created and gold is transferred involves a temporary adjustment of the domestic relative to foreign price level.

Perfect International Capital Mobility

As conventionally postulated, perfect capital mobility means two things. First, there can be no barriers to trade in assets across international boundaries. Second, the assets of the two parts of the world must be perfect substitutes in the portfolios of a sufficient number of domestic and foreign residents to equalise interest rates at home and abroad. The basic equations (4.1) to (4.4) must therefore be supplemented by

$$GS + \overline{GS}^* = GS \tag{4.8}$$

and

$$r = r^* \tag{4.9}$$

The first equation recognises the fact that gold can now be transferred across international boundaries in exchange for assets—the residents of a particular country just buy or sell securities in the international market in return for gold. This transfer of gold can be a one-shot, or once and for all, stock transfer occurring at a point in time. There is no requirement that gold shipments be 'financed' by a difference between exports and imports of goods and services. The second equation recognises the fact that domestic and foreign interest rates must be equal. If domestic rates should happen to be above foreign rates the residents of both countries will try to shift their portfolios from foreign to domestic securities. This will cause domestic asset prices to rise, and foreign asset prices to fall, until the two countries' interest rates are again equal.[15]

Equations (4.5) and (4.6) no longer apply. The trade balance equals

$$B_T\left(Y,Y^*,\frac{P}{P^*}\right) = Y - C(r,Y) - I(r,Y) - GX \tag{4.10}$$

from a simple rearrangement of (4.3) and no longer needs to be zero in long-run equilibrium. When S denotes domestic savings and I total private and government domestic investment,[16] this relationship becomes

$$B_T\left(Y,Y^*,\frac{P}{P^*}\right) = S - I \tag{4.10'}$$

Savings are determined by income and consumption, which in turn depends on income and the world interest rate, while investment depends on income, the interest rate, investment prospects in the domestic economy (incorporated into the form of $I(.)$) and expenditures by the government on investment. Savings represents the flow of purchases of new securities including monetary gold by domestic residents, while investment represents the flow of new issues of securities, including monetary gold, by firms investing in the domestic economy. It is obvious that dGS/dt is only one component of $(S-I)$ and that savings can differ from investment in long-run equilibrium without any gold flow.[17]

When (4.9) is substituted into equations (4.1) to (4.4) to eliminate r^*, the resulting four equations, together with (4.8), solve for the five variables r, GS, GS^*, and either Y and Y^* or P and P^*. The world gold supply $\overline{GS}$, the multipliers γ and γ^*, and the levels of domestic and foreign government expenditure GX and GX^* are all exogenous. In solving the system, the conditions of asset equilibrium can be consolidated by substituting (4.1) and (4.2) into (4.8) and noting that $r = r^*$.

$$\overline{GS} = \frac{P \cdot L(r,Y)}{\gamma} + \frac{P^* \cdot L^*(r,Y)}{\gamma^*} \tag{4.11}$$

This expression can be rearranged in the form

$$r = A(\overline{GS}, P, P^*, Y, Y^*, \gamma, \gamma^*) \tag{4.12}$$

Equation (4.12) gives the world interest rate as a function of the world gold stock, domestic and foreign prices and incomes, and the domestic and foreign money multipliers. The world interest rate consistent with asset equilibrium is thus determined by the combined domestic and foreign demands for what amounts to a homogeneous world asset— once both countries' residents hold their desired stocks of money, they must also have a zero excess demand for the world asset, so demand and supply functions for the latter need not appear explicitly in the model.

Equation (4.12) now plugs into (4.3) and (4.4) to determine the equilibrium values of P and P^* or Y and Y^*, depending upon whether Keynesian or classical assumptions are used. The world interest rate determined by the simultaneous solution of these three equations then substitutes into (4.1) and (4.2) to yield the allocation of the world gold stock between the two countries. As noted above, that allocation is brought into equilibrium simply by an exchange of gold and securities on the part of the two countries' residents.

It is important to notice that the system solves for the levels of GS and GS^*, not their rates of change as in the perfect capital immobility case. The rates of change of GS and GS^* through time can be obtained by differentiating the static solution of the system with respect to time. Since the rates of change of the exogenous variables do not appear in the solution of the system for Y, Y^*, P, P^*, r^* or GS and GS^*, the levels of income, prices and world interest rates are unaffected by the rate at which the world gold stock or any other exogenous variable is growing.[18] Hence, the balance of trade $B_T(.)$ is not directly related to the movement of gold between the two economies either at a point in time or through time. International gold flows are thus in no way 'financed' by changes in exports relative to imports. Since by the same reasoning the relative price variable P/P^* is also unrelated to gold movements, the traditional classical specie flow mechanism (where a disequilibrium allocation of gold leads to relative price changes, a shift in the trade balance, and gold flows) does not apply when capital is perfectly mobile internationally.

Consider now the comparative statics effects of some of the exogenous forces affecting the model.[19] First, take the case of an increase in the world gold stock. The discovery, for example, of a new addition to the gold stock in one of the countries would lead its residents to convert at least part of their newly found treasure into other assets. Asset prices will be bid up and the world interest rate bid down in equation (4.12) until someone is willing to hold the additional world stock of gold at the initial levels of domestic and foreign incomes and prices. The lower interest rate will expand consumption and investment in equations (4.3) and (4.4). Aggregate demand, income and prices will expand in both countries. In the long-run, of course, output in each country will return to the full-employment level. Since nothing has happened to change the relative demand or supply of domestic as compared to foreign goods, the price ratio P/P^* will not change. Full employment in both countries and an unchanged price ratio implies that the interest rate in equations (4.3) and (4.4)—i.e. the world interest rate—must return to its original level. Prices in both countries will thus rise in proportion to the increase in the world gold stock. The increment to that stock will be distributed between the two countries through exchanges of gold for assets until both countries' residents are in portfolio equilibrium. As noted, this will involve a movement of gold from the domestic to the foreign economy.

The effects of an increase in the money multiplier in one of the countries are a little more complex. An increase in γ means that domestic residents now have a larger stock of money associated with their initial gold holdings. They will try to convert this money into assets, bidding down the world interest rate in equation (4.12). Since the lower interest rate will induce foreigners to trade assets for money there will be a once and for all shift of gold from the domestic to the foreign economy. The lower world interest rate will lead to increases in domestic and foreign output and prices, and so forth—the effects on these variables are the same as occurred when the stock of gold increased. The interesting conclusion is that a willingness of the residents (or the banking system) in one country to economise on gold will lead to a loss of gold to the other country and an increase in the world money supply.

Finally, consider the effects of a real sector shift, represented by an increase in the government expenditure variable GX. This leads to excess aggregate demand in the domestic economy and increases in output and prices which in turn cause the trade balance to deteriorate. The deterioration of the trade balance frees labour and capital resources to be absorbed by the additional government expenditure. The surplus in the trade balance abroad leads to an expansion of aggregate demand and increase in output and prices there. As world output prices rise, the demand for nominal money balances goes up, leading to a rise in the world interest rate. This chokes off investment in both countries. The decline in investment abroad permits a trade balance surplus to remain permanently, while the decline in domestic investment offsets some but not all of the aggregate demand effect of the increase in government expenditure. The remainder is offset by the deficit in the domestic trade balance. An excess of investment over savings occurs in the domestic economy combined with an excess of savings over investment abroad—there is thus a net capital flow out of the foreign economy and into the domestic one equal to the trade-balance deficit. The effect on the gold flow cannot be signed without information about the two economies. Both countries' demand for money is reduced by the rise in the world interest rate. The domestic price level rises but the foreign price level may rise or fall depending on whether the interest rate effect on consumption and investment falls short of or exceeds the relative price effect on the trade balance. If the foreign price level falls the foreign demand for money necessarily declines relative to the domestic demand and gold flows from the foreign to the domestic economy. But if the foreign price level rises and the foreign demand for money is very interest inelastic as compared to the domestic demand for money, gold could flow from the domestic to the foreign economy.

In concluding this discussion it is worthwhile to emphasise the fundamental differences between the results under perfect capital mobility and those under perfect capital immobility. When capital is completely immobile between countries the system is brought into equilibrium by gold movements induced by adjustments of domestic relative to foreign prices. Long-run portfolio equilibrium is brought about through protracted adjustments of the balance of trade. This is the standard classical price–specie–flow mechanism. When capital is perfectly mobile, real equilibrium occurs unaided by gold flows—the interaction of the real sectors in the two countries determines long-run equilibrium interest rates, output, and relative prices. Absolute prices are determined by the world gold stock, together with the institutional arrangements in both countries that determine the amount of money the world gold stock will support. The allocation of the world gold stock between the two countries is accomplished simply by an international exchange of gold for interest-bearing assets. Gold movements are not necessarily accompanied by shifts in the balance of trade.

Imperfect International Mobility of Capital

According to the current literature, capital mobility is imperfect when domestic and foreign interest rates are not always equal. This is imprecise. Capital—i.e. ownership of assets—is clearly perfectly mobile internationally whenever domestic and foreign residents are free to buy and sell assets of the other country at will. But perfect mobility in this sense does not lead to equality of domestic and foreign interest rates. It implies that the interest rates on domestic securities are the same for both countries' residents, as are the interest rates on foreign securities. However, interest rates on domestic securities will not be the same as interest rates on foreign securities unless a substantial number of residents of one or other country regard the two countries' assets as perfect substitutes for each other. Restrictions on the terms at which domestic and foreign assets can be exchanged will make them imperfect substitutes. But the absence of such restrictions does not make them perfect substitutes—risk differences are extremely important.

As long as restrictions on international trade in assets are not comprehensive—i.e. do not prevent capital from moving at all—their fundamental effect is to make domestic and foreign assets less-perfect substitutes. For example, a prohibition of foreign ownership of shares in the domestic banking industry merely diverts domestic capital to the banking industry from somewhere else, and foreigners end up owning the assets that domestic residents would otherwise have owned. The net amount of assets owned by each country's residents is not changed by such a law. Nor is the on-going international flow of capital stopped, though it may be reduced. To stop capital from moving entirely it is necessary to impose restrictions on all capital transactions as might be done, for example, in a comprehensive system of foreign exchange controls.

So in the presence of non-comprehensive restrictions on transactions in capital assets across international boundaries we merely operate under the assumption that domestic and foreign assets are not perfect substitutes in portfolios. This assumption is appropriate anyway because domestic and foreign assets have different degrees of risk.

The essence of the imperfect mobility—or better, imperfect substitutability—case is that domestic and foreign interest rates are not equal. Gold is freely mobile at each point in time between the domestic and foreign economies in exchange for capital assets, with once and for all stock adjustments as well as continuous flow changes being possible as in the perfect mobility case. But equation (4.9) must be modified to incorporate the factors determining the difference between r and r^*.

Starting with the interest parity theorem, we have

$$r = r^* + \phi(.) \tag{4.13}$$

where $\phi(.)$ is the risk factor that determines the difference between domestic and foreign interest rates when the forward discount is zero (as the result of rigidly fixed exchange rates).[20] The question is: What are the arguments in the function $\phi(.)$?

To answer, assume the existence of outstanding stocks of the two types of securities, domestic and foreign. These stocks must at all times be willingly held by world wealth owners—the prices of the two assets, and their interest rates, will adjust until this is the case. The question then is: what determines the willingness of world residents to hold domestic as compared to foreign assets? Think of the factors that would cause the relative demands for the two assets to shift.

Suppose for example, that there is a miraculous one-shot transfer of gold from the foreign to the domestic economy in a situation where the international distribution of gold is initially in equilibrium. Domestic residents find themselves with excess money holdings and will try to exchange money for non-monetary assets. Foreigners will experience a deficiency of money holdings and will try to sell non-monetary assets to replenish their money stock. Gold will thus flow from the domestic to the foreign economy. Since domestic residents hold the major part of their non-monetary wealth in domestic assets, and foreigners hold the major part of their's in foreign assets, domestic residents will want to purchase a greater ratio of domestic/foreign assets than foreigners will want to sell, and the interest rate on domestic assets will fall relative to the foreign interest rate (at the initial levels of domestic and foreign outputs and prices).

The same result will occur if there is an international shift of gold resulting from changes in the demand for money. For example, suppose that there is an increase in γ, the ratio of money to gold in the domestic economy. The resulting excess supply of money in domestic hands will lead to a purchase of domestic and foreign assets by domestic residents from foreigners. Gold will flow out and domestic interest rates will fall relative to foreign rates, just as occurred when the international distribution of gold stock equilibrium was exogenously disturbed. Similarly, suppose that as a result of developments in the real sector of the economy the domestic price level increases. This will increase the nominal value of transactions and hence the domestic demand for nominal money balances, which will in turn cause a sale of domestic and foreign assets by domestic residents to foreigners and an inflow of gold. The domestic interest rate will rise relative to the foreign rate.

It is evident from the above discussion that one argument in the function $\phi(.)$ is the cumulative stock of gold transferred between the two economies. In the present context where the world stock of gold is constant, this can be represented simply by the domestic gold stock, *GS*—any change in that stock represents an international transfer of gold.[21]

Since it is customary to view the interest rate consistent with asset equilibrium as dependent on wealth or income, the income variables obviously must appear as determinants of the domestic/foreign interest differential. There are two questions: first, do world interest rates rise as world wealth and income grow, holding $\overline{GS}$ constant? And second, do domestic interest rates rise more or less than foreign rates under these circumstances?

The first question can be answered affirmatively by noting that from the demand functions for money, (4.1) and (4.2), a rise in income requires that interest rates rise if the money stock is held constant—otherwise the demands for money would not equal the supplies in the two countries. The second question is more difficult because it concerns the effect of income changes on the demands of world residents for domestic relative to foreign non-monetary assets. Since both types of asset are presumably held by each country's residents, both interest rates are part of the opportunity cost of holding money. The demand for money functions must therefore be rewritten.

$$GS = \frac{P \cdot L(r, r^*, Y)}{\gamma} \tag{4.1'}$$

and

$$GS^* = \frac{P^* \cdot L^*(r, r^*, Y^*)}{\gamma^*} \tag{4.2'}$$

We know that under conventional assumptions r and r^* must rise as Y and Y^* increase. What we do not know from (4.1') and (4.2') is whether r will rise by more than r^* or less. The purpose of the function $\phi(.)$ is to provide this information, so obviously Y and Y^* belong as arguments in it. The usually stated reason why a rise in income increases interest rates is the tendency of the private sector to try to convert assets into money—the wealth or income elasticity of demand for money is positive. Since each country's residents hold the largest part of their non-monetary wealth in local assets, one would expect that a rise in domestic income would create a bigger excess supply of domestic rather than foreign assets, and cause r to rise by more than r^* holding the international distribution of gold constant. By a similar argument, a rise in foreign income would increase r^* by more than r. Thus Y enters $\phi(.)$ with a positive partial derivative and Y^* enters with a negative one.

Equation (4.13) can now be rewritten

$$r = r^* + \phi(GS, Y, Y^*) \tag{4.13'}$$

where $\phi_{GS} > 0$, $\phi_Y > 0$ and $\phi_{Y^*} < 0$. This equation, together with (4.8), (4.1') and (4.2') solve for r, r^*, GS^*, and GS, given γ, γ^*, P, P^*, Y, and Y^*. The reduced form equations are

$$r = r \overset{(-)}{(\ \gamma} \overset{(-)}{,\ \gamma^*} \overset{(+)}{,\ P} \overset{(+)}{,\ P^*} \overset{(+)}{,\ Y} \overset{(+)}{,\ Y^*)} \qquad (4.14)$$

$$r^* = r^* \overset{(-)}{(\ \gamma} \overset{(-)}{,\ \gamma^*} \overset{(+)}{,\ P} \overset{(+)}{,\ P^*} \overset{(+)}{,\ Y} \overset{(+)}{,\ Y^*)} \qquad (4.15)$$

$$GS = G \overset{(-)}{(\ \gamma} \overset{(+)}{,\ \gamma^*} \overset{(+)}{,\ P} \overset{(-)}{,\ P^*} \overset{(+)}{,\ Y} \overset{(-)}{,\ Y^*)} \qquad (4.16)$$

The world gold stock $\overline{GS}$ is constant and incorporated into the forms of the functions. A change in GS involves an equal and opposite change in GS^*. The signs over the arguments in the functions are the expected signs of the partial derivatives—these signs can easily be established intuitively.

An increase in γ raises the supply of money in the domestic economy and causes gold to flow out and world interest rates to fall as domestic residents convert part of these increased money holdings into non-monetary assets by exchanging with foreigners. The domestic interest rate will tend to fall relative to the foreign rate. An increase in P increases the demand for nominal money balances, leading to a flow of gold into the domestic economy from abroad and a rise in world interest rates. Again, domestic rates will tend to rise relative to foreign rates. A rise in Y increases the domestic and foreign demands for money. The effect on the domestic demand is likely to be greater, so gold will flow in. World interest rates will rise with the increase in the domestic rate again being greater because domestic residents hold a bigger fraction of their wealth in domestic securities than foreigners do. Increases in γ^*, P^* and Y^* have symmetrical effects to those of γ, P, and Y.

Equations (4.14), (4.15) and (4.16) now solve simultaneously with (4.3) and (4.4) to obtain r, r^*, GS, and either P and P^*, or Y and Y^*, depending on whether classical or Keynesian price flexibility conditions are imposed. The relevant exogenous variables are γ, γ^*, GX and GX^*. It should be noted that the net capital flow arises out of this solution—it represents the difference between saving and investment in each country—and does not bear any functional relationship to the differential between domestic and foreign interest rates. The absence of a 'response' of capital flows to interest rate differentials is a consequence of the portfolio equilibrium approach to the asset sector and represents a point of departure from many conventional treatments. A fuller exposition of the fallacy involved in treating capital flows as dependent on interest rate differentials is presented in Appendix II.

The comparative statics effects of changes in the exogenous variables are pretty much what one would expect and are not worth elaborating here. An increase in the money multipliers in either country leads to increases in output or prices in both countries with gold flowing out of the economy whose monetary system is economising on it. A fiscal or other real expansion in one country causes gold to flow into that country and increases output and prices in both countries. The only essential difference between these results and those under perfect capital mobility is that here domestic and foreign interest rates are not necessarily equal.

The very important conclusion that emerges from this analysis— indeed, it is the main reason for developing the imperfect capital mobility model—is that international gold movements are portfolio adjustments, as in the perfect capital mobility case, and are not brought about through a mechanism of relative price adjustments. The classical price–specie–flow mechanism thus applies *only* to the case where there is no international capital mobility at all. When capital is mobile, however imperfectly, gold is transferred simply by exchange for non-monetary assets. An adjustment of the trade balance brought about by changes in the domestic relative to foreign price level is neither necessary nor sufficient to transmit gold from deficit to surplus countries.

Mathematical Notes

1.   The short-run results are obtained by differentiating (4.1) to (4.4) holding Y and Y^* constant, and setting $dGS^* = -dGS$ and $d\gamma^* = dGS^* = 0$. This yields

$$dGS = \frac{L(.)}{\gamma} dP + \frac{L_r}{\gamma} dr - \frac{L(.)}{\gamma} \frac{d\gamma}{\gamma} \tag{4.1'}$$

$$dGS = \frac{-L^*(.)}{\gamma^*} dP^* - \frac{L_r^*}{\gamma^*} dr^* \tag{4.2'}$$

$$0 = (C_r + I_r) dr + dGX + B_{TR}(dP - dP^*) \tag{4.3'}$$

$$0 = (C_r^* + I_r^*)dr^* - B_{TR}(dP - dP^*) \tag{4.4'}$$

where $(C_r + I_r) < 0$, $(C_r^* + I_r^*) < 0$, $L_r < 0$, $L_r^* < 0$, and $B_{TR} = \partial B_T/\partial P/P < 0$. The results are further simplified by choosing the units of output so that P and P^* are initially equal to unity, and assuming that $B_T(.)$ is initially zero.

These four equations solve simultaneously to yield the price level equations

$$dP =$$
$$\left(\frac{\gamma(C_r+I_r)L^*(.)(C_r^*+I_r^*)-B_{TR}[\gamma(C_r+I_r)L_r^*-\gamma^*(C_r^*+I_r^*)L_r]}{DD^*-L_rL_r^*(B_{TR})^2} \right) dGS$$

$$+ \frac{D^*L_r}{DD^*-L_rL_r^*(B_{TR})^2}dGX + \frac{D^*L(.)(C_r+I_r)}{DD^*-L_rL_r^*(B_{TR})^2}\frac{d\gamma}{\gamma} \qquad (\text{M4.1})$$

$$dP^* =$$

$$-\left(\frac{\gamma^*(C_r^*+I_r^*)L(.)(C_r+I_r)-B_{TR}[\gamma^*(C_r^*+I_r^*)L_r-\gamma(C_r+I_r)L_r^*]}{DD^*-L_rL_r^*(B_{TR})^2} \right) dGS$$

$$- \frac{L_rL_r^*B_{TR}}{DD^*-L_r^*L_r(B_{TR})^2}dGX - \frac{L_r^*B_{TR}(.)L(.)(C_r+I_r)}{DD^*-L_r^*L_r(B_{TR})^2}\frac{d\gamma}{\gamma} \qquad (\text{M4.2})$$

where

$$D = L(.)(C_r+I_r) - L_rB_{TR} < 0$$

and

$$D^* = L^*(.)(C_r^*+I_r^*) - L_r^*B_{TR} < 0$$

It can easily be shown that $DD^* - L_rL_r^*(B_{TR})^2$ is positive. Moreover, if the interest elasticities of consumption, investment, and the demand for money are the same in the two countries, and the ratios of money to income and money to gold are also the same, $\gamma(C_r + I_r)L_r^* - \gamma^*(C_r^* + I_r^*)L_r = 0$. Thus, the effect of GS on P is positive and the effect of GS on P^* is negative as long as the countries are not too different in basic structure. It is also easily seen that rises in γ and GX raise the price levels in both countries.

Rearrangement of (4.1') and (4.2') yields

$$dr = \frac{\gamma}{L_r} dGS - \frac{L(.)}{L_r} dP + \frac{L(.)}{L_r} d\gamma \qquad (\text{M4.3})$$

$$dr^* = - \frac{\gamma^*}{L_r^*} dGS - \frac{L^*(.)}{L_r^*} dP^* \qquad (\text{M4.4})$$

Since rises in γ and GX increase P and P^* from equations (M4.1) and (M4.2) they also increase r and r^* in (M4.3) and (M4.4) because the coefficients of dp, $d\gamma$, and dP^* in these equations are positive. An increase in GS lowers r directly in (M4.3), but increases it indirectly via its positive effect on P. And it lowers r^* directly in (M4.4), but increases it indirectly via its negative effect on P^*. The question is whether the net effects on r and r^* are negative and positive respectively.

When we simplify matters by assuming that the structures of the two economies are the same, the coefficient of *GS* obtained by substitution of (M4.1) into (M4.3) equals

$$\frac{\gamma}{L_r}\left(1 - \frac{L(.)(C_r + I_r)L^*(.)(C_r^* + I_r^*)}{DD^* - L_r L_r^*(B_{TR})^2}\right)$$

which can be expanded to yield

$$-\frac{\gamma}{L_r}\left(\frac{L(.)(C_r+I_r)L_r^*B_{TR}+L^*(.)(C_r^*+I_r^*)L_rB_{TR}}{DD^*-L_rL_r^*(B_{TR})^2}\right)$$

which is clearly negative. A rise in *GS* therefore reduces *r*. Substituting (M4.2) into (M4.4) and expanding, we can similarly show that a rise in *GS* raises r^*.

The short-run effect on the balance of payments can be obtained by substituting (M4.1) and (M4.2) into the derivative of (4.5). The latter equals

$$d\left(\frac{dGS}{dt}\right)= B_{TR}(dP-dP^*) \tag{M4.5}$$

Since an increase in *GS* causes *P* to rise and P^* to fall it necessarily deteriorates the trade balance and causes gold to flow out of the unstarred economy. Since increases in γ and *GX* increase both *P* and P^*, the situation is more complicated. When we subtract (M4.2) from (M4.1) the coefficients of *dGX* and *dγ* become respectively

$$\frac{L_r}{DD^* - L_rL_r^*(B_{TR})^2}[D^* + L_r^*B_{TR}]$$

and

$$\frac{L(.)(C_r + I_r)}{DD^*-L_rL_r^*(B_{TR})^2}[D^* + L_r^*B_{TR}]$$

From the definition of D^*, the term in the square brackets above can be shown to equal $L^*(.)(C_r^* + I_r^*)$. The two coefficients are therefore positive. Increases in *GX* and γ thus increase *P* relative to P^* and deteriorate the balance of trade, causing gold to flow out of the unstarred economy.

In the long run, the outflow of gold will lower *GS* and will thus reverse all the effects of the initial one-shot increase in *GS*. The gold flow will continue until $B_T(Y, Y^*, P/P^*) = 0$. The total differentials of (4.3) and (4.4) under this long-run assumption are

$$0 = (C_r + I_r)dr + dGX \tag{4.3''}$$

$$0 = (C_r^* + I_r^*)dr^* \tag{4.4''}$$

It follows from these equations that dr^* must equal zero and

$$dr = \frac{-1}{C_r + I_r} dGX \qquad (M4.6)$$

Moreover, since $B_T(.)$ is zero and Y and Y^* are fixed at the full-employment level, dP must equal dP^*. From substitution of these results into (4.1′) and (4.2′), it is evident that

$$dP = \frac{L_r/\gamma(C_r + I_r)}{[L(.)/\gamma] + [L^*(.)/\gamma^*]} dGX + \frac{L(.)/\gamma}{[L(.)/\gamma] + [L^*(.)/\gamma^*]} \frac{d\gamma}{\gamma} \quad (M4.7)$$

so GX and γ both affect P (and P^*) positively in the long run. The coefficient of $d\gamma/\gamma$ is the ratio of $M/(M + M^*)$ where M and M^* are the two countries' money supplies. An increase in the ratio of money to gold in one country thus increases the world price level in proportion to the share of that country in the world money supply.

2. As in the zero capital mobility case we assume full employment and choose the units of output so that the price levels in both countries initially equal unity. We also simplify by assuming that the net capital flow between the countries is initially zero. The total differentials of (4.3), (4.4), and (4.12) are (4.3′) and (4.4′) above (with $r^* = r$) and

$$dr = \frac{L(.)}{\gamma[(L_r/\gamma) + (L_r^*/\gamma^*)]} \frac{d\gamma}{\gamma} - \frac{L(.)}{[(L_r/\gamma) + (L_r^*/\gamma^*)]} dP$$

$$- \frac{L^*(.)}{\gamma^*[(L_r/\gamma) + (L_r^*/\gamma^*)]} dP^* + \frac{1}{[(L_r/\gamma) + (L_r^*/\gamma^*)]} d\overline{GS} \quad (4.12')$$

Substitution of (4.12′) into (4.3′) and (4.4′) yields two equations which can be solved simultaneously for dP and dP^*. The solutions are

$$dP = \frac{-\gamma^*}{\Delta\Delta^*\overline{\Delta}} [(C_r + I_r) + (C_r^* + I_r^*)] \left[B_{TR} L(.) \left(\frac{L_r}{\gamma} + \frac{L_r^*}{\gamma^*} \right) \right] \frac{d\gamma}{\gamma}$$

$$- \frac{\gamma\gamma^*}{\Delta\Delta^*\overline{\Delta}} [(C_r + R_r) + (C_r^* + I_r^*)] \left[B_{TR} \left(\frac{L_r}{\gamma} + \frac{L_r^*}{\gamma^*} \right) \right] d\overline{GS}$$

$$+ \frac{\gamma}{\Delta\Delta} \left(\frac{L_r}{\gamma} + \frac{L_r^*}{\gamma^*} \right) dGX \qquad (M4.7')$$

$$dP^* = \frac{-\gamma^*}{\Delta^*\Delta\overline{\Delta}} [(C_r + I_r) + (C_r^* + I_r^*)] \left[B_{TR} L(.) \left(\frac{L_r}{\gamma} + \frac{L_r^*}{\gamma^*} \right) \right] \frac{d\gamma}{\gamma}$$

$$\frac{-\gamma\gamma^*}{\Delta^*\Delta\overline{\Delta}} [(C_r + I_r) + (C_r^* + I_r^*)] \left[B_{TR} \left(\frac{L_r}{\gamma} + \frac{L_r^*}{\gamma^*} \right) \right] d\overline{GS}$$

$$-\frac{\gamma^*}{\Delta^*\Delta\overline{\Delta}}\left[(C_r^*+I_r^*)L(.)+\gamma\left(\frac{L_r}{\gamma}+\frac{L_r^*}{\gamma^*}\right)B_{TR}\right]\left(\frac{L_r}{\gamma}+\frac{L_r^*}{\gamma^*}\right)dGX \quad \text{(M4.8)}$$

where

$$\Delta = (C_r+I_r)L(.)-\gamma B_{TR}\left(\frac{L_r}{\gamma}+\frac{L_r^*}{\gamma^*}\right)<0$$

$$\Delta^* = (C_r^*+I_r^*)L^*(.)-\gamma^* B_{TR}\left(\frac{L_r}{\gamma}+\frac{L_r^*}{\gamma^*}\right)<0$$

$$\overline{\Delta} = \frac{-B_{TR}}{\Delta\Delta^*}\left(\frac{L_r}{\gamma}+\frac{L_r^*}{\gamma^*}\right)[(C_r+I_r)+(C_r^*+I_r^*)][\gamma^*L(.)+\gamma L^*(.)]>0$$

It should be noted that the coefficients of $d\gamma/\gamma$ are positive and equal in (M4.7) and (M4.8), as are the coefficients of $d\overline{GS}$. The coefficient of dGX is positive in (M4.7) and either positive or negative in (M4.8). The ambiguity of the latter sign arises because an increase in GX raises the world interest rate, which reduces aggregate demand in the asterisked country, and at the same time improves that country's balance of trade, which increases its aggregate demand.

The effect on the world interest rate can be obtained by substituting (M4.7) and (M4.8) into (4.4') to yield

$$dr = \frac{B_{TR}}{\Delta\overline{\Delta}\Delta^*}\left(\frac{L_r}{\gamma}+\frac{L_r^*}{\gamma^*}\right)[\gamma L^*(.)+\gamma^* L(.)]dGX \quad \text{(M4.9)}$$

Changes in γ and $\overline{GS}$ have no effect on the world interest rate because they affect P and P^* in proportion. Changes in GX cause the world interest rate to increase.

If we assume that the entire increase in the world gold stock was allocated to the country not asterisked, the gold transfer between the countries will be given by the total differential of (4.2),

$$dGS^* = \frac{L_r^*}{\gamma^*}dr+\frac{L^*(.)}{\gamma^*}dP^*, \quad \text{(M4.10)}$$

after substitution of (M4.8) and (M4.9). Since P^* rises in response to increases in both γ and $\overline{GS}$, while r remains unaffected, the asterisked country's gold stock increases. Gold flows from the non-asterisked to the asterisked country when the former economises on gold or is the beneficiary of an increase in the world gold stock. An increase in GX increases the world interest rate and may increase or decrease the asterisked country's price level. The effect on the gold flow cannot be signed. It depends on whether the effect of the rise in the world interest rate on the asterisked country's demand for money exceeds or falls short of the effect of the possible rise in that country's price level on its demand for money.

Appendix I: The Basic Income–Expenditure Model[22]

The cornerstone of the income–expenditure model is the notion that the aggregate demand for the output of the economy must equal the aggregate supply. We can think of the economy as producing a homogeneous output Y, which can be interpreted in the simplest cases as the level of current income. This output is absorbed by the economy for purposes of consumption, investment, the provision of government services and, in the case where the economy is open to international trade, net exports. The equality of aggregate demand and aggregate supply can be expressed

$$Y^S = Y = Y^D = C + I + GX + B_T \qquad\qquad (A4.1.1)$$

where Y^S and Y^D are aggregate output supplied and demanded, C and I are private-sector consumption and investment, GX is absorption through government current and capital expenditure, and B_T is the balance of trade, defined as exports of goods and services minus imports. The equation $Y = C + I + GX + B_T$ is in one sense an equilibrium condition—the various determinants of consumption, investment, the trade balance, and output supplied, must adjust until what the aggregate output producers want to produce equals the amount the community wants to buy. In another sense it is an identity—all output produced must be disposed of somehow, if necessary as the inventory investment component of I.

We can expand (A4.1.1) by incorporating functions determining the various components of aggregate demand. Consumption is generally held to depend on wealth or permanent income, interest rates, the age structure of the population, and taxes. Consumers tend to consume a more or less constant fraction of their permanent income, defined as the amount they can expect to earn with their resources in an average year net of random year-to-year transitory fluctuations. Permanent income tends to be directly related to current income—high levels of current income generally imply that permanent income is also high, though permanent income is less variable than current income.

Higher interest rates imply that the savings resulting from present levels of current income and consumption will yield a higher level of future consumption. This means that wealth and permanent income are higher. It is reasonable to expect that some part of this increase in permanent income will be used to increase current consumption. At the same time, higher interest rates also imply that a marginal sacrifice of current consumption will yield a greater addition to future consumption than otherwise. There will thus be a substitution effect away from current consumption toward future consumption. These two effects of interest rates on consumption work in opposite directions—the net effect may be an increase or decrease.

The age structure of the population affects the fraction of permanent income consumed. People tend to save early in life to educate their children and provide for later retirement. Thus, the larger the fraction of the population that is older the bigger aggregate consumption will tend to be. Tax changes bring about changes in consumption to the extent that they alter the public's actual or perceived wealth and permanent income.

We are not interested here in the finer points of the theory of the consumption function or in questions of government tax and expenditure policy—our concern is with the basic structure of world macroeconomic equilibrium. It is thus convenient to treat consumption simply as a function of current income and the interest rate—$C(r, Y)$.

The level of investment too can be expressed as a function of current output and the rate of interest—$I(r, Y)$. At each point in time, all potential investment projects in the economy can be ranked according to the rate of return they yield. This ranking is shown by the curve II in Figure 4.1.1.[23] As we move down the curve, progressively lower-yielding projects are added to aggregate investment. A level of investment I_m exhausts all projects with a positive yield. Those projects yielding a return above the market rate of interest will be undertaken—at interest rate r_0 the level of aggregate investment will thus be I_0. As the market interest rate falls additional, lower-return projects will be undertaken and aggregate investment will increase.

The level of aggregate output affects investment because in the short run an expansion of output is accompanied by an increase in employment, with the capital stock in the economy constant. This increase in the labour/capital ratio leads to an increase in the marginal product of capital which increases the yield from all investment projects. The curve II thus shifts upward and the level of aggregate investment increases at each rate of interest. Output thus affects investment positively and the interest rate affects it negatively.

Government demand for goods and services is established exogenously by the authorities. In sophisticated models, the analysis of changes in GX must take account of whether the government is adding to the nation's capital stock or merely providing current services. However, we adopt a simplistic view because we are not interested in the finer points of government expenditure policy. Changes in GX have the same effect on the model as any exogenous

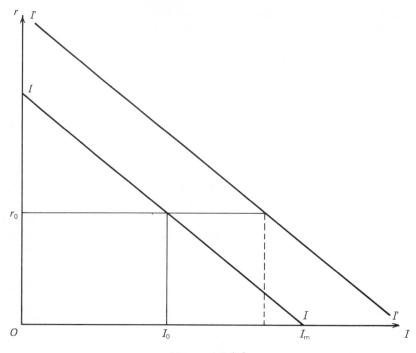

Figure A4.1.1

shift in the aggregate demand for domestic output—the variable should thus be broadly interpreted as a real sector shift variable.

Exports are directly related to the level of income abroad and imports to the level of income at home. A rise in domestic income thus deteriorates the balance of trade, while a rise in foreign income improves it. Exports and imports are also affected by the relative price of domestic in terms of foreign goods, denoted by $P/\pi P^*$, where P and P^* are the prices of domestic and foreign output and π is the domestic currency price of foreign currency. An increase in $P/\pi P^*$ switches expenditure away from domestic and toward foreign goods, increasing imports and reducing exports and thereby deteriorating the balance of trade. Similarly, a fall in $P/\pi P^*$ improves B_T. The balance of trade can thus be formally expressed as $B_T(Y, Y^*, P/\pi P^*)$.

Upon substitution of these behavioural relations, (A4.1.1) becomes

$$Y^S = Y = Y^D = C(r, Y) + I(r, Y) + GX + B_T(Y, Y^*, P/\pi P^*) \quad \text{(A4.1.2)}$$

The terms on the right can be formally consolidated to express domestic aggregate demand as the function

$$Y^D = E(r, GX, Y^*, P/\pi P^*) \tag{A4.1.3}$$

where the signs of the partial derivatives are $E_r < 0$, $E_{GX} > 0$, $E_{Y^*} > 0$ and $E_{P/\pi P^*} < 0$. The negative sign of E_r implies that C_r is either negative or insufficiently positive to make $(C_r + I_r)$ positive. This is always assumed to be the case in the literature. We simplify matters throughout this book by arbitrarily assuming that $C_r < 0$.

The analysis of aggregate supply must now be developed further. What are the determinants of the level of output supplied? One extreme case—the classical full-employment case—postulates that output supplied is exogenously determined at a level dictated by full employment of the economy's resources. Aggregate demand must be brought into line with aggregate supply by adjustments in wages and prices. Another extreme case—the Keynesian case—postulates that wages and prices are sticky and never adjust to demand and supply changes in the length of run relevant for our analysis. In this case, aggregate supply is perfectly elastic at a fixed price level. Aggregate output simply adjusts to whatever level is required to satisfy the aggregate demand for it. The classical case can be imposed by specifying $Y = Y_f$ and the Keynesian case by imposing the constraint $P = P_f$.

Before proceeding further we should inquire why wages and prices would not adjust immediately if people are wealth maximisers. Does a failure of wages and prices to respond instantaneously to supply and demand shifts falsify fundamental propositions of economics about how participants in the economy behave? In answering we should first note that rigidity is usually ascribed to wages rather than prices— prices fail to move primarily because wages and costs are sticky. Whatever the level of competition in product markets, profit maximising behaviour on the part of firms requires that prices be adjusted at least partially in response to changes in costs. It is hard to believe that there is much rigidity of prices independently of rigidity of costs in the absence of an increase in the extent of market imperfection. In addition, there is little reason to believe that those costs other than labour would be rigid—wealth maximising behaviour on the part of a resource owner would seem to dictate that he cut price rather than leave the resource unemployed.

But why would labour be different from any other resource? If workers have a choice of cutting wages and earning less or maintaining wages and earning nothing, why would they not reduce wages? Two reasons have been suggested.[24] First, it has been argued that firms make an implicit contract with their workers under which they guarantee stable wages to established and proven senior workers at the expense of variable employment for junior, unproven workers. They can obtain better workers at lower lifetime wage profiles by guaranteeing this security because workers are willing to pay a price for it. This means that when demand falls firms lay off workers rather than cut wages, and when demand rises they hire more workers rather than increase wages.

Second, it has been noted that labour is not a homogeneous commodity, so an unemployed worker cannot be certain how long it will take to find a job at any given reservation wage. A lower asking wage will result in a shorter waiting time but will also lead to lower earnings when a job is found. An unemployed worker must choose a reservation wage that will maximise utility with respect to the trade-off between a higher wage and a longer waiting time. For both the above reasons, positive unemployment will exist even in good times.

The problem is that the reservation wages of unemployed workers, and the wages offered and agreed to by firms, will depend on their expectations as to what the equilibrium wage is. If everyone knows that equilibrium wages in the economy are rising, wage offers and reservation wages will rise accordingly and layoffs and waiting times will remain at their equilibrium levels. But if equilibrium wages in the economy are rising and workers and firms do not perceive this, the level of wages will fall below equilibrium—firms will employ more workers than they anticipated, workers will find jobs more quickly than they expected, and unemployment rates will be below normal. By the same token, if aggregate demand falls and the equilibrium wage declines without workers and firms realising what has happened, wages will be above equilibrium levels. Firms will hire fewer workers than normal and the unemployed will find themselves waiting longer than expected to find jobs.

As time passes, above or below normal unemployment levels will provide information to workers and firms about the true state of economic conditions. Wage offers and reservation wages will then adjust to levels consistent with normal unemployment rates and long-run labour-market equilibrium.

These general principles of price adjustment can be expressed more formally in terms of the aggregate supply equation

$$Y^S = Y_f + \emptyset(P - P^e) \tag{A4.1.4}$$

where P^e is the expected or anticipated level of prices. If expectations are rational—that is, if economic agents use all information available to them at the time an expectation is formed—the expected price level will be that which equates aggregate supply with expected aggregate demand at normal levels of employment. A fully anticipated increase in aggregate demand will lead to an increase in the price level expected by workers and firms and cause them to raise wages immediately to their new anticipated equilibrium level. As wage increases are passed on into prices, actual and expected prices will rise in proportion, with output remaining at the full employment level. An increase in aggregate demand that is not anticipated by workers and firms will not lead to any change in P^e. As firms hire more labour and workers find jobs more quickly than they anticipated output rises above the full (or normal) employment level. Actual prices rise for two reasons: first, as labour employed increases with the capital stock constant, diminishing returns set in and costs rise. These get passed on in the form of higher prices. Second, as pressure appears in the labour market, wages in some areas of the economy will increase immediately. These wage increases also get passed on into prices. A rise in the actual above the expected price level is thus accompanied by an increase in output and employment above normal. By the same argument, an unanticipated decline in aggregate demand will lead to a decline in actual relative to expected prices, and a decline in output and employment.

Even though market participants use all available information in forming expectations, their anticipations may be wrong. But the actual change in aggregate demand can still be broken down into anticipated and unanticipated components—the error in prediction merely appears as the unanticipated part of the aggregate demand shift.

When all aggregate demand changes are fully—i.e. correctly—anticipated, P always equals P^e and we get the classical case with $Y = Y_f$. When all changes in aggregate demand are unanticipated we get the Keynesian case. The price level becomes a linear function of Y, as can be seen by rearranging (A4.1.3) as follows

$$P = \frac{1}{\emptyset}(Y^S - Y_f) = P^e \qquad (A4.1.3')$$

The crude case where $P = P_f$ results from an assumption that $\emptyset \to \infty$ — namely, that an expansion of Y can occur with an insignificant increase in costs and prices. This violates the notion of diminishing returns to labour on the economy's fixed capital stock and can therefore be rationalised only as a convenient approximation. Workers and firms will always set wages in this case to yield an actual price level equal to the expected one—thus, $P = P^e = P_f$.

In this study we are interested in the basic structure of world monetary equilibrium and not the dynamic path to equilibrium. Accordingly it is convenient to restrict ourselves to the two extreme

cases, classical and Keynesian. A full analysis of the true path of
output, prices, etc. in response to policy changes requires detailed
incorporation of dynamic elements. This would utilise (A4.1.4) along
with some theory of the formation of expectations about the level of
aggregate demand.

The condition of real goods-market equilibrium, given by the
equality of Y with Y^D in (A4.1.3), can be presented as the curve IS in
Figure 4.1.2. This curve gives the combinations of r and Y for which
aggregate demand would equal aggregate supply. It is downward
sloping because a fall in r leads to an expansion of consumption and
investment (as can be seen from (A4.1.2)) which expands aggregate
demand and the level of output which will satisfy that demand. An
increase in government expenditure or an exogenous increase in
consumption or investment shifts the IS curve to the right. The curve
also shifts to the right on account of an increase in foreign output Y^*, or
a decline in the relative price of domestic goods in world markets
$P/\pi P^*$, both of which improve the balance of trade and increase
domestic spending. When classical wage and price flexibility rules,

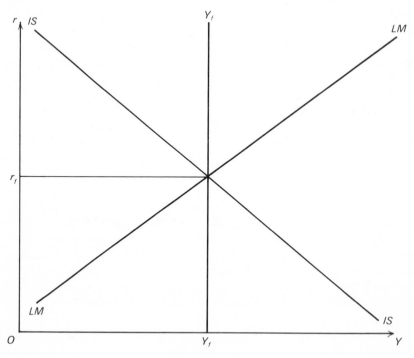

Figure A4.1.2

output cannot adjust passively to changes in aggregate demand. A full employment constraint on aggregate supply is imposed—namely $Y = Y_f$. This appears in Figure 4.1.2 as the vertical line Y_f. Given the level of aggregate demand specified by IS, this constraint implies a full employment interest rate r_f.

Full equilibrium of the economy also implies that the asset markets be in equilibrium—that wealth owners be willing to hold the existing stocks of all assets. Assets can be classified into three broad categories: human capital, physical capital, and money. Since human capital is always held by the person in whom it is embodied and cannot be traded, the supply of it always equals the demand regardless of what else is going on in the economy. This category of assets therefore need not concern us further. Physical capital can be owned either directly or indirectly via bonds or equity shares. Bonds can also represent indirect claims on human capital—much government debt, for example, represents a claim on the taxing power of the state and thereby an indirect claim on labour earnings. It is convenient for us to simplify matters by representing all tradeable non-monetary assets by a single bond-equity bearing real interest at the rate r and/or nominal interest at the rate i. The difference between the real and nominal interest rates is, of course, the expected rate of inflation—that is, $i = r + Ep$, where Ep is the expected inflation rate. Holders of assets having fixed nominal coupon yield and value at maturity must be compensated for the expected decline in their real value due to inflation. Additional interest equal to the expected rate of inflation will compensate for this decline.

The third type of asset, money, performs the role of making exchange. Since money does not bear interest, the cost of holding it equals the real interest that could have been earned had bonds or equities been held plus compensation for the decline in the real value of money due to inflation. The cost of holding money thus equals the nominal rate of interest. The greater the level of output in the economy, the larger the volume of transactions and the greater the demand for money.

Under the above assumptions, asset equilibrium can be presented in terms of a single equation. Wealth owners can hold their non-human wealth in only two forms—bond-equities and money. If the quantity of money demanded equals the quantity supplied, then there must also be zero excess demand for non-monetary assets. Equilibrium in the market for money,

$$\frac{M}{P} = L(i, Y) \tag{A4.1.5}$$

is thus sufficient to describe asset equilibrium in general. M is the nominal money stock, M/P is the real money stock (i.e. the quantity of money measured in terms of the amount of output it will command), and $L(.)$ is the demand function for real money balances.[25] The nominal interest rate can be eliminated from (A4.1.5) by substituting $i = r + Ep$. Since an increase in income increases the number of transactions and hence the demand for money, $L_y > 0$. A rise in the nominal rate of interest increases the cost of holding money and reduces the quantity demanded, so $L_i < 0$.

Asset equilibrium is represented on Figure 4.1.2 as the LM curve, which gives the combinations of r and Y for which the demand for real money balances equals the supply. It is positively sloped because a rise in Y increases the real quantity of money demanded above the quantity supplied, requiring an increase in the real interest rate at any given expected rate of inflation to choke off this excess demand. An increase in the money supply requires a fall in the rate of interest at each level of output to get the public to hold it—the LM curve thus shifts to the right. A rise in the price level reduces the real money supply and shifts LM to the left. An increase in Ep reduces the quantity of money demanded at each level of the real interest rate— LM shifts to the right because a lower real interest rate is now required at each level of Y to get the public to hold the existing stock of money.

Equilibrium of the system occurs at the intersection of the IS and LM curves. In the crude Keynesian case where the price level is fixed, this equilibrium can occur at a level of income above or below Y_f. If $Y > Y_f$ eventual upward pressure on prices will arise. As prices increase the LM curve will shift to the left, leading to a rise in r and a fall in Y. This process will continue until $Y = Y_f$. If $Y < Y_f$ there will ultimately be downward pressure on prices which will shift LM to the right until $Y = Y_f$. In the classical full-employment case, therefore, equilibrium will occur at the intersection of IS and the vertical Y_f line. The price level will adjust to drive LM through this intersection.

When there is no foreign sector and $B_T(.)$ therefore does not appear in the income–expenditure equation (4.1.2), the two equations representing the IS and LM curves plus a constraint that either $P = P_f$ or $Y = Y_f$ give the full macroeconomic equilibrium of the economy. In an open economy where $B_T(.)$ is not necessarily zero, additional specifications must be made concerning capital flows and the balance of payments. These are the subject of the text of Chapters 4, 6, and 8 and it would be redundant to pursue them here. My purpose has been simply to provide the reader with the necessary background to grasp these open economy modifications as they are presented.

Appendix II: Capital Flows and Interest-Rate Differentials

The modelling of international capital movements as a response to differentials between domestic and foreign interest rates has a long tradition in the literature. Yet it is a classic example of a fallacy of composition—the assertion that what is true of a part is, on that account alone, necessarily true of the whole.[26]

The notion that capital movements respond to interest-rate differentials is an improper generalisation of the well-known fact that individuals will shift their portfolios towards securities whose interest rates increase and away from securities whose interest rates decline. As a statement about individual behaviour this is well founded in economic theory. But the same relationship does not apply to all individuals taken together.

Consider a two-country world in which for some accidental reason interest rates in one country rise and those in the other fall. Standard portfolio theory tells us that all individuals in both countries will try to shift their portfolios away from the securities of the country whose interest rates have fallen towards those of the country whose interest rates have risen. Capital cannot flow from the former country to the latter, however, because everyone wants to sell the former country's assets but no one wants to buy, and everyone is trying to buy the latter country's assets while no one wants to sell. Asset prices will be bid down in the country whose interest rate is low and up in the country whose interest rate is high. Interest rates will thus be brought back together until the differential is whatever it was before the accidental disturbance to interest rates occurred. Thus, while individual wealth owners by themselves respond to interest rate changes by shifting portfolios, interest rates are determined by the portfolio decisions of wealth holders in the aggregate. It therefore makes no sense to think of aggregate capital movements as a response to interest rate changes.

The correct way to model capital flows is as the difference between saving and investment. For the world as a whole, income and interest rates always adjust to drive aggregate saving into equality with aggregate investment. Thus,

$$S + S^* = I + I^* \tag{A4.2.1}$$

which implies that

$$S - I = I^* - S^* \tag{A4.2.2}$$

The net capital outflow of the domestic (non-asterisked) country equals the excess of its saving over its investment which in turn equals the excess of investment over saving and the net capital inflow of the foreign economy. Investment depends on world interest rates and the potentialities for future profit in the two economies, while saving (which equals income minus consumption) depends on the levels of income and world interest rates. Interest rates differ in the two economies because domestic and foreign securities are not equally attractive.[27] A shift in relative interest rates would not necessarily result in a change in saving in either country because the net advantage of future relative to present consumption is not necessarily affected— the interest rate changes merely compensate for the perceived changes in the quality of the assets. Only an increase in the general level of world interest rates unaccompanied by an equivalent increase in risk would necessarily cause a substitution of future for present consumption.

On the investment side, higher domestic relative to foreign interest rates will cause a shift of world investment away from the domestic economy—higher interest rates reflect the fact that domestic assets are less attractive and sell at lower prices. The decline in investment accompanied by an unchanged level of saving would make the net capital inflow smaller in response to a rise in domestic interest rates, not larger as the capital flow–interest differential argument would imply.

This argument assumes that the shift in interest-rate differentials is caused by a change in the perceived attractiveness of domestic compared to foreign assets at given levels of domestic and foreign investment. Alternatively, in a longer-run growth context, the shift in interest rate differentials could be caused by a shift in profit opportunities and investment prospects from the foreign to the domestic economy. Suppose, for example, that vast new investment opportunities opened up in the domestic economy. These would be reflected in an increased supply of new securities coming on the market. When the supply of assets having particular characteristics expands, it is reasonable to suppose that the prices of these assets will have to fall to get world investors to hold them. Thus, if the new domestic investment opportunities absorb a significant amount of the world's flow of saving and investment they would lead to a relative rise in domestic interest rates. The higher domestic interest rates would be associated with a greater net capital inflow as conventional arguments imply. But this result applies to long-run capital movements arising from differential domestic and foreign growth prospects and not to short-run movements resulting from a scarcity of money (gold) in one part of the world.

A scarcity of money in, say, the domestic economy would lead to a tightness in world capital markets and a rise in world interest rates as wealth owners try to sell assets to acquire money. Since domestic residents in the aggregate can increase their money holdings by selling assets to foreigners in return for gold, there will be a capital inflow. But this will be a one-shot portfolio adjustment and not a steady-state flow. And the inflow of capital will be exactly offset by the outflow of gold so no net wealth transfer will occur. The ratio of domestic to foreign assets domestic residents are trying to sell will exceed the ratio of domestic to foreign assets held by foreigners (since the portfolio mix held by each country's residents will be skewed towards home assets) so domestic interest rates will tend to rise relative to foreign rates to maintain equlibrium in the market for domestic securities. A rise in domestic interest rates will thus be associated with an inward movement of capital as conventional wisdom would suggest. But the capital movement and the interest rate differential occur simultaneously as part of an overall portfolio adjustment—the capital movement does not 'respond' to the change in domestic relative to foreign interest rates. And the capital movements is a one-shot shift of ownership and not an increased continuous steady-state flow—it is therefore in no way connected to the difference between saving and investment. Moreover, in a fundamental sense capital is really not moving at all because the sale of assets is exactly offset by a purchase of gold—the composition of national wealth changes, but not its level.

Notes

1 The theory developed here is an extension of the standard income expenditure (IS–LM) model with which most readers will be familiar. Those who are not can refer to Appendix I following this chapter for a brief review of the substance of that model.

2 Some non-monetary assets, in particular human capital, are not tradeable because they are embodied in the persons owning them. We can ignore them here without damage to our results.

3 It is useful to think of the economy as subject to two constraints—a stock constraint and a flow constraint. The stock constraint is that the existing stock of wealth must be held in the form of either non-monetary assets or money. The flow constraint is that the existing flow of income from wealth must be either consumed or added to the stock of wealth.

4 The real quantity of money is the amount of money measured in terms of the amount of some bundle of goods the money can buy. This bundle is the set of commodities used to construct the price index, P.

5 Actually, the appropriate price level for calculating the real money stock is the price index of goods absorbed by the economy rather than produced

by it. This price index would contain the price level of foreign goods produced weighted by the share of imports in total absorption. We ignore this refinement here, however, because it complicates the analysis without altering the basic conclusions.

6 The nominal interest rate includes a compensation for anticipated inflation and is usually expressed

$$i = r + Ep$$

where i is the nominal interest rate and Ep is the expected rate of price inflation. The holder of a bond has to be paid the amount Ep to compensate him for the fact that the real value of the bond declines every year by the rate of inflation. To this must be added the rate of return, r, which compensates the bond holder for the real (inflation compensated) return he could earn on alternative investments. Since the value of money declines with inflation, the opportunity cost of holding money is i rather than r.

7 This conversion is based on the fact that

$$P \cdot B_T = -\pi \cdot P^* \cdot B_T^*$$

where π is the domestic currency price of foreign currency and is assumed equal to unity. This equation says that a domestic trade-balance surplus must equal the foreign trade-balance deficit when both are measured in the same currency units.

8 The effect of the interest rate on consumption is generally regarded as ambiguous. A higher interest rate induces a substitution of future for present consumption which reduces C. At the same time, it implies that current savings yields a larger future income stream, raising wealth. The higher level of wealth will be spread over both present and future consumption, increasing C. This ambiguity of the overall effect is simply ignored here by assuming the effect on C to be negative. This makes no difference to our results. A positive interest rate effect on consumption would cause us problems only if

$$\frac{\partial C}{\partial r} + \frac{\partial I}{\partial r} > 0$$

but this is always ruled out in macroeconomic models.

9 Expectations-augmented supply curves would take the form

$$Y_t = \hat{Y} + \emptyset(P_t - P_t^e)$$

where $\hat{Y}$ is normal or full employment output and P_t^e is the expected price level. When expectations are rational, the expected price level is the level of prices at which full or normal employment would hold. Anticipated changes in the money supply or other exogenous variables will lead to equal adjustments in both P_t and P_t^e so that output remains at full employment. Unanticipated changes will lead to changes in P_t but not P_t^e and employment will respond positively to movements in the price level.

Keynesian conditions arise, in effect, when all exogenous changes are unanticipated, and classical conditions occur when they are fully anticipated.

10 The balance of trade must be multiplied by P to convert it to nominal terms—the gold flow is measured in domestic currency and thus depends on the difference between exports and imports measured in domestic currency.

11 Hume, David (1969) 'Of the balance of trade', reprinted in Richard N. Cooper (ed.), *International Finance: Selected Readings*, Penguin Books.

12 The analysis that follows in the remainder of this section is presented more rigorously in Mathematical Note 1 at the end of this chapter.

13 It should be noted that excess money holdings in the above analysis are spent entirely on assets and not at all on goods. The reason for this is that a portfolio disequilibrium leads to a change in the interest rate to the point where asset markets are in equilibrium—any excess money holdings are thus eliminated by an instantaneous adjustment of interest rates before goods markets can be directly affected. Goods markets are affected later when the change in the interest rate induces changes in consumption and investment.

14 An increase in the demand for gold in a very small country has a proportionally small percentage effect on the world demand for gold and leads therefore to a trivial effect on the world price level.

15 The analysis that follows would be the same if domestic and foreign interest rates differ by a constant.

16 It is convenient to assume for expositional purposes that government expenditures finance investment only.

17 There is, of course, no reason why savings would not differ from investment permanently. As world technology expands investment opportunities will not grow evenly in all countries. It should therefore be no surprise to find differences between the level of investment in a country and savings generated in that country. There is no reason to assume that a stationary state will eventually be reached.

18 This is necessarily true because the growth rates do not appear in the equations of the model.

19 These are worked out rigorously in Mathematical Note 2 at the end of this chapter.

20 The interest parity theorem states that the domestic interest rate must exceed the foreign interest rate, after an adjustment for risk, by the forward discount on domestic currency in the forward exchange market. If the domestic currency is not expected to devalue or appreciate the forward discount will be zero so interest rates will differ by the risk premium on domestic securities. An elementary discussion of these issues is contained in the Appendix to Chapter 8.

21 The assumption that the world gold stock is constant is important here. The analysis changes in substance, though not in spirit, if on-going production of gold in one or both countries is introduced.

22 For a fuller development of the ideas reviewed below see Laidler, David

W. (1969) *The Demand for Money: Theories and Evidence*, International Textbook Company, pp. 3–20; Bailey, Martin J. (1971) *National Income and the Price Level*, 2nd edn., McGraw Hill, pp. 3–42; Parkin, M. and Bade, R. (1982) *Modern Macroeconomics*, Prentice Hall.

23 The fact that an internal rate of return criterion might lead to a different ranking of projects than a present value rule is ignored here. The basic analytical framework is not affected by this simplification.

24 For an amplification of these arguments and others relevant to the theory of price adjustment see Gordon, Donald F. (1974) 'A classical theory of Keynesian unemployment', *Economic Inquiry*, 12 Dec., pp. 431–459; Gordon, Donald F. and Allan Hynes, J. (1974) 'On the theory of price dynamics' in E. S. Phelps (ed.) *Microeconomic Foundations of Inflation and Employment Theory*, W. W., Norton, pp. 369–393; Friedman, Milton (1968) 'The role of monetary policy', *The American Economic Review*, vol. 58, March, pp. 1–17; Lucas, Robert E. Jr. (1973) 'Some international evidence on output–inflation tradeoffs', *The American Economic Review*, Vol. LXIII, No. 3, pp. 326–334; Phelps, Edmund S. and Taylor, John B. (1977) 'Stabilizing powers of monetary policy under rational expectations', *Journal of Political Economy*, Vol. 85, Feb., pp. 163–190.

25 Ideally the price level used to convert nominal money balances into real balances should be the price index of goods absorbed by the economy. This index would include the price of imports—i.e. the foreign price level—as a component. This refinement is ignored here, however, because it avoids needless complexity without changing our fundamental results.

26 Samuelson, P. A. (1970) *Economics*, 8th edn., McGraw Hill, pp. 11–12.

27 It is well known from the capital-asset pricing model that securities differ in attractiveness because they differ in degree of risk. An asset bears no risk premium, regardless of the variability of its return, if that return is uncorrelated with movements in world economic activity, because the variance in earnings can be diversified away by holding the asset in common with other assets whose returns fluctuate randomly. A risk premium arises because the returns to the asset are correlated with movements in the returns to a diversified collection of all other assets— the market portfolio. This risk cannot be diversified away by holding the asset in common with others. The degree of risk premium will depend on the amplitude of fluctuations in the asset's return, in comparison with the amplitude of fluctuations in the return to the market portfolio. Assets whose returns fluctuate by large amounts in conjunction with world economic activity will bear a larger risk premium than those whose returns fluctuate by a small amount.

5

The Gold Standard:
An Evaluation

This chapter evaluates the gold standard as a system of international monetary organisation. After presenting a brief history of the gold standard we examine the problem of liquidity crises that plagued the system throughout its existence. Then we consider the real resource costs of using gold as money both from the point of view of the world as a whole, and from the perspective of a small country operating in a gold standard world. The existence of fractional gold backing of the money supply raises the possibility of sterilisation—i.e. of not allowing gold movements into and out of the economy to affect the money supply. This problem—the unwillingness of countries to submit to the gold standard discipline—is then examined, followed by an analysis of the reasons why the gold standard broke down. It is suggested that the discipline imposed by the gold standard was the discipline of fixed exchange rates and could not be avoided by attempts at sterilisation when capital was internationally mobile. Indeed, we argue that under capital mobility sterilisation is impossible. The gold standard, therefore, could not have broken down as a result of sterilisation. Rather, we suggest, it broke down because of structural changes in international relative prices. Countries chose to abandon fixed exchange rates rather than let their nominal price levels adjust in response to changes in the real value of their goods relative to foreign goods in world markets. The chapter ends with a discussion of whether the gold standard was a good system.

A Short History of the Gold Standard

Gold was used as money from the earliest of times. Coins of gold, silver, copper and alloys, minted by monarchs and merchants in a variety of places, circulated widely throughout most of the civilised world. The European countries gravitated quite early to bimetallic gold and silver standards in which silver coins circulated in local use and gold was used in international transactions. The smallest gold coins were too valuable for most local transactions. This, combined with seigniorage, and other transactions costs, together with existing market prices for gold in relation to silver, allowed coins in the two metals to exist simultaneously, unimpeded by Gresham's Law.[1] There was also a tendency for gold coins to be traded at exchange rates equal to the value, in terms of silver, of their gold content.

England drifted onto a gold standard in the first half of the eighteenth century when it became profitable to mint gold coin and ship silver abroad. This followed a rather substantial decline in the market price of gold related to silver.[2]

In America, a variety of foreign coins circulated widely before the War of Independence, the most important of these being the Spanish dollar.[3] After independence, a system of bimetallism was established in the USA. The monetary value of gold was set at fifteen times that of silver. Within a few years the market value of silver in terms of gold had fallen relative to its monetary value and there was an incentive to melt down gold coins and export the gold or exchange it for silver to be minted into silver coins. As a result gold coins had all but disappeared from circulation by 1818. Then in 1834 the mint ratio was adjusted to sixteen to one. This made gold more valuable as money relative to silver than in the free market, and there was an incentive to melt down or export silver coins and take gold to the mint. By the onset of the American Civil War, the only silver coins left in circulation were fractional coins containing less silver than their face value.[4] During the Civil War, paper notes called 'greenbacks' were issued by the north to finance its war effort. Being inconvertible, these traded at a discount in terms of gold coins, which continued to circulate. Since the silver in the fractional coinage was worth more in the market than it was in greenbacks (which exchanged for coins at face value) these fractional coins were melted down and disappeared.[5] In 1879 the US resumed convertibility of the dollar into gold at the pre-war ratio. Since free coinage of silver had been abolished in 1873, the country was effectively on a gold standard. This was officially recognised in an Act of Congress in 1900.[6]

The golden age of the gold standard began around 1870. Germany, Holland, and the Scandinavian countries went on it in the early 1870s, Switzerland, Belgium, and France in 1878, Austria in 1892, Japan in 1897, Russia in 1899 and Italy in 1900. Some countries converted to gold from silver or bimetallic standards while others, such as Russia, Austria-Hungary and Italy, went onto gold off inconvertible paper standards. By the turn of the century, the only important country remaining on a silver standard was China.[7]

The gold standard reigned supreme until the outbreak of the First World War. England and the other belligerents allowed the fixed relationship between their currencies and gold to lapse as gold flowed into the US to purchase war goods. When the US entered the war in 1917, gold began to flow in the opposite direction and an embargo was placed on gold exports. The public's right to redeem paper currency in gold was also suspended. The important countries all remained off the gold standard until the 1920s. Then, one by one, they went back on gold—Germany in 1924, England in 1925, France in 1928—until by 1930, the major industrial countries were all back on gold.[8] The resumption of the pre-war parities, especially in Britain, was held responsible by many for the deflationary atmosphere that prevailed in the late 1920s and led into the severe depression of the 1930s.[9]

This new gold standard was somewhat different than the one that existed prior to 1914. Paper currency was, for the most part, redeemable in bullion, not coin, and many countries, rather than redeeming their currencies directly in gold, tied them to other currencies that were redeemable in gold. Under this system, the world stock of gold supported a much larger volume of currency and credit than before. Moreover, there was a distinct unwillingness in a number of countries, particularly the USA, to allow changes in the gold stock to influence the money supply and, hence, employment and prices.

With the onset and deepening of the Great Depression, the international gold standard again fell apart. Britain went off in 1931 and other countries followed until, by the beginning of the Second World War, the only major country still on gold was the USA. In the early 1930s the USA began manipulating the market price of gold, finally setting it at $35 per oz in 1934. (This compared to $20.67 per oz, which had ruled since before the American Civil War.) It should be noted, however, that though the price of gold was fixed, the stock of money in the USA bore essentially no relationship to the country's gold reserves, and domestic residents were not even allowed to hold gold, let alone redeem domestic currency for it.

After the Second World War, the Bretton Woods Agreement established fixed parities of most currencies in terms of the US dollar, and the dollar remained pegged to gold at the parity established in 1934. Gold was an international reserve asset, used to cover the balance-of-payments disequilibria, but no country's money supply was tied to it. This is what Friedman called the pseudo-gold standard—

a system in which gold was supported in price the world over, but had no real monetary function other than settling inter-governmental claims.[10] Since the world price of gold was supported by the US Government's willingness to exchange it for dollars at $35 per oz, and the dollar was the intervention currency for most countries (the one they bought and sold to fix their exchange rates), US dollars were a convenient substitute for gold as an international reserve. As the volume of world trade increased, and with it the demand for reserves, the bulk of reserves came to be held in US dollars. The realisation that there was not enough gold to redeem all holdings of dollar reserves lead to repeated speculation that the dollar would be devalued in terms of gold—that is, that the USA would raise the price of gold above $35 per oz. This resulted in a number of runs against gold leading in 1968 to the abandonment of any official support of the private gold market.[11] A two-tier system was established in which central banks exchanged gold among themselves in return for US dollars at $35 per oz, but gold was not sold to private individuals at that price. All other transactions in gold took place in the private market at a free-market price which turned out to be above $35. By 1971, conversions of dollar liabilities into gold had drastically reduced the US gold stock and gold continued to flow out. Moreover, despite recent upward re-evaluations of a number of countries' currencies in terms of the dollar (and gold) it was clear that official exchange rates were still out of line. These problems were aggravated by the inflationary policies that were followed in the USA in connection with financing the Vietnam war—a level of world inflation was being generated that a number of the European countries were unwilling to accept. On 25 August 1971 the US Government announced that it was no longer willing to buy and sell gold, even from other central banks, though $35 per oz remained the official price. The last remnant of the gold standard thus disappeared. The fixed parities of other currencies in terms of the dollar were adjusted in accordance with the Smithsonian Agreement struck by the ten major industrial countries in December 1971, but these parities, and the widened margins around them in which exchange rates were allowed to fluctuate, proved also to be unworkable and by 1973 all major countries were on floating exchange rates. The official price of gold was raised to $38 per oz, then to $42, and finally in 1976 was abolished altogether.

Was the gold standard a useful international monetary system? What were its strengths and weaknesses? What caused it to break down? We turn now to these questions.

Liquidity Crises in the Gold Standard System

Liquidity crises were a prominent feature of the gold standard years. They result from two facts: first if every deposit and note holder wanted gold instead there would not be enough gold to satisfy all the demand. Second, because note issue is restricted by a requirement of gold backing, there are not enough notes to enable the banking system to convert all deposits into notes on demand. An attempt by the public to convert deposits into notes leads the banking system to try to sell assets and recall loans to obtain the necessary cash. Since the whole system is trying to sell assets, and no one wants to buy, asset prices fall and the market value of banks' assets falls relative to liabilities, making the weaker banks in the system insolvent. The fall in asset prices, of course, implies an increase in market interest rates, especially short-run rates, as the scramble for liquidity raises its price. If the public's desire for cash is persistent, and the central bank does not discount (i.e. purchase) assets from the banking system to make the necessary cash available, the system will have to suspend convertibility of deposits into notes. Two moneys are then in circulation, notes and deposits, with the latter trading at a discount in terms of the former.

The effect of a run on gold by the public is essentially the same. The banking system as a whole tries to sell assets to acquire gold. Asset prices fall (and interest rates rise), impairing the solvency of weaker banks. The central bank can moderate the crises by selling gold to the banking system in return for assets, thereby reducing the ratio of its gold holdings to its note and deposit liabilities to the banking system. If the crisis continues beyond some point the banking system and the central bank are forced to suspend convertibility of notes and deposits into gold and the country is forced off the gold standard.

Although a great many US banks were forced to suspend convertibility of deposits and notes into gold in 1837, and again in 1847 and 1857 (there was no central bank in the USA at that time), the gold standard was maintained continuously from the resumption in 1879 until the First World War. In Britain the gold standard was maintained continuously (that is, the Bank of England maintained convertibility of its notes and deposits into gold) from the end of the Napoleonic Wars in the early nineteenth century until the First World War.[12] The suspension of convertibility of deposits into notes was quite common in the USA, having occurred in 1882, 1893, and 1907.

Suspension of convertibility of deposits into notes is not a problem peculiar to the gold standard. It can arise any time that the note issue of the banking system is restricted. Note issue is restricted under the gold standard because issues beyond some fixed amount must be backed by gold so the quantity of notes is limited by the size of the gold stock. In the absence of a gold standard, note issue is restricted by the central bank—usually, it is the stock of high-powered money that is restricted and note circulation is therefore limited to the stock of base money minus the reserves of the banking system. Thus, a desire of the public to convert deposits into notes can lead to a currency crisis and a suspension even when the monetary system has no gold backing. This in fact occurred in the USA in the early 1930s when, though technically on a gold standard, the country had severed the link between gold and the nominal money supply. The easy cure for this type of financial crisis is deposit insurance—a guarantee by the government that all deposits under a specified maximum in any one bank will be paid in notes in full if the bank has to suspend payment. A less easy cure is a commitment of the central bank to liberally discount securities for the banking system to provide the notes necessary to meet the demands that would arise from a run on the system. The advantage of deposit insurance is that it makes such a run impossible.

There is no defence against a persistent world-wide run on gold in an international gold standard system. There simply is insufficient gold to redeem all liabilities, and once world asset holders get the feeling that convertibility is in jeopardy there are expected profits to be made by shifting assets into gold. And as central bank reserves in the major countries get smaller because of the drain, the probability of suspension and the expected profits from switching to gold get higher.

However, in a world of international capital mobility an individual country, particularly a small one, can protect itself quite easily against a run on gold. By restricting credit creation—that is, reducing the amount of securities discounted or selling securities on the open market—the central bank can reduce the amount of money in private hands below what the public wants to hold. Private residents will tend to re-establish portfolio equilibrium (replenish their money balances) by selling assets abroad, creating a balance of payments surplus which will lead ultimately to an inflow of gold as the domestic currency appreciates above the gold import point. Or, if the exchange rate is being maintained by purchase and sale of foreign currency, the central bank acquires foreign exchange reserves which it can redeem directly in gold. If capital is highly mobile and domestic and foreign assets are good substitutes, this accumulation of gold can occur without much effect on domestic prices and employment. The central bank could acquire gold even more easily by simply selling assets to foreigners in return for it. If the country is small, this is unlikely to have much effect on the rest of the world's gold supply, though if pursued in sufficient volume, the policy could lead to a rise in domestic interest rates (that is, the interest rates world (including domestic) asset holders require to get them to hold domestic securities). Essentially, the central bank of a small country can hold whatever stock of gold it wishes, within reason, without having adverse effects on prices and employment.

If the country is of significant size in relation to the rest of the world, complications arise in that a gold inflow reduces the gold stock abroad sufficiently to create a shortage of gold there. This makes it necessary for foreign central banks to also contract credit. Now foreign as well as domestic residents are trying to re-establish portfolio equilibrium by selling assets and world interest rates are forced up. Ultimately this rise in world interest rates is eliminated by a fall in the price levels in all countries, which increases the real value of the gold stock in terms of goods and eliminates the excess world demand for gold. However, even if the country is quite large—holding, say, 40 per cent of the gold stock—the effect of an increase in domestic gold holdings on its (and the rest of the world's) price level will be relatively modest in relation to the quantity of gold accumulated. The increase in the country's desired gold stock will have an effect only 40 per cent as large as an increase in the entire world's desired gold stock.

The above analysis would seem to explain why the Bank of England, during the gold standard's heyday, operated the British monetary system on a very small gold stock (domestic gold holdings were less than 5 per cent of total monetary liabilities[13]) and maintained its desired gold holdings remarkably easily by occasional adjustments in its discount rate (and presumably also in the volume of paper discounted) without any wrenching effect on domestic economic activity.[14] A key to understanding this phenomenon is the result, derived in Chapter 4 above, that international mobility of capital modifies the standard price-specie flow mechanism to eliminate relative domestic/foreign price level changes as a component of the adjustment process. The world price level will change (all countries' price levels will move together) in response to a significant increase in the world demand for gold emanating from any part of the system, but changes in *relative* price levels do not have to occur for balance of payments adjustments and international gold movements to take place.

The Real Resource Cost of the Gold Standard

Much has been made of the real resource costs of operating a commodity standard. The money stock of most countries ranges between one-quarter and one-half of national income. If world prices are to remain stable, the world money stock must grow at something in the neighbourhood of 2 to 4 per cent per year (the rate of output growth plus (minus) the rate of decline (increase) in the velocity of circulation).[15] Thus, it could easily cost as much as 2 per cent of world income (4 per cent times one-half) to maintain the money stock—a significant cost.

This resource cost can be reduced somewhat by using a fractional gold reserve system in which the gold backing is less than 100 per cent, although the savings will not be as large as one might think. If, instead of using gold exclusively as money, one were to use a system where, say, one dollar of notes and deposits circulates for every dollar of gold, the price level will be twice as high, and the gold stock will still have to grow at 2 to 4 per cent per year (as will notes and deposits). If the stock of gold is the same as with 100 per cent backing, the real resource cost will be the same. But, in general, a somewhat smaller gold stock will suffice, so the equilibrium addition to gold holdings as a fraction of national income will be correspondingly lower.

To see this, start with a given stock of monetary gold and reduce the gold backing from 100 to 50 per cent. The price level will double, reducing the value of gold relative to its cost of production in terms of goods. Gold production will decline and the stock of gold will thus grow at a slower rate than otherwise and the price level will gradually fall until it reaches the point where current gold production just maintains an expansion of the money stock equal to the rate of growth of the demand for money. The growth rate of the stock of gold at this point will be the same as it would have been with 100 per cent backing. But the level of the stock—the base on which the percentage growth is calculated—will be smaller, as will be the percentage of world income devoted to gold production. The use of a fractional system will thus reduce real resource costs in the long-run.

An interesting special case arises where gold can be produced at constant cost in terms of other goods. When the ratio of gold to the money supply is reduced and prices rise, the value of gold falls below its cost of production at all levels of gold output. No new gold will be produced until the price level has fallen to where it was before. At that point the monetary gold stock will have fallen relative to what it otherwise would have been by the reduction in the fraction of gold backing—that is, if we move from 100 to 50 per cent gold backing, the stock of monetary gold, the level of gold production, and the real resource cost of maintaining the gold standard will ultimately also be only half as great.

The real resource saving from moving to fractional gold reserves is also equal to the actual reduction in backing for a small open economy acting independently in a gold standard world. By creating notes and deposits to be used as money in addition to gold, the country's authorities can induce domestic residents to unload money in return for productive assets from abroad. Gold ultimately flows out to pay for these assets. The exchange of gold for assets ceases when the domestic money stock has been reduced to its initial level. But now the money stock is backed only partially by gold. National income increases by the interest earnings on the assets acquired by disposing of part of the nation's gold stock—if gold backing is reduced from 100 to 50 per cent, national income rises by the interest rate times one-half the gold stock.

Of course, as more and more countries reduce the fraction of gold backing, the world price level rises and the gains are reduced. But there is in any case a large short-run increase in government revenues by reducing the gold backing. By reducing the ratio of gold to money from, say, 40 to 30 per cent, the authorities can in effect print an amount of money equal to 25 per cent of the existing money supply. This can be used to acquire goods and services from the public and is equivalent to a tax of 12.5 per cent of national income when, say, the ratio of money to income is one-half. This increased revenue of the authorities is not a saving to the community—it is simply a redistribution. It becomes a real resource saving when gold is disposed of abroad for productive assets, or when labour and capital that were previously being used to produce additions to the gold stock can in some measure be used to produce other goods and services.

Undoubtedly, it was the additional and hidden tax revenues to governments, rather than the real resource saving, that induced them to increase the ratio of money in circulation to gold reserves during the gold-standard period.

Sterilisation and the Problem of Discipline

A distinguishing feature of the post-First World War gold standard was the apparent unwillingness of countries to allow their money stocks to be tied to their gold holdings—an unwillingness to submit to the discipline of the gold standard. Countries therefore tried, many think successfully, to sterilise the effects of changes in gold reserves on their money supplies.

Sterilisation appears from a very different perspective when capital is internationally mobile than when it is not. In the traditional price–specie–flow mechanism, a shift of gold from one country to another reduced the money supply in the former and increased it in the latter, causing the relative price levels to adjust until balance of payments equilibrium was re-established. In that framework, sterilisation (adjustment of domestic credit to offset changes in the gold stock and hold M constant) prevents the relative price adjustments from occurring. The gold flow continues indefinitely—or until the gold supply runs out. Sterilisation in this kind of world prevents the international monetary system from adjusting to exogenous changes that require gold flows.

In the theory developed here that takes capital mobility explicitly into account, a shift of gold from one country to another has no effect on relative price levels and is itself the process by which equilibrium in the balance of payments (more specifically, world asset equilibrium) is re-established. The balance of payments disequilibrium and the shift of gold arises because a change in the domestic demand for money balances has taken place—this could have arisen because of prior changes in outputs, or price levels, as a result of changes in world (including domestic) demand for domestic relative to foreign goods. The flow of gold is the process by which the domestic supply of money is brought back into line with the demand. The authorities cannot really sterilise such a flow of gold. For if they attempt to, say, increase the stock of money back up to where it was before a gold outflow occurred by increasing the ratio of notes and deposits to gold holdings, a further gold outflow will take place until money holdings are again driven down to what the public is willing to hold. The domestic money supply is thus an endogenous variable. The authorities can control the gold stock by creating or destroying credit but they cannot control the money supply unless the country is large enough to significantly affect the world money supply. And thus they cannot sterilise the effects of gold flows on the domestic supply of money.[16]

What then does it mean in a capital mobile world to say that countries are unwilling to submit to the gold-standard discipline? Unless a country is very large it can have little significant effect on its price level by varying the ratio of notes and deposits to gold, and in that case it affects its own price level only by affecting the whole world's price level. Any attempt to manipulate the price level or employment results in a gold flow, with employment and price-level objectives remaining unaccomplished. Under a gold standard, or any fixed exchange-rate system, the domestic price and employment levels are determined by the demands of world (and domestic) residents for domestic output together with the level of prices and employment in the world economy as a whole. The discipline that a fixed exchange rate imposes is the requirement of having to accept a level of prices and employment in the domestic economy determined by external forces. This discipline is imposed no matter what happens to the money supply and the stock of gold. If a country is unwilling to accept that discipline, its only alternative is to let the exchange rate float— attempts to prevent gold flows or to neutralise the monetary effects of them in order to affect prices and employment will be futile.

This would suggest that since capital was quite mobile in the 1920s the abandonment of the 'rules of the game' in the sense that the monetary effects of gold movements were sterilised could not have been the reason for the breakdown of the system. Countries could not effectively sterilise the effects of gold flows on their money supplies, even though they may have thought they were doing so. The breakdown must have occurred because countries were unwilling to accept the movements in their price and employment levels produced by world demand conditions in the face of fixed exchange rates. Attempts at sterilisation and money supply manipulation, though futile, may have reflected a misguided attempt to simultaneously achieve stable prices and fixed exchange rates. But ultimately, adjustments in the relative prices of domestic and foreign goods must take place through domestic and foreign nominal price-level adjustments when the exchange rate is fixed and monetary policy can do nothing to forestall those adjustments, even temporarily, as long as capital is internationally mobile. And if these adjustments are not allowed to take place through relative movements in the domestic and foreign price levels, they must take place through changes in exchange rates.

The Cause of Breakdown of the Gold Standard

This suggests an interesting hypothesis—that the breakdown of the gold standard in the 1930s, and indeed, the inability of many countries to get back on it until the late 1920s, was the result not of sterilisation and monetary mismanagement but of substantial adjustments of international relative prices due to the First World War and the Great Depression. These relative price adjustments put pressure on countries' employment and price levels, and forced them to abandon the fixed exchange rate regime inherent in the gold standard, rather than submit to (additional) inflation or depression.[17] Of course, such exchange rate adjustments were unable to prevent depression in the 1930s because, due to monetary mismanagement centring primarily on inappropriate policies in the USA, the depression was world-wide.

The USA allowed its money supply to contract drastically in the early 1930s.[18] Due to the size of the US economy in relation to the rest of the world, this by itself significantly reduced the world money supply. Other countries, faced with incipient portfolio disequilibria at existing exchange rates, were forced to further reduce their money supplies either directly, or indirectly through a loss of gold reserves. The drastic world monetary decline precipitated the world depression which, we hypothesise, sufficiently altered relative output prices among countries to make it infeasible for them to remain on the fixed exchange rate system implied by an international gold standard.

To test this hypothesis we must observe whether relative prices varied a lot among countries in the 1930s as compared to other periods when a stable fixed exchange-rate system was in force. Two obvious periods of comparison are 1870 to 1914 and 1950 to 1970—both had comparatively fixed exchange rates.

Let us define the jth country's real price ratio (RPR) as

$$\mathrm{RPR}_j = \frac{\pi_j \cdot \mathrm{CPI}_j (1 - \omega_j)}{\sum_i \pi_i \omega_i \mathrm{CPI}_i - \pi_j \omega_j \mathrm{CPI}_j}$$

where CPI is the consumer price index of the jth country in terms of local currency, π_j is the US dollar price of the jth country's currency and ω_i is the share of the ith country in world output.

The real price ratio is the ratio of the domestic price level to the rest of the world's price level where all prices are taken in US dollars (or some other common currency).[19] It purports to measure the ratio of domestic goods prices to foreign goods prices in a common world currency—or in other words, the relative price of domestic goods in the world market. Ideally, one would use the implicit GNP price deflators instead of the consumer price indexes since it is output prices we are interested in. The CPIs are used because GNP deflators are for the most part unavailable. They are preferable to wholesale price indexes because they contain prices of non-traded as well as traded goods while the WPIs are based largely on internationally traded goods. One would not expect the domestic relative to foreign prices of traded goods to vary except in so far as some traded goods are not produced in every country and the weights in the different countries' indexes differ. The WPI is thus a poorer measure than the CPI, which is in turn a poorer measure than the GNP deflator.

Table 5.1 gives the average year-over-year percentage changes, sign ignored, in the real price ratios of various countries for four periods: 1882–1913, 1925–1936, 1952–1970, and 1971–1980. The average percentage changes for all countries and years for each period are given at the bottom of each column. It is obvious that the real price ratios were much more variable in the two periods 1925–1936 and

TABLE 5.1 *Average Year-over-Year Changes in Real Price Ratios, Sign Ignored, Selected Countries*

	1882–1913	*1925–1936*	*1952–1970*	*1971–1980*
US	1.89	6.01	1.62	5.00
UK	2.05	4.51	1.78	6.43
Austria		4.45	2.29	4.09
Belgium		8.02	0.97	4.01
Denmark		5.56	2.16	4.70
France	1.67	8.88	3.06	5.49
Germany	1.79	5.39	1.74	4.59
Italy	1.33	13.93	1.58	3.96
Netherlands		5.53	1.76	4.53
Norway		6.67	1.80	3.58
Sweden		3.40	1.65	2.77
Switzerland		4.41	0.94	7.69
Japan			2.64	8.72
Australia			2.03	6.74
New Zealand			2.36	4.82
Average of all countries	1.75	6.39	1.89	5.10

Sources: Mitchell, B. R. (1980) *European Historical Statistics, 1950–1975*, Macmillan; Board of Governors of the Federal Reserve System (1943) *Banking and Monetary Statistics*, November; International Monetary Fund, *International Financial Statistics*, various issues.

1971–1980 when the fixed exchange-rate world monetary system had broken down than in the first and third periods when the world was on gold and pseudo-gold standards respectively.

Two alternative hypotheses could explain this variability. The first is the one suggested above—real relative price variability forced the world off fixed exchange rates. The second hypothesis would assert that the fixed exchange-rate system broke down for other reasons (for example, monetary instability in the great depression and liquidity shortage in the 1950s) and the resulting variability of exchange rates caused the real price ratio to vary. The philosophy underlying Bretton Woods was based on the second hypothesis—that flexible exchange rates lead to instability of the world monetary system. This survives in contemporary notions that a world-wide agreement on a system of fixed exchange parities is a necessary and sufficient condition for stability of the international financial system.

Obviously the data as presented in Table 5.1 do not permit us to distinguish between these two alternative hypotheses—correlation does not imply causation. The first step in evaluating the opposing interpretations is to determine what can be said on the basis of standard economic theory combined with readily available facts about the structure of the world economy. It can be shown on this basis that except in certain short-run situations a country's real price ratio is determined by real forces of demand and supply for goods and not by the exchange rate. Changes in the equilibrium real price ratio must *result* in either a change in the domestic nominal price level or a change in the exchange rate.

To see this, consider a two-country world in which each country produces and consumes a non-traded good as well as a single-traded good common to both countries.[21] Suppose that the exchange rate between the two countries' currencies is fixed and that there is a switch of home demand off the traded and onto the domestic non-traded good. The result is an excess aggregate demand for domestic production. Traded goods continue to be produced to the point where domestic marginal cost equals the world price, but there is insufficient production of the non-traded good at the initial domestic price level to meet the demand. The domestic price of the non-traded good, and hence the price level, must rise until this excess aggregate demand is eliminated and the non-traded goods market is in equilibrium. To the extent that money wages are inflexible, the rise in prices will reduce real wages and increase employment. If the domestic monetary authorities do not provide the stock of nominal money balances domestic residents wish to hold in the face of the higher levels of employment and prices, domestic asset holders will sell securities in the international market, creating a balance of payments surplus and an inflow of gold until the desired money supply is attained.

Now suppose that the exchange rate is flexible and that the authorities in the two countries maintain stable rates of monetary expansion in the face of the switch of home demand from traded to non-traded goods. The excess demand for non-traded goods must then have as its counterpart an excess supply of traded goods because stable monetary expansion prevents excess aggregate demand from arising by denying the economic system sufficient money balances to finance more output than is currently being produced. The excess supply of traded goods implies an excess demand for domestic currency on the foreign exchange market (more sales abroad than purchases) so the home currency will appreciate. This will be accompanied by exactly the same change in the real price ratio as occurred when the exchange rate was fixed and the domestic price level was allowed to rise. Had the exchange rate been floating but the authorities allowed the rise in the prices of non-traded relative to traded goods to be accompanied by an expansion of the money supply and increase in the domestic price level, the domestic currency would not have appreciated as much, but the rise in the real price ratio would have again been the same.

While the above discussion has focused on a simple shift in demand as the exogenous factor changing the equilibrium real price ratio, it could just as well have assumed a re-allocation of world investment toward the domestic economy, a shift in foreign tastes away from non-traded and toward traded goods, and so forth—the argument is completely general.

The essential point is that the exchange rate adjustment is a consequence of the shift in the equilibrium real price ratio, not a cause of it. There are, however, three circumstances in which a change in the exchange rate could cause the real price ratio to change. The first is a situation where speculators come to believe that the domestic currency will, say, devalue in the future and begin to sell it forward. Domestic interest rates rise to maintain interest parity, reducing the quantity of money demanded and leading to a sale of assets abroad and a spot devaluation of the domestic currency.[22] Since wages and prices are normally slow to adjust, the switch in demand onto domestic goods resulting from the devaluation will tend to increase domestic output in the short run, and only in the long run have its full effect on the domestic price level. The real price ratio will thus fall in the short run, though in the long run it will return to its initial level. The long run is not likely to be reached, however, because these speculative influences are temporary in nature and will tend to reverse themselves. Substantial variability of the exchange rate due to speculation will thus lead to concomitant variability of the real price ratio, but the variability is likely to be short term.

A second short-run influence of the exchange rate on the real price ratio arises from monetary instability. Suppose that the domestic authorities conduct an open-market purchase of bonds, leading to a substantial increase in the domestic money supply. The implications can be seen by focusing on the equation of monetary equilibrium,

$$M = P_U^{\alpha}(\pi P_T^*)^{(1-\alpha)} \cdot L(r, Y) \tag{5.2}$$

where the price level is expressed as a geometrically weighted average of the domestic prices of non-traded goods, P_U, and traded goods, πP_T^* (the latter price equals the domestic currency price of foreign currency (π) times the foreign currency price of traded goods). In the neo-classical price flexible quantity theory world with no international trade—that is, where $\alpha = 1$—an increase in M results in a proportional increase in the price level (represented by P_U in this case) since both r and Y are fixed by the conditions of full employment. In the Keynesian fixed-price model, where $P_U = 1.0$ (α is still equal to unity), monetary equilibrium is initially maintained in the face of an increase in M by a fall in r, and subsequently through the influence of the real sector equilibrium equation by an increase in Y. In the present open-economy analysis it must be assumed that neither output, interest rates, nor the price of non-traded goods can adjust in the very short run—adjustments of output and prices take time, and interest rates are determined in the world capital market independently of domestic forces. The only variable that can adjust immediately is the exchange rate. This adjustment of the exchange rate leads to a proportional change in the price of traded goods and a less than proportional increase in the domestic price level.

The excess supply of money created by the authorities leads domestic residents to try to re-establish portfolio equilibrium by purchasing assets in the world market, which creates an excess supply of domestic currency on the foreign exchange market and leads to a devaluation. The initial devaluation must be sufficient to increase the domestic price level in the same proportion as the increase in M because no other variable on the right hand side of equation (5.2) can adjust. That is

$$\frac{dM}{M} = \frac{dP}{P} = (1 - \alpha)\frac{d\pi}{\pi} \tag{5.3}$$

which implies that

$$\frac{d\pi}{\pi} = \frac{1}{1 - \alpha}\frac{dM}{M} \tag{5.4}$$

The exchange rate must initially rise more than proportionally to the money supply. In the longer run, the devaluation will lead to a shift of demand onto domestic goods and Y will increase, permitting π to reverse direction and domestic currency to appreciate. And in the longest run, P_U will rise proportionally with M, permitting π to further fall until the devaluation is no more than proportional to the increase in M. Thus, the long-run relative change in the exchange rate in response to a relative change in M will equal

$$\frac{d\pi}{\pi} = \frac{dP_U}{P_U} = \frac{dM}{M} \tag{5.5}$$

The initial depreciation in (5.3) must therefore be followed by a subsequent appreciation equal to

$$\frac{1}{1-\alpha}\frac{dM}{M} - \frac{dM}{M} = \frac{\alpha}{1-\alpha}\frac{dM}{M} \tag{5.6}$$

This is what has been called the phenomenon of overshooting. An expansion of the money supply causes the exchange rate to overshoot its long-run equilibrium. To the extent that world asset holders anticipate this overshooting, a forward premium on domestic currency will arise. Interest parity will in turn lead to a temporary fall in domestic interest rates and a resulting increase in the quantity of money demanded that will tend to smooth out the movement in the exchange rate.[23]

The monetary change will not affect the real price ratio if sufficient time has elapsed to allow the price of non-traded goods to fully adjust—P_U and π change in proportion, so $P/\pi P^*$ will remain constant. In the length of run before P_U fully adjusts, however, the devaluation lowers the domestic real price ratio. Erratic and unstable monetary policy will thus lead to temporary shifts in the real price ratio.

Exactly the same effects on the real price ratio will arise in the short run from variability of the demand function for money. The exchange rate bears the brunt of the initial adjustment and there will be overshooting, with the ultimate adjustment again falling on output and eventually non-traded goods prices.

A third potential causal effect of the exchange rate on the real price ratio could result from direct official manipulation of the exchange rate. Suppose that under a fixed exchange rate system the authorities adjust the peg upwards—that is, devalue the domestic currency once and for all. The effect is to switch world expenditure from foreign to domestic goods, leading initially to a rise in domestic output and employment and ultimately to a rise in the prices of non-traded goods in proportion to the increase in the exchange rate. There can be no effect on the real price ratio in the long run since P_U and π rise in proportion. In the short run, however, the full effect on P_U will not be forthcoming and the real price ratio will move in the opposite direction to the exchange rate.

Variability of the supply and demand for money does not affect the real price ratio under fixed exchange rates because any excess or deficiency of money holdings is eliminated through a purchase or sale of securities by domestic residents in the international capital market and is reflected in official holdings of gold and foreign exchange reserves, not output and prices.

It is thus possible that the higher degree of variability of real price ratios in the interwar and post-Bretton Woods periods could have been caused by speculative forces, by instability of money creation by the various national governments or by instability of the demand functions for money in the different countries. The breakdown of the fixed exchange rate systems could have produced real price ratio instability by making domestic money supplies amenable to official mismanagement and thereby producing uncertainty that could have led to instability of the demand for money.

To examine this issue, the real price ratio series for each country in each period was broken down into movements between peaks and troughs. A peak to trough, or trough to peak, movement is defined as one in which the variable moves by more than 3 per cent in one direction—any reversals of less than 3 per cent are thus ignored. The first and last years in each period were regarded as peaks or troughs if they were separated from the neighbouring trough or peak by 2 years or more, and ignored otherwise. For each peak-trough movement the average annual percentage change was calculated. The results are given in Table 5.2. The movements between peak and trough in each of the four periods are distributed as to length. At the bottom of the table, the average annual percentage change, sign ignored, for all movements between peak and trough are given for the respective periods. The average annual percentage changes were 5.9 per cent for the two flexible exchange rate periods and 1.5 per cent and 2.2 per cent respectively for the gold standard and Bretton Woods periods. When movements of 1 year's duration are ignored the average annual percentage changes are reduced but the pattern remains the same. When movements of 1 and 2 year's duration are dropped the pattern is still the same except that the average annual percentage changes in the post-Bretton Woods period increases to 6.1 per cent. The average annual percentage changes for movements longer than 5 years are 1.1 per cent and 2.0 per cent for the two fixed exchange rate periods, and 4.7 per cent and 5.1 per cent for the two flexible rate periods. In the fixed exchange rate periods, eleven out of twenty-six and fifteen out of twenty-eight movements between peak and trough were 6 years or more in duration. In the two flexible rate periods the corresponding figures were ten out of thirty-three and ten out of thirty-nine movements respectively. This indicates that peak-trough movements of 5 years or less were a greater fraction of total movements in the flexible exchange rate periods. However, movements of 6 years or more were not only numerous but much greater in terms of the annual percentage changes involved in the flexible rate period than in the fixed rate period. That is, the long-run exogenous disturbances affecting real relative prices were greater in the flexible exchange rate periods than in the fixed rate ones. It is difficult to believe that these

TABLE 5.2   *Real Price Ratio Changes: Distribution by Years between Peak and Trough. Average Annual Percentage Changes*

Years between peak and trough	Number of occurrences			
	1882–1913	*1924–36*	*1952–70*	*1971–80*
1	2	4	1	8
2	7	10	4	10
3	0	3	4	7
4	4	4	3	4
5	2	2	1	0
6	4	3	1	2
7	1	1	2	3
8	2	3	2	1
9	0	0	3	3
10	1	1	0	1
11	0	0	1	
12	0	2	2	
13	0		1	
14	1		1	
15	0		2	
16	0			
17	1			
18	0			
19	1			

		1882–1913	*1924–36*	*1952–70*	*1971–80*
	Total occurrences	26	33	28	39
Average Annual	All movements	1.5	5.9	2.2	5.9
Per cent Change	Movements longer than 1 yr	1.4	5.6	2.1	5.8
Sign Ignored	Movements longer than 2 yrs	1.3	5.2	1.9	6.1
	Movements longer than 5 yrs	1.1	4.7	2.0	5.1

greater long-run real price ratio adjustments could have been due to monetary and speculative factors. Price flexibility would appear to be a reasonable assumption over periods of 6 years and longer. Such swings in the real price ratio would thus be unlikely to have resulted from exchange-rate movements. They would more likely have caused any associated movements in exchange rates. The weight of the evidence would thus appear to be in favour of the hypothesis that movements in the equilibrium real price ratio forced the world off a fixed exchange rate system in the two occasions examined. Because of swings in the real price ratio, fixed exchange rates could not be maintained. The evidence is also consistent with the hypothesis that

monetary instability, permitted by flexible exchange rates, could have
caused greater short-run variability of the real price ratios during
those periods.

Was the Gold Standard a Good System?

The judgement about whether the gold standard is a good or bad
system can be made on two levels—on the potential for achieving
monetary stability under a gold standard as compared to other
systems, and on the historical evidence as to whether the gold standard
actually produced greater monetary stability than other systems.

On the basis of potential, the gold standard loses. Gold is produced
at increasing cost and the discovery of the metal combined with
technological change in mining and extracting it does not produce a
smooth rate of growth in the world stock. The world price level can
therefore be expected to vary significantly through time. By contrast,
an international central bank, or the central bank of an agreed-upon
key currency country, can produce a steady rate of monetary growth,
year after year and century after century if it wants to. Fiduciary
money is cheaper to produce since its real resource cost is simply paper
and printing charges, and intelligent management can neutralise the
effects of liquidity crises (resulting from changes in the public's desired
ratio of currency to deposits or the banking system's ratio of reserves
to deposits) on the world money supply to prevent catastrophic
deflations as occurred in the 1930s. If the fixed exchange rates implied
by a gold standard or other common currency system are odious,
individual countries can let their currencies float and the individual
central banks can produce constant (though not necessarily uniform)
rates of national money growth, letting exchange rates adjust to take
care of real price ratio changes and any differences between the
desired national inflation rates.

However, when we examine the history of price level movements
under the gold standard as compared to post-First World War
monetary arrangements a different conclusion emerges. Figure 5.1
plots the price level in Britain for the period 1560–1980.[24] Although
there were relative international price adjustments, the inflation and
deflation experienced in Britain was probably indicative of what
occurred in other countries tied to gold.

As expected, there were considerable price level changes prior to
1914 even though the price of gold was relatively constant. The price
level increased about 2.5 times between 1560 and 1660, although this
represents an average annual inflation rate of less than 2.5 per cent.

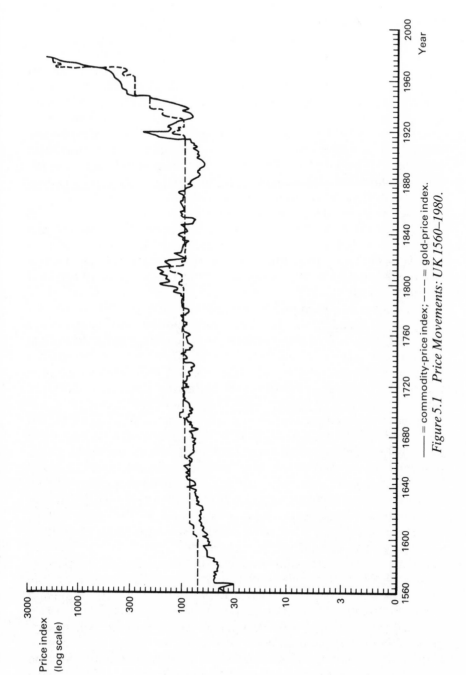

Price index
(log scale)

—— = commodity-price index; − − − = gold-price index.
Figure 5.1   Price Movements: UK 1560–1980.

Year

This inflation resulted from specie discoveries in the new world. In the 60 years between 1660 and 1720 the price level fell about 33 per cent then recovered to almost its level in 1660. Again the average annual deflation and/or inflation rates are less than 2.5 per cent. The price level then fell about 25 per cent between 1720 and 1740, then rose back to its 1720 level in a very few years. It fell 20 per cent and recovered again in the years between 1750 and 1765, then fluctuated within a 5 per cent band on either side of a horizontal trend until the Napoleonic Wars at the end of the century. Britain went off the gold standard and the price level increased around 80 per cent between 1790 and 1810, and then fell back to the 1790 level with the re-establishment of the gold standard after 1816. It varied within a 10 per cent band on either side of a horizontal trend until the mid 1870s, after which a 20 year deflation began that saw the price level fall by nearly 40 per cent. Yet again, this downward price adjustment was small on an average annual basis, being less than 2 per cent per year. With the gold discoveries in the 1890s, a long gradual inflation of prices began which saw them rise back to their level in 1870 by the outbreak of the First World War in 1914.

Though the swings in prices were quite large in the 350 or so years between 1560 and 1915, they were quite modest on a year-to-year basis. The annual year-over-year percentage change exceeded 10 per cent on only thirteen occasions between 1560 and the conversion from loose bimetallism to gold in 1717, and on only twenty-two occasions in the 195 years between 1717 and 1913. The annual inflation or deflation rate thus exceeded 10 per cent about 11 per cent of the time.

These price changes are trivial when compared to what happened after 1914. First, prices more than doubled between 1914 and 1920, then drifted back to below their 1914 level during the 1930s. Then, following the Second World War, a steady inflation began that was never reversed and accelerated after the formal abandonment of gold in 1971. The price level is now about 20 times the 1914 level, which is on an essentially horizontal trend going back to the early 1700s. Moreover, on a year-to-year basis there was also more price-level variability. The annual year-over-year percentage change in price index exceeded 10 per cent on twelve occasions during the periods between 1923 and 1937, and 1948 and 1980—exactly 25 per cent of the time. This was twice as often as during the gold-standard period and the results are biased by ignoring the unstable years of the early 1920s and early post-Second World War period. Since six of the twelve years of more than 10 per cent inflation occurred after 1973 and three more of the years were in the 1930s, one might try to argue that the Bretton Woods years saw better price performance than the gold standard period. There is merit in this view, but it must be realised that all price movements in the Bretton Woods years were in one direction (upwards) and the overall increase in the index between 1948 and 1971 was 320 per cent. The performance after 1973 has been disastrous.

It is obvious that the British money supply got completely out of hand after the last vestiges of the gold standard were abandoned in 1973. By comparison, of course, the British inflation was worse than that of some countries such as the USA, Germany, and Switzerland. But it was less than that of many other countries.

The historical evidence certainly suggests that the gold standard imposed on the world a monetary discipline that has been lacking in recent years. It is one thing for economists to outline what is possible with a fiduciary system and proper monetary management. It is another for monetary institutions to deliver that quality of management given human limitations and the political pressures they face.

Notes

1 See Munro, John H. (1981) 'Mint policies, ratios and outputs in England and the Low Countries, 1330—1420: some reflections on new data', *Numismatic Chronicle*, 8th Series, Vol. I, pp. 77–116.
2 See Jastram, Roy W. (1977) *The Golden Constant,* John Wiley and Sons, Feavearyear, Sir Albert, (1931) *The Pound Sterling: A History of English Money*, Clarendon Press.
3 Jastram, *op. cit.,* p. 13.
4 See Laughlin, J. L. (1885) *History of Bimetallism in the United States*, D. Appleton; and, (1919) *Principles of Money*, Charles Scribner's Sons, pp. 426–7.
5 Laughlin, *Principles of Money, loc. cit.*
6 Friedman, Milton and Schwartz, Anna J. (1963) *A Monetary History of the United States, 1867–1960*, NBER, Princeton University Press, p. 119.
7 See Yeager, Leland B. (1975) *International Monetary Relations,* Harper and Row, 2nd edn., Chapter 15.
8 Jastram, *op. cit.*, p. 17.
9 See Keynes, J. M. (1932) 'The economic consequences of Mr Churchill', *Essays in Persuasion*, Harcourt Brace and Co.
10 Friedman, Milton (1968) *Dollars and Deficits*, Prentice Hall, Chapter 11, pp. 247–265.
11 For an excellent discussion of the issues surrounding this and subsequent international monetary developments see Meier, Gerald M. (1982) *Problems of a World Monetary Order*, Oxford University Press, pp. 77–116.
12 The rigid gold backing requirements for bank notes, established by the Bank Charter Act, 1844, were suspended on a number of occasions in the

nineteenth century. However, this did not involve a suspension of convertibility of notes and deposits into gold.

13 See Yeager, *op. cit.*, p. 302. Walter Bagehot ((1873) *Lombard Street*, pp. 335–336) gives 1872 figures showing the reserve to be 11.2 per cent. See also Viner, J. (1951) *International Economics: Studies*, Free Press, p. 124.

14 See Yeager, *op. cit.*, pp. 302–303.

15 This follows from the fact that the nominal money supply times the income velocity of circulation of money must equal money income.

16 They could only sterilise the effects of, say, gold inflows on the domestic money supply to the extent that they take sufficient gold out of circulation (accumulate official gold reserves) to reduce the world money supply, at which point world interest rates and other variables would have changed so as to induce domestic residents to also hold less money.

17 For a rigorous analysis of issues concerning real relative prices and the exchange rate, see Stockman, Alan C. (1980) 'A theory of exchange rate determination', *Journal of Political Economy*, Vol. 88, No. 4, pp. 673–698, and (1983) 'Real exchange rates under alternative nominal exchange rate systems' *Journal of International Money and Finance*, Vol. 2, No. 2, pp. 147–166.

18 See Friedman and Schwartz, *op. cit.*, pp. 317–318.

19 The term $(1 - \omega_j)$ in the numerator merely converts the jth country's RPR index to the same common base as all countries' CPIs.

20 Canada was not included in these averages because it had a flexible exchange rate throughout the fifties.

21 The two-sector analytical approach that follows in the remainder of this chapter is a departure from the theoretical framework developed earlier. This is necessary because the issues to be considered cannot be properly analysed in a one-sector framework, while the latter approach is much simpler for dealing with the other matters investigated in this book. Fortunately the two-sector analysis that follows is sufficiently elementary that a full-blown detailed model does not have to be developed.

22 The well-known interest parity theorem states that domestic interest rates must exceed foreign rates (after adjustment for differences in risk) by the forward discount on domestic currency—otherwise, arbitrage will occur. When capital markets are efficient in the sense that participants in the market are acting on all the information available to them, the forward discount must equal the market's expectations as to the degree of devaluation expected during the life of the forward contract. An expected devaluation of the domestic currency will thus lead to a forward discount and a rise in domestic relative to foreign interest rates. These issues are considered in more detail in the Appendix to Chapter 8.

23 For an analysis of overshooting that emphasises exchange rate anticipations as an equilibrating device, see Dornbusch, R. (1976) 'The theory of flexible exchange rates and macroeconomic policy', *Scandinavian Journal of Economics*, Vol. 78, No. 2, pp 255–275.

24 The data from 1560 to 1976 was obtained from Jastram, *op. cit.*, and that from 1977 to 1980 is given in *International Financial Statistics* (International Monetary Fund) 1981.

6

World Equilibrium under a Key Currency System

The post-war international monetary system established by the Bretton Woods Agreement of 1944 was essentially a key currency system. The US dollar was the key or central currency with the other currencies—the peripheral currencies—pegged to it. The US authorities did not intervene in the foreign exchange markets to affect the external value of the US dollar,[1] while the other countries adjusted their exchange rates *vis-à-vis* the dollar from time to time as prescribed in the International Monetary Fund rules to correct fundamental balance of payments disequilibria. The system was formally linked to gold in that the US Government was committed to buy and sell gold at $35 per oz. But the supply of money in the USA bore no relationship to the supply of gold. The peripheral countries held foreign exchange reserves in the form of gold and US dollar short-term assets, and added to and ran down those reserves to maintain their currencies at official rates with respect to the US dollar.[2]

The structure of this system can be modelled along lines similar to the gold standard analysis of Chapter 4.[3] Except for one minor modification, the real goods market equilibrium conditions are the same as for the gold standard.

$$Y = C(r, Y) + I(r, Y) + GX + B_T(Y, Y^*, P/\pi P^*) \tag{6.1}$$

$$Y^* = C^*(r^*, Y^*) + I^*(r^*, Y^*) + GX^* - \frac{P}{\pi P^*} B_T(Y, Y^*, P/\pi P^*) \tag{6.2}$$

where Y is output, r is the rate of interest, $C(.)$, $I(.)$ and $B_T(.)$ are the functions determining consumption, investment, and the balance of trade, GX is the level of government expenditure (which can be viewed simply as an exogenous real sector shift variable) and P is the price of output. These equations differ from (4.3) and (4.4) only in that the domestic/foreign relative price term is now $P/\pi P^*$ instead of P/P^* —the exchange rate (π) is no longer assumed equal to unity. This reflects the fact that the exchange rate can now be adjusted under a key currency system. Again it must be noted that a rise in the interest rate in each country reduces investment and (by assumption) consumption, while an increase in income increases them. A rise in the relative price of domestic in terms of foreign goods switches world expenditure from the domestic (non-asterisked) to the foreign economy, reducing $B_T(.)$. The domestic balance of trade improves with an increase in foreign income and deteriorates with an increase in domestic income. Aggregate supply equations relating output and actual and expected prices could again be added but they would contribute nothing to the subsequent analysis—we simply impose Keynesian price rigidity or classical full employment as the situation demands, recognising that a richer, more general analysis would incorporate these extremes as special cases.

The Zero Capital Mobility Case

When capital movements in response to market forces are prohibited, asset equilibrium is given simply by the two countries' demand functions for money,

$$M = P \cdot L(r, Y) \tag{6.3}$$

and

$$M^* = P^* \cdot L^*(r^*, Y^*) \tag{6.4}$$

where M and M^* are the nominal money stocks.[4] The real quantities of money demanded in the two countries, given by $L(.)$ and $L^*(.)$, depend directly on the respective levels of income and inversely on the rates of interest. A rise in the price level in a country increases the demand for nominal money balances in proportion. Again, equality of the demand and supply of non-monetary assets in each country is assured by the equality of the demand and supply of money. Since people can only hold wealth in either of the two forms, an excess demand for money implies an excess supply of other assets and vice versa. The money supplies in the two countries are multiples of their respective stocks of high-powered money in accordance with the appropriate multipliers derived in Chapter 3.

Since there are no private-capital movements, the balance of payments of the peripheral (non-asterisked) country is

$$\frac{dR}{dt} = B_T\left(Y, Y^*, \frac{P}{\pi P^*}\right) \tag{6.5}$$

where dR/dt, the rate of growth of the country's foreign exchange reserves through time, represents a balance of payments surplus.[5] A balance of payments surplus requires that the authorities accumulate an equivalent flow of foreign exchange reserves to keep the domestic currency from appreciating. These reserve accumulations represent an induced capital outflow. (Autonomous outflows of capital are ruled out by our assumption of international capital immobility.) For the balance of payments to be equilibrium the balance of trade and the rate of change of official reserve holdings must be zero. Under the Bretton Woods system, where the US dollar was the key currency and the price of gold was supported at \$35 per oz, official reserves could be held in the form of either gold- or US dollar-denominated assets. When the price of gold is not supported, key currency denominated assets are the only available official reserves.

The five equations, (6.1) to (6.5), solve for the five endogenous variables $r, r^*, dR/dt$, and Y and Y^* or P and P^*, depending on whether we impose Keynesian or classical assumptions. The exogenous variables that drive the model are M, M^*, π, GX, and GX^*. The four equations (6.1) to (6.4) can be solved separately for interest rates and outputs or prices. These solutions then plug into (6.5) to determine the balance-of-payments surplus or deficit and the associated rate of accumulation of foreign exchange reserves.

An increase in one country's money supply causes the domestic interest rate to fall and output to increase in the Keynesian case, and the domestic price level to rise in the classical case. In both cases the balance of trade (payments) deteriorates causing output or prices and the interest rate to rise in the rest of the world. Fiscal (or other exogenous) expansion in one country leads to a deterioration in its balance of payments and a rise in interest rates and outputs or prices in both countries. These results can be demonstrated with reference to Figure 6.1. They are worked out rigorously in Mathematical Note 1 at the end of the chapter.

Diagrammatic Analysis†

(a) Less than full employment Less than full employment conditions are presented in Figure 6.1(a), with the key currency

---

† Readers whose background is such that they fully understood the preceding paragraph can skip this section without missing anything.

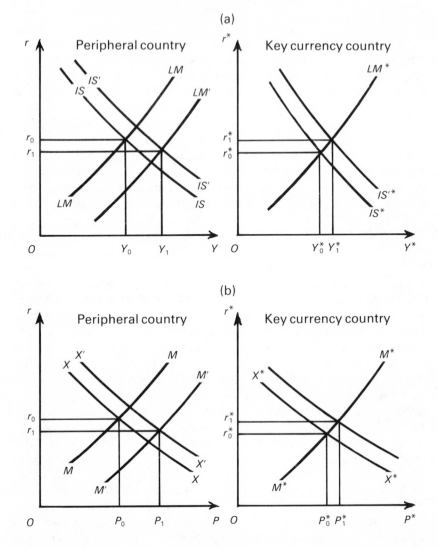

Figure 6.1

country's situation shown on the right and the peripheral country's situation on the left. Each country's *IS* curve gives the combinations of income and the interest rate for which aggregate demand equals aggregate supply. The effects of changes in *r* on *Y*, and *r** on *Y**, as we move down along the respective curves can be obtained by differentiating (6.1) and (6.2) totally with respect to output and the interest rate. This yields

$$\frac{dY}{dr} = \frac{I_r}{1 - C_y - I_y - B_{Ty}} \tag{6.6}$$

together with a corresponding expression for the key currency country. I_r, C_y, I_y, and B_{Ty} are the relevant partial derivatives of the behavioural functions with respect to the variables appearing as subscripts. It should be noted that each country's *IS* curve is drawn holding the other country's output constant. The *LM* curve gives the combinations of output and the interest rate for which asset markets are in equilibrium—these are the combinations for which the demand for real money balances equals the supply. The *LM* curve is positively sloped because an increase in the level of output increases the demand for money, requiring an increase in the interest rate to eliminate this excess demand and keep $L(r, Y)$ equal to M/P. An increase in government expenditure in a country shifts its *IS* curve to the right because aggregate demand increases at each interest rate, requiring a corresponding increase in the level of output. An increase in the nominal money supply in a country or fall in prices (i.e. increase in the real money supply) causes its *LM* curve to shift to the right because a higher level of income is now necessary to get the public to hold these additional real money balances.

An increase in the peripheral country's money supply appears as a rightward shift of the *LM* curve on the left side of Figure 6.1(a). This increases output and lowers the interest rate. But each country's income is an exogenous variable affecting the other country's *IS* curve. Thus, as Y rises IS^* shifts to the right on the right-hand side of Figure 6.1(a)—the key country's aggregate demand increases when its trade balance improves. This leads to an increase in both income and the interest rate in the key-currency country. In turn, the increase in Y^* has a positive effect on aggregate demand in the peripheral country, shifting its *IS* curve to the right, further increasing its income and moderating the fall in its interest rate. The increase in Y then feeds through onto IS^* and so forth with the process continuing until the final equilibrium is reached. This is shown at the intersection of LM' and IS' in the peripheral country, and at LM^* and $IS^{*\prime}$ in the key currency country. Outputs increase in both countries and the interest rate falls in the peripheral country and rises in the key currency country. The net effect of all this on the balance of trade and dR/dt is necessarily negative. The increase in output of the peripheral country deteriorates $B_T(.)$. This deterioration is moderated by the increase in the key currency country's output caused by the positive effect of the decline in $B_T(.)$ on its aggregate demand.

When the key currency country's money supply increases, the

analysis is symmetrical. However, the peripheral country's balance of payments now improves and dR/dt increases—only the peripheral country's authorities intervene in the foreign exchange market. It should also be noted that when the country experiencing the monetary expansion is small in relation to the other country, the feedback effects through the other country's income and balance of trade will be small and of little significance.

We can conclude that a monetary expansion in one country raises output both at home and abroad and deteriorates its balance of payments. If that country is the peripheral one it will have to sell reserves to maintain its fixed change rate. If the expanding country is the key currency country, the peripheral country will have to accumulate official reserves to maintain its exchange rate.

The effect of an increase in government expenditure or other exogenous shift in aggregate demand in one country can be analysed on a graph like Figure 6.1(a). However, since the results should be evident intuitively, the formal demonstration is left to the reader. The fact that the level of each country's IS curve depends on the other country's income means that an increase in, say, GX leads to a rightward shift on both IS and IS^*, with the proportional effect being greater in the case of IS. Interest rates will rise in both countries and the trade balance (and balance of payments) of the peripheral country will deteriorate. Only through a deterioration of the expanding country's balance of trade can income in the other country increase. The peripheral country will thus have to continuously sell foreign exchange reserves to maintain the exchange rate. Had GX^* increased, both countries' incomes would have increased and the peripheral country would have had to accumulate reserves.

(b) Full employment   The full-employment case is shown in Figure 6.1(b)—the left side again gives the situation of the peripheral country and the right side that of the key currency country. The price levels rather than the levels of income are now on the horizontal axes. The XX and X^*X^* curves give the combinations of the price level and interest rate for which aggregate demand equals aggregate supply in the respective countries. Their slopes are obtained from the total derivatives of equations (6.1) and (6.2). The slope of XX is

$$\frac{dr}{dp} = \frac{-B_{TR}}{C_r + I_r} \tag{6.7}$$

It is negative because B_{TR}, the partial derivative of the function $B_T(.)$ with respect to the relative price variable, is negative, as are C_r and I_r.

The negative slope of XX can be seen intuitively from the fact that a rise in P causes world demand to shift off the non-asterisked country's good, reducing its aggregate demand and requiring a fall in the interest rate to increase investment and consumption to maintain aggregate demand equal to full employment output. The corresponding slope of X^*X^* is formally the same. Since each country's aggregate demand is affected by the ratio of home to foreign prices, rather than just by its own price level, P^* is an exogenous variable underlying XX, and P is an exogenous variable underlying X^*X^*. The two countries' curves are interrelated in the same way that IS and IS^* were in the less-than-full-employment case. The MM and M^*M^* curves give the combinations of r and P, and r^* and P^*, for which the respective demands and supplies of money are equal. They are positively sloped because an increase in P reduces the real money supply, requiring an increase in r to reduce equivalently the demand for real money balances and maintain asset equilibrium.

An increase in the money supply in the peripheral country shifts MM to the right since a higher P is necessary to get the public to hold the higher money stock. This leads to a fall in r and a rise in P which causes imports to increase relative to exports and deteriorates the balance of trade. Since the key-currency country's trade balance improves, X^*X^* shifts to the right and the foreign interest rate and price level rise. The rise in P^* in turn shifts XX to the right, which further raises P and moderates the fall in r. The final equilibrium is shown at P_1, r_1, P_1^*, and r_1^*.

The essential result is that an increase in the money supply in the peripheral country causes the price level to rise both at home and abroad, with the effect on the home price level being proportionally greater, and leads to a fall in the home interest rate and rise in the interest rate in the key currency country. The peripheral country's balance of payments deteriorates and it must sell foreign exchange reserves continuously to maintain the exchange rate. Symmetrical results would occur in response to an exogenous increase in the key currency country's money supply, except that the peripheral country must now acquire foreign exchange reserves to maintain the exchange rate.

The effects of a real sector expansion can now be seen intuitively— the interested reader can work them out on graphs similar to Figure 6.1(b). The increase in GX causes the peripheral country's balance of payments to deteriorate, and shifts both XX and X^*X^* up. The price levels and interest rates rise in both countries. An increase in GX^* would have had qualitatively the same effect with the peripheral country's balance of payments now showing a surplus. Prices always rise proportionally more in the country whose government expenditure increases.

These results should all be qualified by noting that if the country whose money supply or government expenditure increase is small in relation to the rest of the world, the resulting relative change in output prices, interest rates, etc. in the rest of the world will be small. And the feed-back effects on the expanding country will be correspondingly small.

Balance of Payments Pressures on Peripheral Countries' Policies

It should also be noted that the peripheral country could offset any effect of key-currency monetary and fiscal policy on its output and price level by conducting an opposite monetary or fiscal policy of its own. However, this will tend to accentuate the balance of payments effect of the key country's policy. Contraction in the key country will deteriorate the peripheral country's balance of payments and an expansion in the latter country will further deteriorate it. Similarly, if the peripheral country initiates a monetary or fiscal expansion which leaks over into the key currency country, the latter could tighten up its monetary and fiscal policy to offset the effects of peripheral-country expansion on its output and employment. This would make the deterioration of the peripheral country's balance of payments from its own expansion much worse. Thus, since the peripheral country is the one responsible for maintaining the exchange rate, it has a strong balance-of-payments incentive to follow the lead of the key currency country on counter-cyclical policy.

Money Creation and Sterilisation

High-powered money in the peripheral country is created through the purchase of either foreign exchange reserves or domestic bonds by the monetary authority. Foreign exchange reserves consist of gold and key currency or key currency denominated bonds. Domestic bonds may be purchased either from the public or the fiscal wing of the government. Thus

$$H = R + D \tag{6.8}$$

where D is the stock of domestic bonds held by the authorities.[6] In the key-currency country, high-powered money is created by the purchase of bonds from the public or fiscal authority (the key currency country does not intervene in the foreign exchange market) and destroyed through the accumulation by the peripheral country of reserves in the form of key currency. By accumulating reserves in the form of currency the peripheral country takes key currency out of circulation. However, if the peripheral country's reserves are held in bonds or gold, there is no effect on the central country's money supply. Thus

$$H^* = D^* - \psi R \qquad (6.9)$$

where ψ is the fraction of the peripheral country's reserves held in cash.[7] It is customary to refer to D and D^* as the domestic source components of the two countries' money supplies and to R and $-\psi R$ as the foreign source components.

When capital is perfectly immobile internationally, R can only change through time through a deficit or surplus in the balance of trade—it cannot change once-and-for-all at an instant of time. Thus, if we differentiate (6.8) and (6.9) at a point in time (i.e. holding time constant) only M, M^*, D, and D^* change. However, if we differentiate with respect to time, we obtain

$$\frac{dM}{dt} = \frac{dR}{dt} + \frac{dD}{dt} = B_T(.) + \frac{dD}{dt} \qquad (6.8')$$

and

$$\frac{dM^*}{dt} = \frac{dD^*}{dt} - \psi \frac{dR}{dt} = \frac{dD^*}{dt} - \psi B_T(.) \qquad (6.9')$$

If the domestic and foreign authorities refrain from open or closed market operations in home-country bonds, a balance of payments deficit in the peripheral country will lead to a decline in its money supply and, if $\psi > 0$, to an increase in the key currency country's money supply. As time passes, this will reduce output or prices in the peripheral country and increase output or prices in the central country until $B_T(.)$ has been driven to zero.

This adjustment process can be forestalled by sterilisation—that is, by positive dD/dt equal to $B_T(.)$ in the peripheral country, and negative dD^*/dt equal to $\psi B_T(.)$ in the key-currency country.

Capital Mobility

The conditions of asset equilibrium change substantially when international capital mobility is introduced. Two conditions must hold for perfect mobility as conventionally defined. First there must be free exchange of domestic for foreign assets. Second, a sufficient fraction of world residents must regard domestic and foreign assets as perfect substitutes in portfolios. These two conditions are sufficient for domestic and foreign interest rates to be the same. The right to transact freely across international boundaries is insufficient to equalise the two countries' interest rates because world wealth owners may perceive one country's assets to be more risky than the other's. The interest rate on domestic assets would be the same for domestic and foreign residents as would the interest rate on foreign assets. But the foreign and domestic interest rates would differ. We concentrate here on the perfect-mobility case. The results are not fundamentally different in the intermediate case where there are restrictions on the international exchange of selected assets and the two countries' assets are not perfect substitutes in portfolios.

When capital is perfectly mobile internationally, the stock of official reserves can change at a point in time. The public can decide that it wants to convert some fraction of its existing stock of money into non-monetary assets and make a once-and-for-all purchase of assets from foreigners. This would create a one-shot balance of payments deficit and an instantaneous reduction in the stock of reserves. Differentiation of (6.8) and (6.9) holding time constant thus leads to a change in R as well as in M, D, M^* and D^*.

Equations (6.8) and (6.9) can be substituted into the demand functions for money, (6.3) and (6.4), to yield

$$D + R = P \cdot L(r, Y) \tag{6.10}$$

$$D^* - \psi R = P^* \cdot L^*(r^*, Y^*) \tag{6.11}$$

Note that the implications of fractional reserve banking are ignored, so that the money multipliers are unity and $M = H$ and $M^* = H^*$.

As noted, the twin assumptions that international transactions in securities can be freely undertaken and that domestic and foreign securities are perfect substitutes in portfolios implies that

$$r = r^* \tag{6.12}$$

After substitution of (6.12), equations (6.10), (6.11), (6.1) and (6.2) solve for the four variables $r(=r^*)$, R, and Y or P, and Y^* or P^*, depending upon whether Keynesian or classical conditions are assumed. The two asset equations solve simultaneously for R and r, and these reduced-form equations then can be solved simultaneously with the income-expenditure equations (6.1) and (6.2) to determine outputs or prices.

To solve the asset equations for r and R, substitute (6.10) into (6.11) to eliminate R. This yields

$$D^* + \psi D = P^* \cdot L^*(r, Y^*) + \psi P \cdot L(r, Y) \tag{6.13}$$

which can be rearranged to give an equation determining the world interest rate of the form

$$r = A(D, D^*, P, P^*, Y, Y^*) \tag{6.13$'$}$$

The stock of reserves is then determined by equation (6.10), which can be rearranged to yield

$$R = P \cdot L(r, Y) - D \tag{6.10$'$}$$

Equation (6.13$'$) can then be substituted into (6.1) and (6.2) to yield two equations in Y and Y^*, or P and P^*, as the case may be. The solutions for r and Y or P then substitute into (6.10$'$) to determine R.

When the peripheral country holds virtually all its foreign exchange reserves in key currency denominated bonds—a highly likely situation in practice—world output and prices are determined entirely by monetary policy in the key-currency country. The parameter ψ becomes zero, equation (6.13) becomes simply the key-currency country's condition of monetary equilibrium, and (6.13$'$) reduces to

$$r = A(D^*, P^*, Y^*) \tag{6.13$''$}$$

This equation substitutes into (6.1) and (6.2) to determine P^* and P, or Y^* and Y, depending upon whether we impose classical or Keynesian assumptions. These equilibrium values then substitute into (6.10$'$) to determine R. Since the equilibrium values of Y or P and r determined in (6.13$''$), (6.1) and (6.2) establish an equilibrium value for $L(.)$ in (6.10$'$), the peripheral country's money supply $(R + D)$ is determined endogenously. It follows that monetary policy in the peripheral country is completely impotent—changes in D simply result in equal and opposite changes in R, with no effect on P or Y or r.

It should be noted that this latter result holds independently of the relative sizes of the key and peripheral countries—if a tiny country like Switzerland were the key currency country, and if other countries held all their official foreign exchange reserves in Swiss bonds, the Government of Switzerland would be the world's monetary authority.

If the peripheral country holds a significant fraction of its foreign exchange reserves in cash, its monetary policy can influence world prices and employment. An increase in D would lead to a loss of R as before, but now the loss of reserves increases the key currency country's money supply and leads to a fall in r, expansion of Y, and Y^* and, eventually, increases in P and P^*. For this influence to be significant, however, the peripheral country's reserves must be substantial relative to the size of the key currency country's money supply. It follows that the USA, making up some 50 per cent of the advanced industrial free-world's output, could have a significant effect on world output employment and prices even if tiny Switzerland were the key currency country. This assumes, of course, that the Swiss authorities do not sterilise the effects of changes in US reserves on their money supply by altering D^* and that the USA holds sufficient cash reserves (deposits in francs in the Swiss central bank) in proportion to the Swiss money supply.

Diagrammatic Analysis—Less than Full Employment†

These results can perhaps be made clearer by presenting them graphically.[8] Simple inspection of the goods-market equilibrium conditions, (6.1) and (6.2), indicates that we can solve them simultaneously for Y and Y^* as functions of the variables r, GX, GX^* and $P/\pi P^*$. The formal solutions are

$$Y = Y\left(r, GX, GX^*, \frac{P}{\pi P^*}\right) \tag{6.14}$$

$$Y^* = Y^*\left(r, GX, GX^*, \frac{P}{\pi P^*}\right) \tag{6.15}$$

In the less-than-full-employment fixed exchange rate case, we can assume that initially $P = P^* = \pi = 1$. These two equations can be presented as the curves IE and IE^* on the right-hand side of Figure 6.2. These are similar to conventional IS curves except that the two countries' outputs are simultaneously determined at each interest rate level. The curves are negatively sloped, of course, because a fall in the world interest rate increases investment, output and aggregate demand in both countries. Increases in GX or GX^* will obviously shift both IE and IE^* to the right since they increase aggregate demand at home leading to an expansion of output and a deterioration of the home trade balance which, in turn, expands aggregate demand and output abroad. On the left side of Figure 6.2, we draw the curve IE_w which gives the effect of changes in the world interest rate on a weighted average of Y and Y^*, denoted by Y_w.

The world asset equilibrium equation (6.13) (or (6.13′)) can be represented as a world LM-type curve, which we denote by AE_w on the left side of Figure 6.2, giving the combinations of the world interest rate and Y_w for which the demand for world non-monetary assets equals the supply.[9] The curve slopes upward to the north-west. An increase in output increases desired money holdings in both countries

---

† Readers with a sophisticated knowledge of international monetary theory can skip directly to (c) Conclusions without sacrificing understanding of later sections.

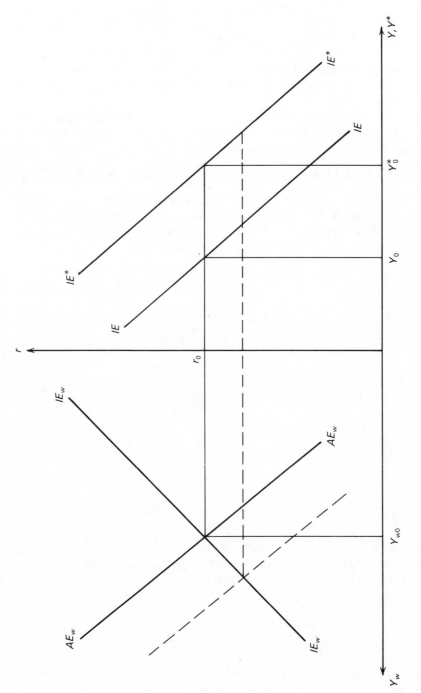

Figure 6.2

and reduces desired non-monetary asset holdings at the old interest rate. The interest rate must thus rise to get world residents to hold the existing stock of non-monetary assets.

The intersection of AE_w and IE_w gives the equilibrium world interest rate on the left side of Figure 6.2. This projects across to the right side to determine the equilibrium levels of output in the two countries.

To proceed further we must determine the weights in the index converting Y and Y^* into Y_w. The first step is to differentiate the asset equilibrium equation (6.13) totally as follows:

$$dD^* + \psi dD = P^*L_r^*dr + P^*L_y^*dY^* + \psi PL_rdr + \psi PL_ydY \quad (6.16)$$

We now divide all terms in the equation by $(D^* + \psi D)$ and multiply and divide each individual term by the variable appearing in the differential for that term—e.g. multiply and divide the first term by D^*, the second by D, the third by r, etc. This yields

$$\frac{D^*}{D^*+\psi D}\frac{dD^*}{D^*} + \frac{\psi D}{D^*+\psi D}\frac{dD}{D}$$

$$=\left(\frac{P^*rL_r^*}{D+\psi D} + \frac{\psi PrL_r}{D^*+\psi D}\right)\frac{dr}{r} + \frac{P^*Y^*L_y^*}{D^*+\psi D}\frac{dY^*}{Y^*} + \frac{\psi PYL_y}{D^*+\psi D}\frac{dY}{Y} \quad (6.16')$$

This expression can be simplified in three ways. First, we can define $\theta = D^*/(D^* + \psi D)$. Second we can utilise the definitions of the interest and income elasticities of demand for money to obtain

$$rL_y^* = \eta^*L^*(r, Y^*)$$
$$rL_r = \eta L(r, Y)$$
$$Y^*L_y^* = \epsilon^*L^*(r, Y)$$

and

$$YL_y = \epsilon L(r, Y)$$

when η^* and η are the interest elasticities and ϵ^* and ϵ the income elasticities of demand for money in the respective countries. Third, we can utilise (6.10) and (6.11) to substitute

$$D^* b \psi R = P^*L^*(r, Y^*)$$

and

$$D + R = P \cdot L(r, y)$$

These simplifications reduce (6.18') to

$$\theta\,\frac{dD^*}{D} + (1-\theta)\,\frac{dD}{D}$$

$$= \left(\frac{\eta^*(D^*-\psi R)}{D^*+\psi D} + \frac{\psi\eta(D+R)}{D^*+\psi D}\right)\frac{dr}{r} + \frac{\epsilon^*(D^*-\psi R)}{D^*+\psi D}\frac{dY^*}{Y^*} + \frac{\psi\epsilon(D+R)}{D^*+\psi D}\frac{dY}{Y}$$

$$(6.16'')$$

Finally, we can further simplify by letting

$$\frac{D^*-\psi R}{D^*+\psi D} = \frac{D^*}{D^*+\psi D} - \frac{\psi R}{D^*}\frac{D^*}{D^*+\psi D} = \theta(1-\psi\lambda^*)$$

and

$$\frac{\psi(D+R)}{D^*+\psi D} = \frac{\psi D}{D^*+\psi D} + \frac{\psi R}{D}\frac{D}{D+\psi D} = (1-\theta)(1+\psi\lambda)$$

where λ^* is the ratio of the stock of foreign exchange reserves outstanding to the domestic source component of the key currency country's money supply, and λ is the ratio of the stock of foreign exchange reserves to the domestic source component of the peripheral country's money supply.

Substituting the above expressions into (6.16″) and rearranging the terms, we obtain

$$\frac{dr}{r} = -\frac{\theta}{\Delta}\frac{dD^*}{D^*} - \frac{1-\theta}{\Delta}\frac{dD}{D}$$

$$+\left(\frac{\epsilon^*\theta(1-\psi\lambda^*)}{\Delta}\frac{dY^*}{Y^*} + \frac{\epsilon(1-\theta)(1+\psi\lambda)}{\Delta}\frac{dY}{Y}\right) \qquad (6.16''')$$

where $\Delta = -[\eta^*\theta(1-\psi\lambda^*) + \eta(1-\theta)(1+\psi\lambda)]$. This latter expression is positive because η^* and η are both negative. Equation (6.16‴) is the total differential of (6.13′) with respect to D^*, D, Y^*, and Y, where the differentials are converted to relative changes.

If we now let the relative change in world output be the last term in (6.16‴), namely,

$$\frac{dY_w}{Y_w} = \left(\frac{\epsilon^*\theta(1-\psi\lambda^*)}{\Delta}\frac{dY^*}{Y^*} + \frac{\epsilon(1-\theta)(1+\psi\lambda)}{\Delta}\frac{dY}{Y}\right)$$

we have in effect defined world output as a geometrically-weighted index of Y^* and Y, with the respective weights being $[\epsilon^*\theta(1-1\psi\lambda^*)]/\Delta$ and $[\epsilon(1-\theta)(1-\psi\lambda)]/\Delta$. This implies that the elasticity of r with respect to Y_w in the relevant range of AE_w is unity. These same weights, of course, must be used to combine (6.14) and (6.15) in obtaining IE_w.

It should be realised that Y_w is not a conventional world output measure but a very special weighted average of the individual countries' outputs. The weights are *not* based on the importance of individual country output in total world output as one might expect in a conventional index. Instead, they are based on the importance of each country in determining the world interest rate—on each country's contribution to world-asset equilibrium. The key term in the weights is θ. This is the ratio of the domestic source component of the key currency country's money supply to the total world domestic source component, where the peripheral country's domestic source component is weighted by the fraction of official reserves held in cash or deposits with key currency authorities. As θ approaches unity the weight assigned to the peripheral country in the output index goes to zero. Since the coefficient of dD/D in (6.16''') also becomes zero, the world interest rate is determined essentially by conditions in the key currency country. Y_w becomes identical with Y^* and AE_w becomes simply the key currency country's LM curve as conventionally defined. And as $\theta \to 0$, the weight of the key currency country in Y_w and in the determination of the world interest rate becomes zero. Y_w becomes identical with Y, and IE_w with IE, and AE_w becomes the peripheral country's conventional LM curve.

Consider the conditions under which θ will go to unity. First, this will obviously occur when the peripheral country is very small relative to the key currency country so that $D/D^* \to 0$ (recall that $\psi \leqslant 1$). In this case, an open-market expansion of credit in the peripheral country has a trivial effect on the total volume of credit in the world as a whole and hence on the world interest rate. Second, θ will go to unity as ψ approaches zero regardless of the relative sizes of the two countries. When ψ is zero, the peripheral country holds all its foreign exchange reserves in key currency denominated bonds. Changes in the stock of official reserves thus have no effect on the key currency country's money supply because they do not put key currency money into and out of circulation. The rate of interest in the key currency country is unaffected. Since the world interest rate must be the same as the interest rate in the key currency country, it also cannot change. Thus an expansion of credit in the peripheral country results simply in a loss of official reserves with no effect on the world interest rate. It should be emphasised that this will occur even if the peripheral country is very large relative to the key currency country.

For the parameter θ to go to zero, the key currency country would have to be very small relative to the peripheral country so that $D^*/D \to 0$. But even if this is the case, θ can only go to zero if $\psi > 0$. Official reserves in the peripheral country must be held in cash or central bank deposits, at least to some significant degree. Casual knowledge of actual practice suggests that ψ would normally be close to zero— official reserves would be held primarily in interest-bearing, key currency denominated debt rather than in non-interest bearing cash, or deposits with the key currency country's authorities. The key currency country thus would have to be miniscule in size before θ would approach zero.

(a) Monetary policy   We can now analyse the effects of monetary policy in the less-than-full-employment case. Suppose that the authorities in the key currency country conduct an expansionary monetary policy by increasing D^*. If the key currency is not tiny in relation to the rest of the world or if ψ is nearly zero, the world money supply will expand. AE_w will shift to the left and r will fall in Figure 6.2, increasing output and employment all over the world. The balance of payments implications are not shown on the figure, but are immediately obvious from inspection of equation (6.10'). When Y rises the quantity of money demanded by peripheral-country residents increases. They re-establish portfolio equilibrium by selling assets abroad, forcing the peripheral country's authorities to provide the desired money holdings by accumulating foreign exchange reserves— that is, by increasing R. The authorities in the peripheral country can prevent this balance of payments effect by expanding D sufficiently to satisfy the increased demand for money holdings without an international portfolio adjustment. Whatever they do, the money supply will necessarily expand to satisfy the increased demand. If changes in official reserves are undesirable, the peripheral country's authorities must acquiesce and follow the credit-expansion policy in the key currency country. As long as official reserves are held almost exclusively in key currency bonds, the key currency country can be quite small and these results will still hold.[10]

Suppose now that the authorities in the peripheral country expand credit by increasing D. When the country is either small relative to the key currency country or holds virtually all its official reserves in key currency bonds—that is, when $\theta \rightarrow 1.0$—AE_w will be unaffected and the world interest rate, and both countries' incomes, will not change. As can be seen from (6.10'), the increase in D will produce an exactly equal decline in R because $L(r, Y)$ does not change. A one-shot balance of payments deficit will result and all the attempted monetary expansion will leak away. The money supplies in both countries will be unaffected.

When the peripheral country is large and holds a significant amount of its official reserves in key currency, or deposits with the key country's authorities, so that ψ is positive and θ is less than unity, the increase in D will increase the world money supply. Domestic residents re-establish portfolio equilibrium by purchasing assets abroad, forcing the authorities to maintain the exchange rate by selling official reserves, thereby increasing the money supply in the key currency country. The world interest rate falls as AE_w shifts to the left. Output and employment expand in both countries. Since the fall in the world interest rate and increase in domestic output leads to an increase in $L(r, Y)$ in equation (6.10′), the peripheral country will not lose reserves to the full extent of the increase in D. It will necessarily lose some reserves, of course, because otherwise the money holdings of the key currency country residents could not increase as required for the world interest rate to fall.

(b) Fiscal policy Consider now the effects of fiscal or other exogenous aggregate demand expansion. First suppose that government expenditure in the key currency country increases. As long as the key currency country is of reasonable size both IE and IE^* shift to the right. IE_w will thus shift to the left. The world interest rate rises and Y_w increases. Output will increase in the key currency country, and either rise or fall in the peripheral country depending on whether the effect of the rightward shift of IE exceeds or falls short of the effect of the rise in r. And, as is evident from a look at equation (6.10′), the peripheral country's balance of payments will deteriorate if Y falls and could improve or deteriorate if Y rises, depending on the relative effects on the demand for money of the simultaneous increases in Y and r.

Now suppose that government expenditure in the peripheral country increases. The curves IE and IE^* will again shift to the right, but the rightward shift of IE^* will be insignificant if the peripheral country is very small—the shift in its trade balance would in this case have an insignificant effect on aggregate demand in the key currency country. Because the peripheral country is small, IE_w is also unaffected, so no world interest rate effect can take place. Output will rise significantly in the peripheral country but not in the key currency country. A one-shot surplus will appear in the peripheral country's balance of payments and the stock of official reserves will increase. If the peripheral country is large in relation to the key currency country, IE_w will shift to the left because both IE and IE^* will shift significantly to the right. There will be a positive effect on the world interest rate, which will moderate the expansion of the peripheral country's output. The effect on the key currency country's output could be positive or negative, depending on the magnitude of the rightward shift of IE^* in relation to the upward movement along the curve due to the rise in the world interest rate.

(c) Conclusions The important general conclusion is that under fixed exchange rates world monetary policy is run by the key-currency country's authorities. In the very likely situation where the bulk of the peripheral country's foreign exchange reserves are held in key currency denominated bonds, the peripheral country cannot affect its output and employment and the world interest rate by monetary expansion—its output will be determined by what happens in the key currency country. Indeed, it cannot even control its money supply—any funds pumped into the economy are lost through the balance of payments. This conclusion holds regardless of the size of the key currency country in relation to the peripheral country. But even if the peripheral country were fairly large and a significant part of its reserves were held in cash or deposits with the key currency country's central bank, so that domestic monetary expansion and contraction would have world interest rate and output effects, balance of payments pressure will in most cases still force the peripheral country's authorities to acquiesce and adjust the domestic source component of the money supply to match expansions and contractions in the key currency country. A peripheral country would have to have a lot of foreign exchange reserve holdings to buck key currency monetary policy for any length of time.

With regard to fiscal policy or other exogenous shifts in aggregate demand, the conclusion is that expansion in the key currency country will increase home output but not necessarily output in the peripheral country. And fiscal expansion in the peripheral country will increase its output but the effect, if any, on the key currency country's output will be ambiguous. Again the balance of payments effect of key currency country expansion or contraction will exert pressure on the peripheral country to engage in acquiescent monetary or fiscal expansion or contraction.

Diagrammatic Analysis—Full Employment Case†

We now turn our attention to the full-employment case which is analysed in Figure 6.3. The graphical approach is somewhat different than in the previous case of less than full employment. The two income–expenditure equations (6.1) and (6.2) now solve for the two variables r and $P/\pi P^*$, given the full-employment levels of output and the exogenous levels of GX and GX^*. The solution is given on the right

---

† Again, readers with good background can proceed directly to (c) Conclusions, without jeopardising understanding of subsequent material. A rigorous treatment is given in Mathematical Note 2 at the end of the chapter.

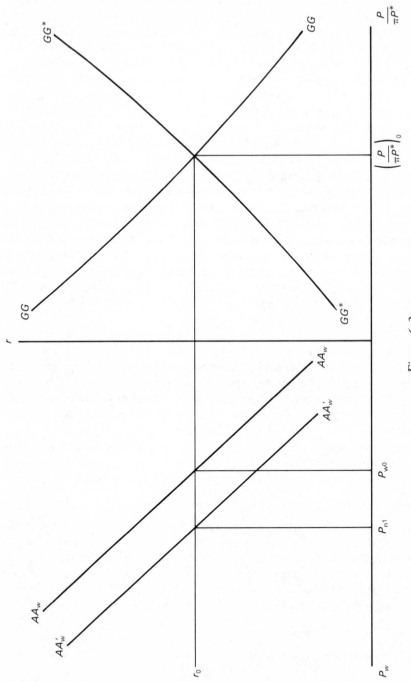

Figure 6.3

side of Figure 6.3. The curve *GG* gives the combinations of *r* and $P/\pi P^*$ for which aggregate demand equals aggregate supply in the peripheral country. It is negatively sloped because an increase in the interest rate reduces aggregate demand requiring a fall in the relative price of the country's goods to bring about a compensating improvement of the trade balance. The GG^* curve gives the combinations of *r* and $P/\pi P^*$ for which aggregate demand equals aggregate supply in the key currency country. It is positively sloped because a rise in the world interest rate reduces aggregate demand requiring a fall in the relative price level of the country to shift a corresponding amount of world demand onto its output. The interest rate and real price ratio $P/\pi P^*$ are determined by the intersection of the two curves. The interest rate thus determined projects across to the right side of Figure 6.3 where we have an index of world prices P_w on the horizontal axis. This world price level will have to adjust to where the aggregate world demand for money equals the world supply.

To investigate the weights in this aggregation we differentiate equation (6.13) totally and translate the differentials into relative changes. We thus obtain

$$\frac{D^*}{D^*+\psi D}\frac{dD^*}{D^*}+\frac{\psi D}{D^*+\psi D}\frac{dD}{D}$$

$$=\left(\frac{rP^*L_r^*}{D^*+\psi D}+\frac{\psi PL_r}{D+\psi D}\right)\frac{dr}{r}+\frac{P^*L^*(.)}{D^*+\psi D}\frac{dP^*}{P^*}+\frac{\psi L(.)P}{D^*+\psi D}\frac{dP}{P} \quad (6.17)$$

Using the same simplifications as in the case of (6.16) we can reduce this to

$$\frac{dr}{r}=-\frac{\theta}{\Delta}\frac{dD^*}{D^*}-\frac{(1-\theta)}{\Delta}\frac{dD}{D}+\frac{\theta(1-\psi\lambda^*)}{\Delta}\frac{dP^*}{P^*}+\frac{(1-\theta)(1+\psi\lambda)}{\Delta}\frac{dP}{P} \quad (6.17')$$

where $\Delta = -[\eta^*\theta(1-\psi\lambda^*) + \eta(1-\theta)(1+\psi\lambda)] > 0, \theta = D^*/(D^*+\psi D)$, $\lambda^* = R/D^*, \lambda = R/D, \eta^*$ and η are the interest elasticities of demand for money, and ψ is the fraction of the peripheral country's official foreign exchange reserves held in the form of currency and deposits with the key-currency country's central bank. Equation (6.17′) is the total differential of (6.13′) with respect to D^*, D, P^* and P.

We can now define the price index P_w as a geometrically weighted average of P^* and P, with the weights being $[\theta(1-\psi\lambda^*)]/\Delta$ and $[(1-\theta)(1-\psi\lambda)]/\Delta$ respectively. This implies of course, that dP_w/P_w equals the two right hand terms of (6.17′), namely

$$\frac{dP_w}{P_w} = \frac{\theta(1-\psi\lambda^*)}{\Delta}\frac{dP^*}{P^*} + \frac{(1-\theta)(1+\psi\lambda)}{\Delta}\frac{dP}{P} \quad (6.18)$$

The weights in the world price index P_w are not the relative contributions of the respective countries to world output, as is usually the case with price indexes. Rather, they are the contributions of the respective countries in determining the world interest rate.

The condition of world asset equilibrium appears on the left side of Figure 6.3 as the curve AA_w, which gives the combinations of the world interest rate and the price index P_w for which world asset markets are in equilibrium. Equation (6.17′), upon substitution of (6.18), gives the total differential of that curve. Its slope is unity in the relevant range.

(a) Monetary policy Now consider the effects of a monetary expansion in the key currency country. If the peripheral country is very small, or if it holds virtually all its reserves in interest-bearing, key currency bonds (i.e. $\psi = 0$) as is likely to be the case, θ becomes unity and the AA_w curve shifts to the right in proportion to the increase in D^*. P_w increases in the same proportion. Since r and $P/\pi P^*$ are unaffected, being determined by real factors on the left side of Figure 6.3, P and P^* both rise in the same proportion as P_w. The balance of payments effect can not be shown on Figure 6.3, but can be seen from equation (6.10′). The differential of that equation yields

$$dR = P \cdot L(.) \frac{dP}{P} + PL_r dr - dD \qquad (6.10'')$$

The rise in P increases the domestic demand for nominal money balances in the peripheral country, causing the public to sell assets abroad. The peripheral country's authorities must increase the stock of foreign exchange reserves to prevent the local currency from appreciating.

If the peripheral country is of significant size in relation to the key currency country and holds a significant part of its official reserves in key currency and central bank deposits, θ will be less than unity and the rightward shift of AA_w and the increase in P_w will be less than proportional to the increase in D^*. Since the interest rate cannot change and $P/\pi P^*$ is unaffected, both P^* and P will rise proportionally with P_w. The accumulation of reserves by the peripheral country will be correspondingly smaller.

In both the above cases the peripheral country can avoid accumulating reserves by simply expanding D appropriately.[11]

Monetary expansion in the peripheral country will have no effect on domestic or world prices as long as $\theta \to 1$. The loss in reserves required to maintain the exchange rate will be exactly equal to the expansion of the domestic source component. If the peripheral country is large and holds some significant portion of its reserves in key currency or central bank deposits, θ will be less than unity and the world money supply will increase. The AA_w curve will shift to the left and world prices—i.e. prices in both countries and the price index P_w—will rise. Since dP/P is positive in (6.10″), not all of the increase in the domestic source component will be lost through the balance of payments. Some will, however, because otherwise the quantity of money held by key currency country residents would not increase as required for the increase in P^* to occur. It would appear that even if the peripheral country is quite large, the balance of payments effects of unilateral credit expansion and contraction are likely to create a strong disincentive for independent policy. The pressure will be to increase and decrease D in proper proportion to D^*, and thereby avoid changes in the stock of reserves.

(b) Fiscal policy   Finally, let us briefly consider the effects of fiscal policy and other real sector shifts. These are considered with reference to Figure 6.4. Take first the case where both the key and peripheral countries are of similar size. An expansion of GX^* will shift the curve GG_0^* upward to GG_1^* because a rise in the interest rate will be required at each level of $P/\pi P^*$ to restrict investment and 'make room' for the additional government expenditure. The equilibrium interest rate–price ratio combination will move from point a to point b and the price index P_w will rise. The key currency country's price level must rise relative to that of the peripheral country. If the peripheral country's authorities hold all their reserves in interest-bearing, key currency denominated bonds (so $\psi = 0$), the parameter θ will be unity and the rise in P^* will be proportional to the rise in P_w. This rise in P^* may or may not be sufficient to reduce $P/\pi P^*$ by the required amount, so the peripheral country's price level may either rise or fall. Either way there will be a deficit in the peripheral country's balance of payments. The effect of the rise in the world interest rate on the demand for money will be roughly the same in the two countries if η^* and η are not too different while the rise in P^* relative to P will increase the demand for money in the key currency country relative to the peripheral country. Key currency country residents will thus end up selling assets to residents of the peripheral country creating for the latter country a balance of payments deficit. If the peripheral country holds significant reserves in key currency or in deposits with the key currency country's authorities, θ will be less than unity and P^* will rise more than proportionally with P_w. Since the magnitude of the increase in P_w is dictated by the slope of AA_w and the equilibrium rise in r and not by the size of θ, P^* will have to increase relatively more than it had to when θ was unity. Since the new level of $P/\pi P^*$ is also determined

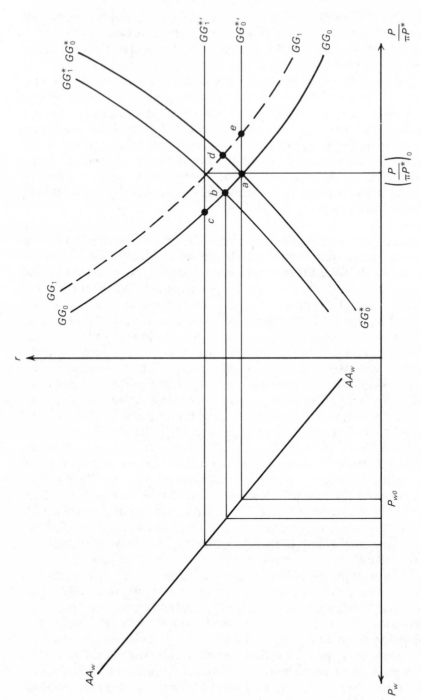

Figure 6.4

independently of θ, it follows that P will have to increase by more, or fall by less, than it did when θ equalled 1.

An expansion of government expenditure in the peripheral country under the above assumptions will have a symmetrical effect to that outlined above. The new equilibrium will be at point d, and P must now rise relative to P^*. In the case where $\theta = 1$, P^* must rise proportionally with P_w so P will have to rise even more. The peripheral country will necessarily experience a balance of payments surplus since the home demand for money will increase relative to the demand for money abroad.

Now consider the case where the peripheral country is extremely small relative to the key-currency country. In this case the key currency country's curve GG^* will be horizontal. A shift in international relative prices will produce a trivial change in that country's trade balance as a fraction of output, so a trivial rise in the interest rate is all that would be necessary to re-establish equality of aggregate demand and supply. An increase in GX^*, exactly equal to that analysed before, will now have a greater effect on the world interest rate and on the price level in the key currency country. Again, P may increase or fall, depending on the required fall in $P/\pi P^*$ in relation to the rise of P^*. The peripheral country will experience a balance of payments deficit for the reasons outlined before. When government expenditure in the peripheral country expands, the equilibrium $(r, P/\pi P^*)$ combination goes to point e. The relative price of the domestic good increases, but nothing happens to the world interest rate or the price level abroad. The domestic price level therefore rises in proportion to $P/\pi P^*$ and a balance of payments surplus results as domestic residents sell assets abroad to acquire the larger stock of nominal money balances demanded at the higher price level.

(c) Conclusions Our conclusions in the full-employment case can be summarised as follows. When the peripheral country holds its official reserves in key-currency denominated bonds, and the key currency country's money supply is therefore not affected by changes in the stock of reserves, the monetary authorities in the key-currency country run world monetary policy. The peripheral country's authorities have no choice but to tag along creating whatever stock of money the public wants to hold by adjusting either the stock of reserves or the domestic source component. And even when the peripheral country is large and does hold some reserves in currency or central-bank deposits in the key currency country, independent monetary policy leads to balance of payments adjustments which will

put pressure on its authorities to produce the same credit conditions as in the key currency country and avoid wide swings in official reserves. On the fiscal policy side, expansion in the key currency country will unambiguously lead to expansion in the peripheral country only if the latter is relatively small. But it creates a deficit in the peripheral country's balance of payments which will have a tendency to put expansionary pressure on its authorities. Expansion in the peripheral country always leads to a rise in its prices and a balance of payments surplus.

Importance of Size of the Key Currency Country

Perhaps the most striking conclusion to emerge from the analysis of both the less than full and full employment cases is that under normal circumstances where official reserves are held in interest bearing debt, the key currency country will run world monetary policy even if it is quite small. However, this does not mean that it makes no difference to world monetary stability if the key currency country is small or large. Private individuals in peripheral countries will normally hold key currency bank balances, and if the key currency country is relatively small in relation to one or more peripheral countries, changes in desired key currency holdings by residents of those countries could significantly shift the key currency country's demand function for money. (It should be recalled that the demand for money function $L^*(.)$ in (6.4) gives the demand for key currency by all holders, wherever they reside.) And a shift in the demand for money has exactly the opposite effect of an equal shift in supply. This would mean, for example, that if Switzerland were the key currency country and the USA a peripheral country, a desire of US residents to shift money balances from dollars into francs in anticipation, say, of a possible devaluation of the dollar in terms of the key (and every other) currency, would have a deflationary effect on the world economy. The excess demand for money in the key currency would cause r to rise, and Y and Y^* and eventually P and P^* to fall. On the other hand, if the USA were the key currency country and Switzerland the peripheral country, a switch from francs into dollars by Swiss residents would not have a significant effect on the world economy because Swiss holdings would be extremely small in relation to the US stock of money. A big key currency country, such as the USA, would dominate all other peripheral countries. Any other country, if it were the key currency country, would be dominated by the USA and possibly other countries, and blocks of countries, as well. Of course, even if the key currency country were large, a problem could arise if speculation arose that all peripheral currencies were going to have to be revalued in terms of the key currency. But normally, fundamental balance of payments disequilibria are likely to arise only in a few countries at any one time and, if these are small in relation to the key currency country, speculative movements of funds are not likely to have much effect on world equilibrium.

Imperfect Capital Mobility

Imperfect capital mobility, as the literature conceives it, means that interest rates in the two countries are not equal. It can arise in two ways. First, the assets of the two countries may not be perfect substitutes in the portfolios of world asset holders. As a result, the two countries' securities may not be regarded as equally risky and wealth owners will capitalise the income streams from the two assets at different rates of interest. Second, the governments of either or both countries may impose restrictions on international transactions in certain types of assets—e.g. foreigners may be prohibited from owning stock in banks and other financial institutions. As long as these restrictions are not comprehensive, as would be the case, for example, under a tight system of foreign exchange controls where all foreign ownership of domestic capital or domestic ownership of foreign assets is prohibited, the basic conclusions of the perfect capital mobility case still hold. International portfolio adjustments would still be possible at a point in time. Balance of payments disequilibria would arise to bring the demand and supply of money into equality and would not necessarily involve changes in the balance of trade. Restrictions on certain types of international asset transactions merely create an additional reason why the assets of the two countries would not be perfect substitutes in portfolios.

When capital mobility is imperfect in the sense outlined above, equation (6.12) must be modified to allow r to diverge from r^*. From the interest parity theorem together with efficient markets,

$$i - i^* = \phi + \frac{\pi' - \pi}{\pi} = \phi + E_\pi \qquad (6.12')$$

where π' is the forward price of the asterisked currency in units of the non-asterisked currency, E_π is the expected rate of depreciation of the non-asterisked country's currency, and ϕ is the risk premium on the non-asterisked country's assets. Utilising the fact that the nominal interest rate equals the real rate plus the expected rate of inflation we can rewrite this as

$$r = r^* + \phi + E_\pi + E_P^* - E_P$$
$$= r^* + \phi - E_q$$

where $E_q = E_P - E_\pi - E_P^*$ is the expected rate of change in the country's real price ratio, defined as $q = P/\pi P^*$. Although doubts about the ability of the authorities to maintain the fixed exchange rate may lead to a situation where E_π will not be zero, it is convenient here to assume that it is zero. In addition, it is useful to assume that $E_q = 0$, so that (6.12′) becomes

$$r = r^* + \phi \tag{6.12″}$$

The question then is: What are the factors determining the magnitude of the risk premium ϕ? In general, these are the factors that change wealth-owners' willingness to hold the securities of one country relative to those of the other. It is well known that as income rises asset holders will tend to shift their portfolios away from non-monetary assets towards money in order to satisfy a transactions demand for additional cash. This will tend to cause interest rates to rise. An effect on international interest-rate differentials will arise when income expands in one country because the residents of that country tend to hold the major part of their portfolios in domestic assets. A shift out of non-monetary assets into money will thus create a bigger excess supply of domestic assets than foreign assets, which will cause the domestic interest rate to rise relative to the foreign rate. The function determining ϕ must thus contain Y and Y^* as arguments, with the partial derivative of ϕ with respect to Y being positive, and that with respect of Y^* being negative.

Changes in the stock of official reserves will also have an effect on the international interest-rate differential. When the non-asterisked authorities accumulate reserves and increases R, they do so in response to a sale of assets by the residents of that country as they attempt to accumulate cash balances to maintain portfolio equilibrium. Indeed, the domestic currency value of the reserves accumulated is exactly equal to the domestic currency value of assets sold by the private sector as well as to the amount of (base) money injected into the domestic economy through the purchase of reserves. When this process takes place, the authorities are accumulating only foreign assets while the private sector is selling both domestic and foreign assets. The result is an excess supply of domestic assets and an excess demand for foreign assets. An increase in R will thus result in a rise in r relative to r^*. Equation (6.12″) can thus be rewritten

$$r = r^* + \phi(Y, Y^*, R) \tag{6.12‴}$$

where
$$\phi_y > 0, \phi_y^* < 0, \phi_R > 0.$$

When the assets of the two countries are imperfect substitutes in portfolios the demand functions for money in (6.10) and (6.,11) must also be modified to incorporate both r and r^* as arguments. Thus we must write

$$D + R = P \cdot \bar{L}(r, r^*, Y) \tag{6.10''}$$

and

$$D^* - \psi R = P^* \bar{L}^*(r^*, r, Y^*) \tag{6.11'}$$

Equations (6.12'''), (6.10'), (6.11'), (6.1) and (6.2) form a five-equation system in the five variables r, r^*, R, and Y or P and Y^* or P^*, depending upon whether we adopt Keynesian or classical labour-market assumptions. The exogenous variables are D, D^*, GX, GX^*, and π.

Little can be accomplished by working through the comparative status results in the imperfect capital mobility case. The process of adjustment is broadly the same as in the case of perfect capital mobility. And the basic conclusion that the key currency country runs world monetary policy remains unimpaired. The perfect capital mobility case is simpler and more tractable and gives a close enough approximation to the truth for the kinds of issues of interest here.

Mathematical Notes

1   Equations (6.1) to (6.4) can be solved for the comparative statics effects on interest rates and outputs or prices without reference to (6.5). The results can then be substituted into (6.5) to obtain the effect on the balance of payments. Differentiate (6.1) to (6.4) totally and choose the units so that $P = P^* = \pi = 1.0$ initially. Assume that trade is also initially balanced. This yields

$$(1 - C_y - I_y - B_{Ty})dY = (C_r + I_r)dr + dGX + B_{Ty}^* dY^* \\ + B_{TR}(dP - dP^* - d\pi) \tag{M6.1}$$

$$(1 - C_y^* - I_y^* + B_{Ty}^*)dY^* = (C_r^* + I_r^*)dr^* - B_{Ty}dY \\ - B_{TR}(dP - dP^* - d\pi) \tag{M6.2}$$

$$dr = \frac{1}{L_r}dM - \frac{L_y}{L_r}dY - \frac{L(.)}{L_r}dP \tag{M6.3}$$

$$dr^* = \frac{1}{L_r^*}dM^* - \frac{L_y^*}{L_r^*}dY^* - \frac{L^*(.)}{L_r^*}dP^* \tag{M6.4}$$

Less than Full Employment

Substituting (M6.3) into (M6.1) and (M6.4) into (M6.2) and letting $dP = dP^* = 0$, we obtain

$$dY = \frac{(C_r + I_r)}{L_r U} dM + \frac{1}{U} dGX + \frac{B_{Ty}^*}{U} dY^* - \frac{B_{TR}}{U} d\pi \qquad \text{(M6.3')}$$

and

$$dY^* = -\frac{B_{Ty}}{U^*} dY + \frac{B_{TR}}{U^*} d\pi \qquad \text{(M6.4')}$$

where

$$U = 1 - C_y - I_y - B_{Ty} + \frac{(C_r + I_r)L_y}{L_r} > 0$$

and

$$U^* = 1 - C_y^* - I_y^* + B_{Ty}^* + \frac{(C_r^* + I_r^*)L_y}{L_r^*} > 0$$

Since the results are symmetrical, we impose exogenous changes in the non-asterisked country only, assuming that dM^* and dGX^* are zero. The above two equations can be solved simultaneously to yield

$$dY = \frac{(C_r + I_r)}{U\bar{U}L_r} dM + \frac{1}{U\bar{U}} dGX - \frac{B_{TR}}{U\bar{U}}\left(1 - \frac{B_{Ty}^*}{U^*}\right) d\pi \qquad \text{(M6.5)}$$

$$dY^* = -\frac{(C_r + I_r)B_{Ty}}{U^* U\bar{U}L_r} dM - \frac{B_{Ty}}{U U^* \bar{U}} dGX + \frac{B_{TR}}{U^*\bar{U}}\left(1 + \frac{B_{Ty}}{U}\right) d\pi \qquad \text{(M6.6)}$$

where

$$\bar{U} = 1 + \frac{B_{Ty}B_{Ty}^*}{U U^*} > 0$$

Since $C_r, C_r^*, I_r, I_r^*, L_r, L_r^*, B_{Ty}$ and B_{TR} are all negative, and B_{Ty}^*, U, U^* and $\bar{U}$ are all positive, it follows directly that increases in the money supply or government expenditure in one of the countries increases both countries' output. A devaluation of a country's currency raises its output at the expense of output in the other country.

Substitution back into (M6.3) and (M6.4) gives the effects on the two countries' interest rates

$$dr = \frac{1}{U\bar{U}L_r}\left[1 - C_y - I_y - B_{Ty} + \frac{B_{Ty}B_{Ty}^*}{U^*}\right] dM - \frac{L_y}{U\bar{U}L_r} dGX$$

$$+ \frac{L_y B_{TR}}{U\bar{U}L_r}\left(1 - \frac{B_{Ty}^*}{U^*}\right) d\pi \qquad \text{(M6.6')}$$

$$dr^* = \frac{(C_r+I_r)B_{Ty}L_y^*}{U^*U\bar{U}L_rL_r^*}dM + \frac{B_{Ty}L_y^*}{UU^*\bar{U}L_r^*}dGX - \frac{B_{TR}L_y^*}{U^*\bar{U}L_r^*}\left(1-\frac{B_{Ty}}{U}\right)d\pi \quad (M6.6'')$$

It is easily seen that an increase in a country's money supply lowers its interest rate and raises the interest rate in the other country, while an increase in its government expenditure raises interest rates in both countries. A devaluation raises the domestic interest rate and lowers the foreign rate.

It is immediately obvious from the above results and (6.5) that an increase in a country's money stock or government expenditure deteriorates its balance of payments, reducing $B_T(.)$.

Full Employment

Substituting (M6.3) into (M6.1), and (M6.4) into (M6.2), letting $dY = dY^* = 0$, we obtain

$$dP = \frac{(C_r+I_r)}{BL_r}dM + \frac{1}{B}dGX - \frac{B_{TR}}{B}dP^* - \frac{B_{TR}}{B}d\pi \quad (M6.7)$$

$$dP^* = -\frac{B_{TR}}{B^*}dP + \frac{B_{TR}}{B^*}d\pi \quad (M6.8)$$

where

$$B = -B_{TR} + \frac{(L(.))(C_r+I_r)}{L_r} \quad >0$$

and

$$B^* = -B_{TR} + \frac{(L^*(.))(C_r^*+I_r^*)}{L_r^*} \quad >0$$

Again, recognising the symmetry of the results, we impose exogenous money supply and government expenditure changes in only the non-asterisked country.

Equations (M6.7) and (M6.8) solve for the comparative statics effects of the money supply and government expenditure changes on domestic and foreign prices,

$$dP = \frac{(C_r+I_r)}{\bar{B}BL_r}dM + \frac{1}{\bar{B}B}dGX - \frac{B_{TR}}{\bar{B}B}\left(1+\frac{B_{TR}}{B^*}\right)d\pi \quad (M6.9)$$

and

$$dP^* = -\frac{(C_r+I_r)B_{TR}}{\bar{B}BB^*L_r}dM - \frac{B_{TR}}{\bar{B}BB^*}dGX + \frac{B_{TR}}{\bar{B}B^*}\left(1+\frac{B_{TR}}{B}\right)d\pi \quad (M6.10)$$

where $\bar{B} = 1 - [(B_{TR})^2/BB^*]$. Since B_{TR}/B and B_{TR}/B^* are both less than unity, $\bar{B}$ is positive. It is directly evident that monetary and fiscal expansion in a country increase both countries price levels, while a devaluation of a particular country's currency increases its own price level and lowers the price level abroad.

The effect of exogenous monetary and fiscal changes on relative domestic and foreign prices is given by

$$dP - dP^* = \frac{(C_r + I_r)^2 L(.)}{\bar{B}BB^*(L_r)^2} dM + \frac{(C_r + I_r)L(.)}{\bar{B}BB^*L_r} dGX$$
$$- \frac{B_{TR}}{B}\left(\frac{B^* + B_{TR}}{BB^*} + \frac{B + B_{TR}}{BB^*} \right) d\pi \qquad \text{(M6.11)}$$

It is directly evident that increases in the money supply, government expenditure, and the exchange rate all increase domestic relative to foreign prices. From this, together with (6.5), it follows that monetary and fiscal expansion worsens a country's balance of payments while a devaluation of its currency improves it.

The effects on interest rates can be obtained by substituting (M6.10) and (M6.10) into (M6.3) and (M6.4).

$$dr = \frac{1}{L_r}\left(1 - \frac{(C_r + I_r)L(.)}{\bar{B}BL_r} \right) dM - \frac{L(.)}{B\bar{B}L_r} dGX$$
$$+ \frac{B_{TR}L(.)}{\bar{B}BL_r}\left(1 + \frac{B_{TR}}{B} \right) d\pi \qquad \text{(M6.12)}$$

$$dr^* = \frac{(C_r + I_r)L(.)B_{TR}}{\bar{B}BB^*L_rL_r^*} dM + \frac{L(.)B_{TR}}{\bar{B}BB^*L_r^*} dGX$$
$$- \frac{L(.)B_{TR}}{\bar{B}B^*L_r}\left(1 - \frac{B_{TR}}{B} \right) d\pi \qquad \text{(M6.13)}$$

It can be easily shown that the coefficient of dM in equation (M6.12) is negative. From this and the signs of the other parameters it follows directly that an increase in the money supply lowers the domestic interest rate and raises the interest rate abroad, while an increase in government expenditure raises both domestic and foreign interest rates. A devaluation raises the domestic interest rate and lowers the foreign one.

2 Less than Full Employment

From (6.16''') the total differential of the world asset equation is

$$\frac{dr}{r} = -\frac{\theta}{\Delta}\frac{dD^*}{D^*} - \frac{(1-\theta)}{\Delta}\frac{dD}{D} + \frac{dY_w}{Y_w} \tag{6.16'''}$$

where

$$\theta = \frac{D^*}{D^*+\psi D}$$

$$\Delta = -[\eta^*\theta(1-\psi\lambda^*)+\eta(1-\theta)(1+\psi\lambda)]>0$$

and

$$\frac{dY_w}{Y_w} = \frac{\epsilon^*\theta(1-\psi\lambda^*)}{\Delta}\frac{dY^*}{Y^*} + \frac{\epsilon(1-\theta)(1+\psi\lambda)}{\Delta}\frac{dY}{Y}$$

To obtain the total differentials of the IE and IE^* curves we first differentiate (6.1) and (6.2) and translate the differentials into relative changes. This yields

$$\frac{dY}{Y} = \frac{\rho}{Z}\frac{dr}{r} + \frac{U_g}{Z}\frac{dGX}{GX} + \frac{\beta}{1-\beta}\frac{U_m^*\xi^*}{Z}\frac{dY^*}{Y^*} + \frac{U_m B_{Tq}}{Z}\frac{dq}{X}\frac{dq}{q} \tag{M6.14}$$

$$\frac{dY^*}{Y^*} = \frac{\rho^*}{Z^*}\frac{dr}{r} = \frac{U_g^*}{Z^*}\frac{dGX^*}{GX^*} + \frac{1-\beta}{\beta}\frac{U_m\xi}{Z^*}\frac{dY}{Y} - \frac{U_m^* B_{Tq}}{Z}\frac{dq}{X}\frac{dq}{q} \tag{M6.15}$$

where $q = P/\pi P^*$, $Z = 1 - C_y - I_y + U_m\xi$, $Z^* = 1 - C_y^* - I_y^* + U_m^*\xi^*$, $\rho = (C_r + I_r)/Y$, $\rho^* = (C_r^* + I_r^*)/Y^*$, $\beta = Y^*/(Y + Y^*)$, U_m and U_m^* are the ratios of imports to output in the respective countries, X is the initial level of exports and imports of both countries since trade is initially balanced, ξ and ξ^* are the respective income elasticities of demand for imports, and U_g and U_g^* are the ratios of government expenditure to output in the two countries. The initial levels of P, P^*, π, and q are unity.

Equations (M6.14) and (M6.15) can be further refined by noting that the ratios of imports to income, U_m and U_m^* will depend on the sizes of the two countries. If one country is extremely large and the other extremely small the large country's ratio of imports to income must be nearly zero— otherwise a small change in its income would produce a swamping effect on imports and income in the smaller country. Suppose that each country's ratio of imports to income approaches U as we shrink it to infinitesimal size and zero as we expand it to infinite size relative to the other country. This is equivalent to writing $U_m^* = (1 - \beta)U$ and $U_m = \beta U$. Substituting these expressions into (M6.14) and (M6.15) we obtain

$$\frac{dY}{Y} = \frac{\rho}{Z}\frac{dr}{r} + \frac{U_g}{Z}\frac{dGX}{GX} + \frac{\beta U\xi^*}{Z}\frac{dY^*}{Y^*} + \frac{\beta U B_{Tq}}{ZX}\frac{dq}{q} \tag{M6.14'}$$

and

$$\frac{dY^*}{Y^*} = \frac{\rho^*}{Z^*}\frac{dr}{r} + \frac{U_g^*}{Z^*}\frac{dGX^*}{GX^*} + \frac{(1-\beta)U\xi}{Z^*}\frac{dY}{Y} - \frac{(1-\beta)UB_{Tq}}{Z^*X}\frac{dq}{q} \quad \text{(M6.15')}$$

It is easy to see from these equations that as one country gets very large relative to the other a change in the small country's income has an insignificant feed-through effect on the large country's income. Moreover, while a change in international relative prices will produce equal and opposite effects on the two countries' trade balances, the percentage effect of the change in the trade balance on the large country's income will be insignificant.

Simultaneous solution of (M6.14') and (M6.15') for dY/Y and dY^*/Y^* yields the total differentials of the IE and IE^* curves.

$$\frac{dY}{Y} = \left(\frac{\rho}{ZZ'} + \frac{\beta U\xi^*\rho^*}{ZZ'Z^*}\right)\frac{dr}{r} + \frac{U_g}{ZZ'}\frac{dGX}{GX} + \frac{\beta U\xi^* U_g^*}{ZZ'Z^*}\frac{dGX^*}{GX^*}$$

$$+ \frac{\beta UB_{Tg}}{ZZ'X}\left(1 - \frac{(1-\beta)U\xi^*}{Z^*}\right)\frac{dq}{q} \qquad \text{(M6.16)}$$

$$\frac{dY^*}{Y^*} = \left(\frac{\rho^*}{Z^*Z'} + \frac{(1-\beta)U\xi\rho}{ZZ'Z^*}\right)\frac{dr}{r} + \frac{U_g^*}{Z^*Z'}\frac{dGX^*}{GX^*}$$

$$+ \frac{(1-\beta)U\xi U_g dGX}{ZZ'Z^*}\frac{dGX}{GX} - \frac{(1-\beta)UB_{Tq}}{Z^*Z'X}\left(1 - \frac{\beta U\xi}{Z}\right)\frac{dq}{q} \quad \text{(M6.17)}$$

where

$$Z' = 1 - \frac{(1-\beta)\beta U^2\xi\xi^*}{ZZ^*} > 0.$$

The total differential of the curve IE_w can be obtained by substituting (M6.16) and (M6.17) into the expression for dY_w/Y_w. This yields

$$\frac{dY_w}{Y_w} = V_r\frac{dr}{r} + V_g\frac{dGX}{GX} + V_g^*\frac{dGX^*}{GX^*} + V_q\frac{dq}{q} \qquad \text{(M6.18)}$$

where

$$V_r = \frac{\epsilon^*\theta(1-\psi\lambda^*)}{\Delta}\left(\frac{\rho^*}{Z^*Z'} + \frac{(1-\beta)U\xi\rho)}{ZZ'Z^*}\right)$$

$$+ \frac{\epsilon^*(1-\theta)(1+\psi\lambda)}{\Delta}\left(\frac{\rho}{ZZ'} + \frac{\beta U\xi^*\rho^*}{ZZ'Z^*}\right) < 0$$

$$V_g = \frac{\epsilon^*\theta(1-\psi\lambda^*)(1-\beta)U\xi U_g}{\Delta ZZ'Z^*} + \frac{\epsilon(1-\theta)(1+\psi\lambda)U_g}{\Delta ZZ'} \gtrless 0$$

$$V_g^* = \frac{\epsilon^*\theta(1-\psi\lambda^*)U_g^*}{\Delta Z^*Z'} + \frac{\epsilon(1-\theta)(1+\psi\lambda)\beta U\xi^* U_g^*}{\Delta ZZ'Z^*} \gtrless 0$$

$$V_q = \frac{\epsilon(1-\theta)(1+\psi\lambda)\beta UB_{Tq}}{\Delta ZZ'X}\left(1 - \frac{(1-\beta)U\xi^*}{Z^*}\right)$$

$$- \frac{\epsilon^*\theta(1-\psi\lambda^*)(1-\beta)UB_{Tq}}{\Delta Z^*Z'X}\left(1 - \frac{\beta U\xi}{Z}\right) \gtrless 0$$

The comparative statics effects of monetary and fiscal policy and exchange rate changes on the world interest rate can be obtained by substituting (M6.18) into (6.16′″). This yields

$$\frac{dr}{r} = -\frac{\theta}{\Delta\Delta'}\frac{dD^*}{D^*} - \frac{(1-\theta)}{\Delta\Delta'}\frac{dD}{D} + \frac{V_g dGX}{\Delta'} \frac{dGX}{GX}$$

$$+ \frac{V_g^* dGX^*}{\Delta'}\frac{dGX^*}{GX^*} + \frac{V_q}{\Delta'}\frac{dq}{q} \qquad\qquad \text{(M6.19)}$$

where $\Delta' = (1 - V_r) > 0$. If the key-currency country is large, with the result that θ and β both approach unity, the peripheral country's monetary and fiscal policy have no effect on the world interest rate. If the peripheral country is large relative to the key currency country, so that $\beta \to 0$, its monetary and fiscal policy will affect the world interest rate as long as $1 > \theta > 0$, which would require that $1 > \psi > 0$. Key currency monetary and fiscal policy will affect the world interest rate under the same circumstances.

The comparative statics effects on output in the two countries can be obtained by substituting (M6.19) into (M6.16) and (M6.17). It can be seen that monetary expansion, where effective, lowers the world interest rate and leads to an expansion of output in both countries. While fiscal expansion in a country always increases domestic output directly through (M6.16) and (M6.17), it also raises the world interest rate when the country is relatively large, leading to a negative secondary output effect. In the case where the key currency country is large—i.e. $\theta \to 1$ and $\beta \to 1$—the domestic output effect of its fiscal policy is given by

$$\frac{dY^*}{Y^*} = \frac{U_g^*}{Z^*}\left(1 + \frac{\rho^*\epsilon^*(1-\psi\lambda^*)}{\Delta'\Delta Z^*}\right)\frac{dGX^*}{GX^*}$$

It is easily seen from simple substitution that the term in the large parentheses is positive. The effect of key currency fiscal policy on the peripheral country's output under these circumstances is given by

$$\frac{dY}{Y} = \frac{U_g^*}{\Delta'ZZ^*}\left(U\xi^* - \frac{\rho\epsilon^*}{\eta^*}\right)\frac{dGX^*}{GX^*}$$

which can be positive or negative, depending on the magnitudes of the parameters. Fiscal expansion in the key currency country has a positive feed-through effect on the peripheral country's output via the trade balance, but it has a negative effect on account of the fact that it increases the world interest rate.

When the key currency country is small so that $\beta \to 0$, the effect of fiscal expansion on its own output is given by

$$\frac{dY^*}{Y^*} = \frac{U_g^*}{\Delta' Z^*}\left[1 + \left(\frac{\rho^*}{Z^*} + \frac{U\xi\rho}{ZZ^*}\right)\left(\frac{\epsilon^*\theta(1-\psi\lambda^*)}{\Delta}\right)\right.$$
$$\left. - \left(\frac{\rho^*}{Z^*} + \frac{U\xi\rho}{ZZ^*}\right)\left(\frac{\epsilon^*\theta(1-\psi\lambda^*)}{\Delta}\right)\right]\frac{dGX^*}{GX^*}$$

Even when $\theta \to 0$ on account of the fact that the large peripheral country holds its key currency reserves in cash, this expression reduces to $U_G^*/\Delta' Z^*$, which is positive. When the peripheral country's foreign exchange reserves are held in interest-bearing debt the secondary terms involving θ cancel out in the above expression. The effect on the peripheral country's output is given by

$$\frac{dY}{Y} = \frac{\rho V_g^*}{Z\Delta'}\frac{dGX^*}{GX^*}$$

which is negative for positive values of θ and zero as $\theta \to 0$. There is no positive feed-through effect into the peripheral country via the trade balance, only a possible negative effect of the rise in the world interest rate that will occur if peripheral-country reserves are held in interest-bearing debt.

Finally, consider the effects of fiscal expansion in the peripheral country. When that country is small—i.e. $\beta = \theta = 1$—the results are simple.

$$\frac{dY}{Y} = \frac{U_g}{Z}\frac{dGX}{GX}$$

and Y^* is unaffected. When the peripheral country is large,

$$\frac{dY}{Y} = \frac{U_g}{Z\Delta'}\left(1 - \frac{\epsilon\theta(1-\psi\lambda^*)\rho}{\Delta Z^*}\right)\frac{dGX}{GX}$$

and peripheral country output always responds positively to domestic fiscal policy. The effect on the key-currency country's output is given by

$$\frac{dY^*}{Y^*} = \frac{U_G^*}{\Delta' ZZ^*}\left(U\xi + \frac{\rho\epsilon(1-\theta)(1+\psi\lambda)}{\Delta}\right)\frac{dGX}{GX}$$

The term in the large parentheses reduces to

$$\left(U\xi - \frac{\rho\epsilon}{\eta}\right)$$

when $\theta \to 0$. Peripheral-country fiscal policy has two effects on key currency country output—a positive feed-through effect via the trade balance and a negative effect due to the rise in the world interest rate. The latter effect is zero if the peripheral country holds all its foreign exchange reserves in bonds and θ therefore becomes unity.

The comparative statics effects of exogenous exchange rate changes can be read directly from (M6.16) and (M6.17) if we ignore the possible aggregation effect of the exchange rate on the world interest rate. A devaluation of the peripheral country's currency raises its income and lowers income in the key currency country. If the net effect on world income is zero—i.e. $V_q \to 0$—there will be no further effects on the countries via world interest rate changes. The conditions for this aggregation to hold are examined in the mathematical notes to Chapter 8.

Full Employment

The income expenditure equations (6.1) and (6.2) can be differentiated totally and the differentials translated into relative changes to yield

$$\frac{dr}{r} = -\frac{U_g}{\rho+\beta U\xi\rho^*/Z^*}\frac{dGX}{GX} - \frac{\beta U\xi^* U_g^*/Z^*}{\rho+\beta U\xi\rho^*/Z^*}\frac{dGX^*}{GX^*}$$

$$-\frac{\beta U\beta_{Tq}}{(\rho+\beta U\xi\rho/Z^*)X}\left(1-\frac{(1-\beta)U\xi^*}{Z^*}\right)\frac{dq}{q} \qquad \text{(M6.20)}$$

$$\frac{dr}{r} = -\frac{U_g^*}{\rho^*+\beta U\xi\rho/Z}\frac{dGX^*}{GX^*} - \frac{(1-\beta)U\xi U_g/Z}{\rho^*+\beta U\xi\rho/Z}\frac{dGX}{GX}$$

$$+\frac{(1-\beta)UB_{Tq}}{(\rho^*+\beta U\xi\rho/Z)X}\left(1-\frac{\beta U\xi}{Z}\right)\frac{dq}{q} \qquad \text{(M6.21)}$$

These can be solved simultaneously for dq/q and dr/r as functions of dGX/GX and dGX^*/GX^*,

$$\frac{dq}{q} = -\frac{W_g}{W_q}\frac{dGX}{GX} + \frac{W_g^*}{W_q}\frac{dGX^*}{GX^*} \qquad \text{(M6.22)}$$

$$\frac{dr}{r} = -\left(\frac{U_g Z^*}{Z^*\rho+\beta U\xi\rho^*} - \beta\bar{N}\frac{W_g}{W_q}\right)\frac{dGX}{GX}$$

$$-\left(\frac{\beta U\xi U_g Z^*}{Z^*\rho + \beta U\xi\rho^*} + \beta\bar{N}\frac{W_g^*}{W_q} \right)\frac{dGX^*}{GX^*} \tag{M6.23}$$

where

$$W_g = \frac{U_g Z^*}{Z^*\rho + \beta U\xi^*\rho^*} - \frac{(1-\beta)U\xi U_g Z}{Z\rho + \beta U\xi\rho}$$

$$W_g^* = \frac{U_g^* Z}{Z\rho^* + \beta U\xi\rho} - \frac{\beta U\xi^* U_g^* Z^*}{Z^*\rho + \beta U\xi\rho^*}$$

$$W_q = \beta\bar{N} + (1-\beta)\bar{N}^*$$

$$\bar{N} = \frac{UB_{Tq}}{X(Z^*\rho + \beta U\xi^*\rho^*)}(Z^* - (1-\beta)U\xi^*) > 0$$

$$\bar{N}^* = \frac{UB_{Tq}}{X(Z\rho^* + \beta U\xi\rho)}(Z - \beta U\xi) > 0$$

If we assume that the two economies are similar in structure so that $U_g = U_g^*$, $\rho = \rho^*$ and $\xi = \xi^*$, we can easily demonstrate that W_g and W_g^* are negative for values of β approaching zero, unity, and one-half. Under these circumstances a rise in GX clearly raises q while a rise in GX^* lowers it. Also an increase in GX^* raises the world interest rate as β becomes significantly greater than zero while an increase in GX raises it as long as β is significantly less than unity.

From the fact that

$$\frac{dq}{q} = \frac{dP}{P} - \frac{dP^*}{P^*} - \frac{d\pi}{\pi} \tag{M6.24}$$

it is evident that fiscal expansion in a country increases its price level relative to the foreign price level. The effect on the world price level can be obtained from (6.17′) upon substitution of (6.18).

$$\frac{dP_w}{P_w} = \frac{dr}{r} + \frac{\theta}{\Delta}\frac{dD^*}{D^*} + \frac{1-\theta}{\Delta}\frac{dD}{D} \tag{M6.24}$$

The world price level will rise if the country undertaking fiscal expansion is of significant size.

First, let us focus on the effects of fiscal policy in the key currency country. When that country is large so that β and θ both approach unity,

$$\frac{dP^*}{P^*} = \frac{dP_w}{P_w} = \frac{dr}{r} = -\left(\frac{U\xi U_g Z^*}{Z^*\rho + U\xi\rho^*} + \frac{U_g^* Z}{Z^*\rho + U\xi\rho} \right.$$

$$\left. - \frac{U\xi U_g^* Z^*}{Z^*\rho + U\xi\rho^*} \right)\frac{dGX^*}{GX^*} = -\frac{U_g^* Z}{Z\rho^* + U\xi\rho}\frac{dGX^*}{GX^*}$$

and

$$\frac{dP}{P} = \frac{dP^*}{P^*} + \frac{dq}{q} = \left[\frac{U_g^* Z}{Z\rho^* U\xi\rho} \left(1 - \frac{X(Z^* p + U\xi^* \rho^*)}{U\beta_{Tq} Z^*}\right) \right. $$
$$\left. + \frac{U\xi^* U_g^* X}{U\beta_{Tq}} \right] \frac{dGX^*}{GX^*}$$

An increase in government expenditure in the key-currency country always increases that country's price level. It may increase or decrease the price level of the peripheral country depending upon the magnitude of $\rho(= \rho^*)$ in relation to β_{Tq}—that is, upon whether the world interest rate effect exceeds or falls short of the relative price (balance of trade) effect.

As the key currency country becomes small and $\beta \to 0$, the effect of GX^* on r vanishes as does the effect on the world price level. It is evident from (6.18) that if θ also goes to zero (i.e. the peripheral country's foreign exchange reserves are held in cash), $dP/P = dP_w/P_w = 0$. The effect on the key currency country's price level is given by $dP^*/P^* = -(dq/q)$.

Since q necessarily falls in response to an increase in GX^*, the price level in the key currency country necessarily rises. If the peripheral country's foreign exchange reserves are held in interest-bearing government debt, so $\theta \to 1$,

$$\frac{dP^*}{P^*} = \frac{dP_w}{P_w} = 0$$

from (6.18), and

$$\frac{dP}{P} = \frac{dq}{q}$$

The price level in the peripheral country falls as a result of the fiscal expansion in the key currency country. The key currency country has no weight in determining the world interest rate because it is so small, but it is the sole determinant of asset equilibrium regardless of its size. It therefore forces a price-level reduction on the (large) peripheral country.

It is easily seen by symmetry that a fiscal expansion in the peripheral country will leave the world interest rate unaffected as that country becomes small and will positively affect the world interest rate as it becomes large. If the country is small θ necessarily goes to unity so its price level necessarily increases as its trade balance deteriorates to 'make room' for the additional demands on domestic resources resulting from fiscal expansion. If the country is large θ could go to zero or unity, depending on whether or not its foreign exchange reserves are held in government bonds.

If $\theta \to 0$,

$$\frac{dP}{P} = \frac{dP_w}{P_w} = \frac{dr}{r}$$

The domestic price level will rise because r is positively affected. The key currency country's price level will be determined by

$$\frac{dP^*}{P^*} = \frac{dP}{P} - \frac{dq}{q}$$

and will be ambiguously affected depending on the relative magnitudes of the interest rate effect and the trade balance effect— this result is symmetrical to the effect of fiscal expansion in the key currency country when it is large.

If $\theta \to 1$,

$$\frac{dP^*}{P^*} = \frac{dP_w}{P_w} = \frac{dr}{r}$$

Fiscal expansion in the peripheral country raises the price level in the key currency country. The effect on its domestic price level is given by

$$\frac{dP}{P} = \frac{dr}{r} + \frac{dq}{q}$$

and will be positive since both q and r increase.

It is clear from (M6.22) and (M6.23) that monetary expansion in either country has no effect on the relative price levels of the two countries or on world interest rates. Thus it is evident from (M6.24) that monetary expansion in a country increases the world price level in proportion to that country's weight in determining world asset equilibrium.

It follows directly from the (M6.24), and the invariance of q with respect to monetary factors, that a devaluation of the peripheral country's currency raises its price level relative to the key-currency country's price level in proportion to the increase in π.

Appendix: The Balance of Payments

The balance of payments is an accounting statement that summarises a nation's transactions with the rest of the world. Purchases of goods, services and assets abroad appear in the accounts as debits and sales of goods, services and assets appear as credits. Because of the nature of double-entry bookkeeping, the sum of all debits in the balance of payments must equal the sum of all credits—that is, the balance of payments must balance. This will be explained in more detail as the discussion proceeds.

The balance of payments is divided into two accounts—the current account and the capital account. The current account contains all transactions that involve the production and disposal of, and claims on, current output. These include exports and imports of commodities and of services such as freight, insurance, etc. Payments and receipts of interest on investments are also current transactions because they involve claims against current output that represent the income from capital used in the production process. The balance on account of interest payments to and from foreigners is called the *debt service balance*. The balance on account of exports and imports of commodities and other services is called the *trade balance*. The sum of the trade balance and the debt service balance equals the *current account balance*.

The capital account contains all transactions that involve claims against future domestic or foreign output. A purchase of bonds or equity shares from foreigners or a direct investment abroad is the acquisition of a claim against future foreign output. It represents a capital outflow from the domestic economy because capital, in the sense of past savings or foregone consumption, is being lent abroad to produce output there. A sale of bonds or equity to foreigners or a direct investment by foreigners in the domestic economy is the acquisition by foreigners of a claim against future domestic output and represents a capital inflow. Foreign savings are borrowed for use in domestic production. It should be noted that a purchase of foreign currency or other international reserves by domestic residents either privately or through the actions of their government represents the acquisition of a claim against future foreign output and a capital outflow. And the purchase of domestic currency by foreign individuals and governments represents the acquisition by foreigners of a claim against future domestic output and represents a capital inflow.

The components of the balance of payments accounts are summarised in Table A6.1. Items in the first column on the left, the debt items, enter negatively. The credit items in the middle column enter positively. The horizontal sum of the items in the left and middle columns give the corresponding balances in the right column. The sum of all items in the debit column plus the sum of all items in the credit column must equal zero. Correspondingly the balance of trade plus the debt service balance—i.e. the current account balance—plus the

TABLE A6.1   *Balance-of-Payments Transactions: A Summary*

Debits (−)	Credits (+)	
Imports of commodities	+ Exports of commodities	⎫
+	+	⎬ = Balance of trade
Imports of services such as freight and insurance	+ Exports of services such as freight and insurance	⎭
+	+	+
Payments of interest and dividends to foreigners	Receipts of interest + and dividends from foreigners	⎫ ⎬ = Debt-service balance ⎭
=	=	=
Imports of goods and services	+ Exports of goods and services	⎫ ⎬ = Current-account balance ⎭
+	+	
Purchases of equities, bonds, foreign currency etc., from foreigners and direct investment abroad (capital outflows)	Sales of equities, bonds, domestic currency + to foreigners and foreign direct investment in domestic economy (capital inflows)	+ ⎫ ⎬ = Capital-account balance ⎭
=	=	=
TOTAL DEBITS	+ TOTAL CREDITS	= ZERO

capital account balance must equal zero. A current account deficit must be offset by a capital account surplus and vice versa.

The fundamental reason why the balance of payments always balances relates to the way in which the various transactions are entered in the accounts. Suppose, for example, that a domestic importer buys $1000 worth of goods abroad and his supplier gives him 30 days to pay. This appears as a $1000 debit under imports and $1000 of borrowing abroad which enters as a credit in the capital account. When the importer pays off the account, borrowings abroad and holdings of foreign currency are both reduced by $1000. The reduction of borrowings reduces the middle column and the reduction of foreign currency holdings reduces the left-hand column by the same amount, so that balance is preserved. The foreign currency in the importer's account was perhaps acquired by selling domestic currency for it on the foreign exchange market. This increase in domestic holdings of foreign currency would appear as an increase in the debit column and the increase in foreign holdings of domestic currency would appear as an equal increase in the credit column—again, as always, balance is preserved.

As the above discussion indicates, debit transactions generally involve the conversion of domestic currency into foreign currency on the foreign exchange market while credit transactions involve the conversion of foreign currency into domestic currency. The fact that the balance of payments always balances means simply that all foreign currency obtained from the sale of goods and services and securities is used somehow—either spent on goods, services and securities or held as an asset. And all domestic currency relinquished in the purchase of goods, services and securities is either held in reserve by foreigners or used to purchase goods, services, and securities from domestic residents.

The equality of the current-account surplus with the capital account deficit can be treated as an *ex ante* equilibrium relationship as well as *ex post* identity. We can write

$$B_T(Y, Y^*, P/\pi P^*) = NCO \tag{A6.1}$$

where NCO is the net capital outflow and the function $B_T(.)$ gives the trade balance as defined in the text. For simplicity, we assume that the debt service balance is zero. The net capital outflow equals the excess of domestic resident's purchases of securities over sales of securities by domestic firms. The purchase of securities, broadly defined, by domestic residents equals domestic savings, while the sales of securities by firms equals domestic investment. (A6.1) can therefore be rewritten.

$$B_T(Y, Y^*, P/\pi P^*) = S' - I' \tag{A6.2}$$

where saving and investment is taken to include asset accumulation and investment by government as well as on private account. Savings equals income minus consumption (both private and government) so we can write

$$B_T(Y, Y^*, P/\pi P^*) = Y - C' - I' \tag{A6.3}$$

This expression can be rearranged to yield

$$Y = C' + I' + B_T(Y, Y^*, P/\pi P^*) \tag{A6.4}$$

which is, of course, the standard income–expenditure equation. This equation is in one sense an identity and in another sense an equilibrium relationship. It is an identity in the accounting sense—all income must be either consumed or saved and total receipts abroad must always equal total payments. It is an equilibrium equation in the sense that for markets to be in equilibrium desired savings minus desired investment must equal desired exports minus desired imports—otherwise, income, prices, the exchange rate, or some other variable will change. The equation must hold *ex ante* in the sense that if aggregate demand does not equal aggregate supply the system is out of equilibrium and something must change, and *ex post* in the sense that either inventory adjustments or changes in prices, outputs, etc. will always ensure that output produced will equal output absorbed.

The equilibrating process can be illustrated most simply in the full-employment case where capital is perfectly mobile internationally. In this case the domestic interest rate is determined in the world as a whole and output is fixed at the full-employment level. Savings are determined by the community's choices between present and future consumption and investment is determined by the decisions of world investors as to the allocation of investment among countries. Given the (positive or negative) net capital inflow thus determined there is an equilibrium level of the balance of trade. If the trade balance is above this equilibrium level, there will be excess aggregate demand. The equilibrium relative price of domestic goods—the real price ratio, $P/\pi P^*$—must rise to switch world expenditure from domestic to foreign goods.[12] This will reduce the trade balance in line with the net capital outflow. If the trade balance is below its equilibrium level there will be excess aggregate supply in the domestic economy and a fall in the real price ratio will be required to switch world expenditure onto domestic goods and bring the trade balance into line with the net capital outflow.

Under less than full employment conditions the equilibrating process is more complicated because excess aggregate demand or supply in the domestic economy will lead to changes in domestic output which will change both the trade balance and (through the income effect on savings) the net capital flow.

The fact that the balance of payments balances and aggregate demand equals aggregate supply does not imply that there is balance of payments equilibrium. The equality of receipts and payments implies balance of payments equilibrium only if none of the transactions are undertaken by government for the purpose of manipulating the exchange rate. All transactions must be *autonomous*—that is, undertaken for their own sake as a result of actions of private individuals and government in the ordinary course of business. When the government buys or sells foreign currency in order to maintain a given level of the exchange rate or cause the exchange rate to change it is making an *induced* transaction. This permits an imbalance between autonomous receipts and payments to occur.

When autonomous payments exceed autonomous receipts there is an excess supply of domestic currency on the foreign exchange market. If the government does nothing, the domestic currency will depreciate to drive autonomous payments and receipts back into line. This depreciation will lead, of course, to changes in domestic prices and output to keep aggregate demand equal to aggregate supply in equations (A6.2) to (A6.4). The government can prevent the domestic currency from depreciating by selling foreign currency out of its reserves and buying up the excess supply of domestic currency. When this happens there is a *balance of payments deficit*. An induced diminution of official foreign exchange reserves brings total (autonomous plus induced) receipts into equality with total payments without a change in the exchange rate.

Similarly, when autonomous receipts exceed autonomous payments there is an excess demand for domestic currency on the foreign exchange market and upward pressure on the external value of the domestic currency. The government can present an appreciation from occurring by accumulating foreign exchange reserves in return for domestic currency. When the government does this there is a *balance of payments surplus*.

The relationship between equilibrium in the balance of payments and equilibrium of aggregate demand and supply can be seen with reference to equation (A6.2). Domestic savings, which equals the total accumulation of assets by domestic residents both privately and through the intermediation of government, can be decomposed into two parts—autonomous asset accumulation on the part of both the public and private sectors, and induced asset accumulation by the government in connection with foreign exchange market intervention. We can thus write

$$S = AAC + \frac{dR}{dt} \tag{A6.5}$$

Where AAC is autonomous asset accumulation and dR/dt is the rate of change through time of the stock of official foreign exchange reserves. Substituting this equation into (A6.2) and rearranging the terms we get

$$\frac{dR}{dt} = B_T(Y, Y^*, P/\pi P^*) - (AAC - I) \tag{A6.6}$$

This says that the balance of payments surplus equals the current-account balance, which is autonomous and represented here by the balance of trade, minus the autonomous net capital outflow. The equality of aggregate demand and supply is implied by equation (A6.6) at all magnitudes of dR/dt. Balance of payments equilibrium occurs only when dR/dt is zero.

Notes

1 There was nevertheless great concern in the USA throughout the 1960s about the fact that other countries were running surpluses and the USA was therefore running a deficit. This concern was translated into various policy actions designed to reduce the apparent deficit, but these fell short of actual intervention in foreign exchange markets.

2 There were exceptions of course. Canada had a flexible exchange rate with all currencies throughout most of the 1950s; and some other countries maintained apparent balance of payments equilibrium by exchange restrictions and imposed multiple exchange rates. But the majority of countries followed the International Monetary Fund rules.

3 A very simply exposition of the basic income–expenditure model, on which the theory developed in this chapter is based, can be found in Chapter 4, Appendix I. The development in this chapter is self-contained and need not require prior familiarity with the text of Chapter 4.

4 Ideally, the price levels in the demand for money equations should be the price indexes of goods absorbed. These price indexes would depend on both P and P^*. However, the analysis is simplified at no cost in terms of our conclusions, by ignoring this.

5 For an elementary discussion of the concept of balance-of-payments disequilibrium, see the Appendix to this chapter.

6 To be correct, R in (6.8) should equal all past increments (positive or negative) to the stock of reserves, with each increment multiplied by the exchange rate existing at the time it occurred. The variable D should be calculated in the same way, with each past increment being evaluated at the price of bonds existing at the time. The variables R and D should not be viewed as the present values in the context of (6.8) because a change in the exchange rate or the interest rate and the capital gains or losses involved should not result in a change in the stock of high-powered money. High-powered money changes only when a *transaction* occurs. This refinement of (6.8) is not made here because it complicates our analysis without changing the conclusions.

7 Actually, only key currency or deposits with the key-currency country's central bank constitute a deduction from M^*. Deposits with commercial banks in the key-currency country, even if inactive, provide reserves for expansion of the banking system and should be considered as part of the central country's money supply.

8 They are presented rigorously in Mathematical note 2 at the end of the chapter.

9 Since the assets of the two countries are perfect substitutes in portfolios there is in effect a single homogeneous world non-monetary asset.

10 In the unrealistic case where the key currency country is small and ψ is, say, close to unity, the increase in D^* will have no effect on AE_w and on the world interest rate or world output. Official reserves in the peripheral country will increase as key country residents sell assets abroad, but the percentage increase will be infinitesimal because the peripheral country is so large relative to the key currency country.

11 In the case where R is to be maintained constant, D must be expanded in proportion to D^*.

12 The real price ratio is discussed on pp. 70–77 and in Chapter 5, Note 3. It is further discussed on p. 177.

7
The Liquidity Problem— Paper Gold and Special Drawing Rights

Nothing pre-occupied international monetary economists more in the 1960s than the liquidity problem. A common view was that the liquidity needs of the world were not being satisfied because the stock of monetary gold was not growing as fast as the volume of trade. Reserve accumulations in the form of US dollar short-term assets instead of gold were viewed as inappropriate because the gold stock was inadequate to redeem such assets if presented to the US authorities—a financial crisis endangering world economic stability could erupt at any time.

A related matter of concern was the perception of continuing US balance of payments deficits. An excess of purchases of goods, services, and long-term securities over sales was being financed by accumulations of dollar-denominated, short-term assets by other countries. The European countries objected that these accumulations were inflationary, but were not willing to revalue their currencies to eliminate the supposed surpluses. Rather they put pressure on the USA to curtail excess spending abroad by restricting aggregate demand. There was even pressure for the USA to raise the price of gold on the grounds that it would devalue the dollar and improve her balance of payments. This view was mistaken in that a rise in the price of gold would not devalue the US dollar in terms of other currencies as would be required for an effect on the balance of trade. The apparent balance of payments adjustment problem was thus confused with the liquidity problem. Countries like France deliberately converted assets into gold, or threatened to do so, in order to force the USA to do something about its alleged balance-of-payments deficit.

A further complication was the major industrial countries' concern that the USA was unjustly dominating the world monetary system and exploiting other countries as a result. This concern about domination was shared by many in the US who felt that their country's central role in the system caused problems in implementing domestic policy and any benefits from being the world's banker were not worth the cost.

Several solutions to these problems were suggested at the time. One alternative was to increase liquidity by raising the price of gold—at $70 per oz instead of $35, the existing gold stock would finance twice the volume of trade. Another was to allow exchange rates between countries to be determined by the demand and supply of the respective currencies in the foreign exchange market. This would involve a flexible price in the non-dollar currencies in terms of gold, and of the dollar in terms of gold as well if the USA ended its commitment to buy and sell gold at $35 per oz. Still another alternative was to go on a pure dollar standard by demonetising gold—this could be done by simply ending the US policy of buying and selling gold at a fixed price. Other countries' foreign exchange reserves would then be held entirely in dollars which they could accumulate to satisfy liquidity needs by simply running balance of payments surpluses with the USA. This option appeared unacceptable on grounds that it strengthened the role of the USA. Finally, there was the suggestion that the International Monetary Fund issue a gold substitute that would take the place of an increase in the world gold stock and permit countries to hold less of their reserves in dollars. This would reduce the dominant role of the USA and permit a truly internationally managed system, a paper standard with agreed-upon rules for adjusting the exchange rates of the various currencies, including the dollar, in terms of the international currency unit.

This chapter presents an analysis of these issues in terms of the theory developed in Chapter 6. We first consider the key currency nature of the Bretton Woods system. It is suggested that gold was a destabilising rather than a stabilising feature of the system because of the potential for the dollar price of gold to be changed. Had the USA abolished its commitment to buy and sell gold at $35 per oz nothing essential to the functioning of the system would have changed—the only effect would have been to eliminate the speculation in gold.

We next turn to consider the problem of liquidity and conclude that a liquidity shortage should not have been a problem. The problem was a shortage of gold not liquidity. It arose because of the unsuccessful attempt of the Bretton Woods conferees to make gold rather than the US dollar the key element of the international monetary system.

This leads to the third topic for analysis in this chapter—the nature and causes of the so-called US balance of payments deficit. Our conclusion is that the deficit reflected a desire of other countries to accumulate US dollar reserves rather than a fundamental disequilibrium of the system. It therefore should not have been viewed as a problem.

Finally, we consider the efforts that were made to create an international paper asset to replace gold. The problems involved in reorganising the international monetary system around such an asset are examined and the rather limited efforts in that direction that have been made are noted.

The Key Currency Nature of the Bretton Woods System

The Bretton Woods Conference set up what has been billed as a gold exchange standard in which gold was at the centre of the international monetary system. Gold was the reserve money with which nations were to settle their balance of payments accounts. In fact, however, the system was really a key currency standard with the US dollar as the key currency. The commitment of the key currency country to buy and sell gold at $35 per oz was a disturbing complication rather than a cornerstone of the monetary order that was in fact set up. The system was a key currency one because the dollar was the intervention currency used by all participants—countries pegged their currencies to the dollar by agreeing to purchase and sell it at an official rate established in accordance with the rules of the International Monetary Fund. Under these circumstances the US balance of payments surplus or deficit was the sum of the deficits or surpluses of all countries pegging to the dollar, and the USA had no control over either its balance of payments or its foreign exchange rate. Since the US economy was large in relation to the rest of the world and the bulk of the official reserves of the peripheral countries was held in interest-bearing, dollar-denominated assets, world monetary policy was determined by the Federal Reserve System. An expansion of the US money supply, for example, tended to create an excess demand for non-monetary assets, driving down world interest rates. This led in turn to an expansion of aggregate demand in all countries and to an increase in output, employment, and ultimately, prices. Other countries were forced to expand their money supplies to finance these lower interest rates and higher output and price levels, doing so by purchasing either domestic securities or US dollar assets (foreign exchange reserves) redeemable in gold. If they did not supply the necessary funds by domestic open-market operations or other domestic money-creating devices, they were forced to do so by increasing their stock of official reserves. A monetary contraction in the USA tended to force a contraction on all the peripheral countries through the same mechanism. The only way one of these countries could insulate itself from world monetary policy as established by the USA was to let its exchange rate with the dollar (and hence other currencies pegged to it) float freely. Periodic adjustments of exchange rate were not a satisfactory insulating device. Balance of payments surpluses and deficits arise only after income and/or prices have changed enough to create a discrepancy between the supply and demand for money. Domestic output and prices would thus have already changed significantly as a result of US policy developments by the time the need for adjustment had become apparent.

Since the price of gold was fixed in terms of the dollar, gold and dollars were virtually perfect substitutes for each other as foreign exchange reserves—imperfect substitutability only arose to the extent that the dollar price of gold could potentially be changed, and because dollar reserves (i.e. US short-term securities) bore interest while gold did not. Table 7.1 gives the stock of foreign exchange reserves held by all countries as well as the stock held by countries other than the USA.[1] These totals are broken down into gold and non-gold reserves—the latter include non-dollar currencies and reserves at the International Monetary Fund as well as short-term dollar assets. The gold component of reserves is not shown after 1970 because the official price of gold was meaningless in that no trades were required to occur at it. It is evident from the table that the ratio of gold to total reserves of the peripheral countries declined almost steadily from 1959 on.

Though gold holdings of the peripheral countries were part of their official reserves, albeit a decreasing part as the years passed, gold was not really crucial to the system, especially in the later years. Had the USA terminated the commitment to buy and sell gold at a fixed price, nothing would have happened to the everyday functioning of the international monetary system. Countries would simply have held their reserves entirely in dollars rather than partly in gold. Those countries with open capital markets could accumulate dollar reserves painlessly by tightening up domestic credit—domestic residents would then sell non-monetary assets abroad to maintain desired money holdings and the authorities would acquire the dollar proceeds of this sale by selling domestic currency for dollars on the foreign exchange market. Those with comprehensive restrictions on capital mobility would have to maintain either a lower value of their currencies in terms of the dollar or a lower price level as compared to the rest of the world in order to accumulate desired dollar reserves.

TABLE 7.1   *World Liquidity (Billions of $US)*

	All countries			All countries but the USA			
	Total reserves	Total reserves minus gold	Gold	Total reserves	Total reserves minus gold	Gold	Gold as percent of total
1953	51.2	17.2	33.9	27.7	15.9	11.8	42.6
1954	52.9	18.3	34.5	29.9	17.1	12.8	42.8
1955	53.6	18.6	35.0	30.8	17.6	13.2	42.9
1956	55.9	20.0	35.9	32.4	18.4	13.8	42.6
1957	56.4	19.3	37.1	31.6	17.4	14.2	44.9
1958	57.4	19.7	37.8	34.9	17.6	17.2	49.3
1959	57.1	19.4	7.8	35.6	17.4	18.2	51.1
1960	60.0	22.1	37.9	40.6	20.5	20.1	49.5
1961	62.0	23.3	38.7	43.3	21.5	21.8	50.3
1962	62.9	23.7	39.2	45.6	22.5	23.1	50.6
1963	66.8	26.6	40.2	50.0	25.4	24.6	49.2
1964	69.1	28.4	40.7	52.4	27.2	25.2	48.1
1965	71.2	29.4	41.8	55.7	28.0	27.7	49.7
1966	72.8	32.0	40.8	57.9	30.4	27.6	47.7
1967	74.5	35.1	39.4	59.7	32.4	27.4	45.9
1968	77.8	39.0	38.8	62.1	34.2	27.9	44.9
1969	78.7	39.8	39.0	61.8	34.7	27.1	43.8
1970	93.3	56.3	37.0	78.8	52.8	25.9	32.9
1971		94.6			92.5		
1972		120.5			117.8		
1973		140.8			138.0		
1974		176.6			172.3		
1975		185.9			181.3		
1976		217.0			209.8		
1977		275.2			267.6		
1978		318.1			311.1		
1979		356.3			348.5		
1980		410.2			394.7		

Source: International Financial Statistics, International Monetary Fund.

The peg to gold was a complicating feature of the system because it created the potential for the dollar price of gold to be changed, leading to speculative pressures. Since the stock of gold was not growing as fast as total world monetary reserves, a desire of the peripheral countries to hold a significant proportion of their reserves in gold would eventually lead to an exhaustion of the gold holdings of the USA, and impair that country's ability to maintain the price of gold at $35 per oz. This was complicated by the fact that until 1968 the US authorities were required by law to maintain a 25 per cent gold backing of domestic currency. The amount of gold available to support the $35 peg was therefore substantially less than the amount actually held by the USA. The speculation therefore was that the dollar price of gold might eventually be raised. The result was recurring runs on gold in the major world financial centres which led to the establishment of the two-tier gold market in 1968. Thereafter central banks exchanged gold among themselves at $35 per oz, and private individuals traded at the free-market price which was above $35. No gold was allowed to move from official reserves into private hands. The gold-dollar peg was abolished entirely in 1971. Much wasted effort by politicians, administrators, traders, and policy advisors could have been prevented by doing this 15 years earlier.

Was there a Liquidity Shortage?

Since there can be no liquidity shortage under a key currency system, which the Bretton Woods system essentially was, a shortage of international reserves should not have been a problem. Why, then, was there so much concern among economists and policy makers throughout the 1960s.

There appear to have been two reasons for this concern. First, there was certainly a gold shortage and many international financial problems were caused as a result of it. Since gold was a form of liquidity, it was easy to make the step from gold shortage to liquidity shortage. Second, the actual functioning of the international monetary system was substantially at variance with the perceptions of economists and policy makers alike as to how it was supposed to function. The objective of the Bretton Woods conferees and the system they designed was to make gold the centre of the international monetary system. All currencies were *equal* participants in the system. Had each country pegged its currency directly to gold, and had every subsequent adjustment to the peg been an adjustment of the price of gold in terms of that currency, and had balance of payments deficits actually been cleared by exchanges of gold, had the USA been a smaller country and a less significant one in world trade, and had the US dollar not enjoyed the status of a strong currency in the early post-war period, things might have been different. The dollar would have been one currency of many. Countries would have held reserves of various currencies as substitutes for gold, with the reserve status of the different currencies shifting according to the likelihood they would be devalued or revalued in terms of gold.

This system would have had a serious liquidity problem. The gold stock would not have expanded fast enough to finance the needs of trade. Individual countries would have had to reduce domestic credit expansion to create balance of payments surpluses that would lead to inflows of gold reserves. As all countries tried to do this the world price level would have fallen. Alternatively countries might have tried to produce the necessary balance of payments surpluses by devaluing their currencies in terms of gold. In this case speculation in favour of gold and against individual currencies would have been rife. Had this been the system, it surely would not have worked very well.

Clearly, if this is the kind of system that was wanted, there were inadequate reserves to permit it to exist. The world essentially backed into a key-currency dollar standard because the idealised system of Bretton Woods was non-functional. The USA was a large country whose currency was strong and given the role of intervention currency in the practical design of the system. The USA held a large fraction of the world's gold stock and was given the responsibility of pegging the price of gold. It would appear that those of influence at the time did not want a key currency dollar standard, did not want to recognise politically that the system was in fact a dollar standard, and felt that anything less than the idealised gold exchange standard with the dollar one currency among equals was inadequate for world financial stability and prosperity. A shortage of liquidity thus appeared as the factor preventing the ideal system from being attained and the fiction of gold backing world money being maintained. The myth that gold was the centre of the system could not survive unless the convertibility of the dollar into gold could be maintained and there was obviously not enough gold to maintain it indefinitely. This led to the attitude that if only a gold substitute could be found the harsh reality of a dollar standard could be prevented.

A US Balance of Payments Deficit?

Table 7.2 gives the US liquidity position between 1953 and 1980. The penultimate column gives the US balance of payments surplus according to the liquidity definition, and the last column, the surplus according to the official settlements definition. The remaining columns give the stock of liabilities of the USA to foreign governments and individuals. The balance of payments surplus figures give the increase in US reserve holdings minus the increase in liquid liabilities

TABLE 7.2   The US Liquidity Position (Billions of $US End of Period)

	Total external liabilities	To central banks	To other banks and foreigners	Of which short term to banks	All short term	Percentage short term	US gold holdings	Gold holdings/ all short-term liabilities	Gold holdings/ liabilities to central banks	Liquidity surplus[a]	Official settlements surplus[b]
1953	11.36	6.48	4.35	2.57	10.55	92.8	22.1	2.09	3.41	-1.64	-1.52
1954	12.45	7.52	4.37	2.57	11.71	94.0	21.7	1.85	2.89	-0.70	-0.93
1955	13.52	8.26	4.76	2.98	12.22	90.3	21.7	1.88	2.63	-0.89	-0.01
1956	15.29	9.15	5.44	3.41	13.99	91.4	22.1	1.57	2.41	0.76	1.18
1957	15.82	9.14	5.72	3.47	14.40	91.0	22.9	1.59	2.50	-3.56	-2.80
1958	16.84	9.64	5.95	3.52	15.66	92.9	20.6	1.31	2.14	-2.79	-1.51
1959	19.43	10.12	7.62	4.68	17.42	89.6	19.5	1.12	1.93	-4.64	-3.13
1960	21.03	11.09	7.60	4.82	18.80	89.3	17.8	0.95	1.60	-0.53	-1.33
1961	22.94	11.83	8.35	5.48	20.73	90.3	16.9	0.81	1.43	-2.88	-2.52
1962	24.27	12.91	8.36	5.35	22.07	90.9	16.1	0.73	1.25	-1.59	-1.99
1963	26.39	14.43	9.21	5.82	23.29	88.2	15.6	0.67	1.08	-2.51	-1.53
1964	29.36	15.78	11.05	7.30	25.62	87.2		0.60	0.99	-1.09	-1.28
1965	29.57	15.82	11.48	7.42	25.50	86.2	14.1	0.55	0.89	-2.19	0.36
1966	31.02	14.89	14.21	9.94	27.12	87.4	13.2	0.49	0.89	-2.84	-3.35
1967	35.67	18.19	15.76	11.08	29.91	83.8	12.1	0.40	0.66	-0.18	1.72
1968	38.47	17.34	19.38	14.47	30.96	80.4	10.9	0.35	0.63	-7.24	2.60
1969	45.91	15.99	28.23	39.45	85.9	11.9	11.9	0.30	0.74	-4.42	-8.32
1970	46.96	23.77	21.77	17.17	41.39	88.1	11.1	0.27	0.47		
1971	67.81	50.64	15.09	10.95	55.18	81.3				—	—
1972	82.86	61.53	19.71	14.67	60.70	73.2				-4.97	-10.34
1973	92.49	66.85	23.62	17.69	69.07	74.6				-8.30	-5.25
1974	119.16	76.83	39.02	30.11	94.77	79.5	c			-24.20	-8.48
1975	126.55	80.71	40.22	29.52	94.34	74.5		c	c	+1.37	-3.48
1976	151.36	91.98	50.90	37.33	108.99	72.0				-12.13	-8.04
1977	192.29	126.08	58.61	42.50	124.26	64.6				-14.88	-33.66
1978	244.36	156.84	79.98		169.43	69.3				-45.73	-31.37
1979	267.97	143.11	117.07		189.20	70.6				-18.97	+14.53
1980	295.35	156.93	131.45		209.05	70.9				-12.03	-8.44

a Calculated from IMF, International Financial Statistics — total reserves minus all short-term external liabilities prior to 1971, and total reserves less gold minus all short-term external liabilities after 1971. The figures presented are year-end to year-end changes.

b Calculated from IMF, International Financial Statistics — total reserves minus gold minus external liabilities to central banks and governments prior to 1971 and total reserves minus gold minus external liabilities to central banks and governments after 1971. The figures presented are year-end changes.

c Gold was in effect demonetized in 1971. Dollar reserves could no longer be converted into gold at a fixed price. The official price of gold after that year is therefore meaningless.

to foreign governments in the official settlements balance and minus the increase in liquid liabilities to both foreign governments and private individuals in the liquidity balance. By both definitions the surplus was negative (i.e. a deficit) during most years from the early 1950s until 1971. It is interesting to note that in the 1970s, when important countries were on flexible exchange rates with respect to the dollar, there was also a substantial accumulation of US dollar, short-term liquid liabilities by foreign central banks and private banks and individuals.

The US official settlements deficit can be interpreted as the sum of the balance-of-payments surpluses of all other countries. But there is a real question as to whether these accumulations of dollar liabilities by foreigners represented balance of payments disequilibria, given the key-currency nature of the system as it in fact operated. Since the volume of trade was expanding, the peripheral countries' authorities needed to increase their stocks of foreign exchange reserves through time. The only way they could do this was to run what would appear to be balance of payments surpluses. Such reserve accumulations are costless in terms of domestic policy objectives because all they require is a tightening of the domestic source component of the money supply, leading to an almost equal expansion of the foreign source component—effectively, the size of the domestic money supply is beyond the peripheral country's control.[2] A country might object to imported inflation, but this is a consequence of the fixed exchange rate in conjunction with the key currency country's monetary policy and need not either lead to an increase in official reserves, or be caused by one.

The accumulation of foreign official dollar holdings should thus be interpreted as a deliberate attempt to expand official reserves—if these countries had not wished to add to their reserves, they could have avoided it by faster expansions of their domestic source components. In a properly functioning key currency system, the central country has no responsibility for balance of payments disequilibria. It does have responsibility for world monetary policy. Stable domestic policies were in the US interest, and the key currency system enabled foreign countries to 'free ride' on this stability until the late 1960s. Had they objected to US monetary policy, they could have let their exchange rates float and handled monetary policy on their own. Or they could have pegged their currencies to that of another country which had more stable internal policies than the USA and a floating rate with respect to the dollar. Were this widespread, the USA would have lost its key currency status to some other country. Free choice and natural selection by individual countries would thus lead to the most suitable country being selected as the key currency country—indeed there could be more than one key currency with flexible exchange rates between them. So there is a real question whether the accumulation of official dollar reserves by foreign authorities should be regarded as a US balance of payments deficit.

One way to pose the question of whether the US balance of payments was in deficit is to ask oneself whether world exchange rates would have moved significantly during the 1960s if they had been allowed to float and the monetary, fiscal and other policies of all countries had been what they in fact were. Other countries would have less need for official reserves than they in fact had, and any monetary expansion resulting from reserve accumulations would have had to be replaced by expansion of the relevant domestic source components. Were this done, it is unlikely that exchange rates would have moved much. The price levels in the various countries would have been roughly the same as they in fact were because money growth (and fiscal policy) would have been, by assumption, the same. And the real factors affecting trade would not have been much different. Since the external value of a country's currency is its nominal price ratio divided by its real price ratio,[3] it is unlikely to have changed much on account of the introduction of flexible exchange rates under the conditions posited.

If the case is weak for treating the official settlements balance as a balance of payments deficit, it is even weaker for treating the liquidity balance as a deficit. Private acquisitions of short-term dollar assets were clearly the result of voluntary autonomous transactions. So why would anyone want to call them balance of payments disequilibria, as was in fact done by many people at the time?[4]

The key currency nature of the system, as it actually functioned, makes it inappropriate to call these accumulations deficits in the US balance of payments. But they were, nevertheless, an important problem in that all these dollar assets could be redeemed in gold within 1 year.[5] When the securities matured, their foreign holders could simply convert the dollars received into gold by directly or indirectly redeeming them with the US authorities. The total stock of such short-term, dollar-asset accumulations by private residents and central banks abroad was thus a potential run on the US gold stock. As long as the goal was to maintain convertibility of the dollar into gold this stock of liquid dollar liabilities was a matter of great concern. And the notion of a liquidity deficit was an attempt to measure what was happening to this stock on a year-by-year or quarter-by-quarter basis—to measure whether the problem was getting worse or better.

It is likely that these private short-term dollar holdings would have expanded whether or not the dollar was tied to gold. As Despres, Kindleberger, and Salant noted at the time,[6] a process of intermediation was occurring. Savings in the USA exceeded investment and capital was flowing abroad almost continuously from 1955 until 1968. But while US residents were accumulating long-term foreign debt foreigners were accumulating short-term US debt. These accumulations were the result of on-going market forces together with the special economic circumstances of the countries at the time. The USA was a capital exporter because domestic investment opportunities fell short of savings. Foreigners wanted to accumulate short-term, US-dollar assets on both private and public account to obtain liquidity to finance trade, a large part of which was denominated in dollars. Indeed these private and official reserve accumulations continued throughout the 1970s when the important exchange rates were flexible. It would certainly have been inappropriate to regard the US balance of payments as being in deficit during that period.

Special Drawing Rights—Paper Gold?

In 1970 the International Monetary Fund began issuing special drawing rights (SDRs), an international asset to be used to settle balance of payments disequilibria in the same way as gold. It was hoped that this would make it less necessary for countries to rely on dollar reserves.

Purists would have envisioned a system in which the IMF, acting as a world central bank, would issue a new currency, the SDR, pegged to gold and a perfect substitute for it in international exchange. All countries including the USA would peg their currencies to the SDR and would devalue or revalue with respect to it to correct fundamental disequilibria in their balances of payments. The system would be, in essence, a gold standard with a paper supplement to the gold stock. If countries maintained rigidly fixed exchange rates in terms of SDRs, domestic price levels would have to be determined by world conditions as domestic credit expansion in all countries is adjusted to permit the desired accumulation of gold and SDR reserves. Any country whose money supply expanded too fast would lose reserves to the rest of the world. All countries together would thus be forced to expand the world money supply at a rate consistent with the expansion of the total stock of gold and SDRs and the growth of aggregate, desired, international reserve holdings.[7]

The first problem posed by such a system is that of deciding how fast to expand the total stock of reserves. Is this decision to be made by the IMF or by some other international institutional arrangement? Too fast an expansion would lead to world inflation, too slow a growth to depression. Are individual countries willing to let such important decisions be beyond their control? Establishment of the desired rate of monetary expansion is a serious problem in many countries where political institutions are well established—it would be impossible in an international setting where there are no rules for setting priorities and making decisions. In the key currency system established by the Bretton Woods Agreement, this problem was handled by letting the US Federal Reserve system set world monetary policy. Of course, no one intended this to happen and few recognised that it was happening.

A second problem is the political one of deciding who gets the seigniorage from reserve-money creation.[8] The IMF could create SDRs simply by a stroke of the pen, that is, by giving them to countries. Does it give these reserves to all countries equally? According to population? According to a country's share in world trade? Or according to income, with poorer countries getting the greater share? Alternatively, the IMF could create SDRs by buying bonds in the open market. Which country's bonds should it buy? In this case the incentive for a country to sell bonds to the IMF would be tempered by the fact that it has to pay interest on them—if the bonds were sold at market prices (and interest paid at market rates) there would be no advantage to the individual country at all. But the IMF would then be earning a large income equal to the interest received on the bonds purchased through the process of creating SDRs. What should it do with this income? One possibility is to dispose of the revenue by paying interest on SDRs at the market rate. In this case there would be no seigniorage but each country would benefit to the extent that the social value it placed on intra-marginal reserve holdings exceeded the marginal cost to it of acquiring them—where interest is paid at market rates, this marginal cost will be zero.[9] Under the Bretton Woods system, the USA got the seigniorage. However, to the extent that countries held their reserves in interest-bearing, dollar-denominated, short-term assets rather than non-interest-bearing cash, there was little seigniorage to be had. Any benefit to the US Government from creating international money is offset by the interest that had to be paid on the bonds purchased to create it. Again, of course, the individual countries gain to the extent that the social value of intramarginal reserve holdings exceeds their cost.[10] The political problem of deciding whether there is to be seigniorage from SDR creation and, if so, who is to get it seems insurmountable. The Bretton Woods system again solved this problem inadvertently with little realisation on the part of the participants as to what was happening.

Finally, there would also be the problem in this ideal system of speculation between the SDR and gold. If countries do not regard the SDR and gold as perfect substitutes (there might be anticipations that the price of gold in terms of SDRs would someday be changed) they might wish to accumulate part of their reserves in gold and part in SDRs. This being the case, the world gold stock will eventually become inadequate as the volume of world trade expands and the convertibility of the SDR into gold could become in doubt. The IMF could solve this problem by abandoning gold as an international money, refusing to peg the SDR price of it. The system would then become a pure paper-gold system. This would pose no problem to world economic stability as long as a well-defined mechanism exists for regulating the growth of the world supply of SDRs. Unfortunately, however, it is unlikely that international agreement on such a mechanism could be reached.

The actual introduction of SDRs fell far short of this ideal system. These special drawing rights were created by the stroke of a pen and were allocated to countries in proportion to the sizes of their quotas in the IMF.[11] One SDR was valued at $US1 at the time of issue in 1970 and the asset bore interest at a minimal rate. While SDRs were a substitute for gold in the Bretton Woods system, the dollar was still the key currency. Within some range, nations had the option of holding SDRs instead of dollars or gold, but the rules prevented them from converting their SDR allocations into the other two assets beyond some point. If countries had been free to exchange their SDRs for dollars they might well have done so since dollar assets bore higher interest rates than the SDR. The dollar was still the intervention currency and was still the major currency in international trade—SDRs could not be held privately and were good only in exchanges between central banks. The stock of SDRs issued was quite small, comprising 3.3 per cent of total world reserves in 1970 and the same percentage in 1980.

The analysis of Chapter 5 suggests that the breakdown of the Bretton Woods system in the early 1970s was due not to a shortage of liquidity but to a shift in the relative price of various countries output. Had the problem been simply one of liquidity, the demonetisation of gold, through President Nixon's decision to stop converting dollars into gold at a fixed price, would not have led to an adjustment in exchange rates—the system would simply have continued as a key currency dollar standard.

With the advent of flexible exchange rates after 1971 the IMF began valuing the SDR in terms of a weighted average of sixteen currencies. Interest was paid on it according to a formula based on the interest rates in five major countries—USA, UK, Germany, France, and Japan. In 1981 the currency basket determining the value of the SDR was revised to include only the five major currencies—the same five that determine the interest paid on the SDR.[12]

In 1976 the Jamaica Conference formally introduced changes in the IMF Articles of Agreement to recognise that individual countries may choose to let their exchange rates float, or to peg to the SDR or some other national currency. The official price of gold (at which the USA would neither buy nor sell it in return for US dollars) was abolished and member countries are now free to buy and sell it at market or any other prices they choose.

Notes

1 There is a real question whether US holdings of gold and other currencies should be called foreign exchange reserves because, as the system operated, they would never have been used to support the exchange rate between the dollar and other currencies.
2 The foreign source component would expand by exactly the same amount as the domestic source component contracts—i.e. the money supply would remain unchanged—only if there is perfect capital mobility. Otherwise the money supply would decline to some degree.
3 It will be recalled from Chapter 5 that a country's real price ratio (RPR) is the ratio of its price index, adjusted for changes in the dollar value of its currency, to the rest of the world's price index, also adjusted for changes in the dollar value of the other countries' currencies. The nominal price ratio can be defined as the ratio of a country's price index to the rest of the world's price index as compared to some base, i.e.

$$NPR_j = \frac{CPI_j(1-\omega_j)}{\sum_i \omega_i CPI_i - \omega_j CPI_j}$$

The implicit external value of a country's currency (EV) is thus

$$EV_j = \frac{NPR_j}{RPR_j}$$

and is an index of the exchange rates of its currency with the other currencies in the world.
4 See, for example, Cohen, Stephen D. (1970) *International Monetary Reform, 1964–69*, Praeger Publishers; and Bergsten, C. Fred (1972) *Reforming the Dollar: An International Monetary Policy for the United States*, Council on Foreign Relations. See also *The Balance of Payments*

Mess, Hearings before the Subcommittee on International Exchange and Payments of the Joint Economic Committee, 92nd Congress, 1st Session, 16 June 1971.

5 Short-term assets are defined as assets maturing within 1 year.

6 Depres, Emile, Kindleberger, C. P. and Salant, Walter S. (1960) 'The dollar and world liquidity: A minority view', *The Economist*, February pp. 526–529. See also Salant, Walter S. (1972) 'Financial intermediation as an explanation of enduring "Deficits" in the balance of payments' in Machlup, Fritz *et al.* (eds) *International Mobility and Movement of Capital*, pp. 609–659, and Kindleberger, C. P. (1981) *International Money*, George Allen and Unwin.

7 The world money supply would be the sum of the money supplies of the individual countries measured in SDR units.

8 In this context, seigniorage can be thought of as revenue from money creation. In the days of gold coinage the sovereign or government charged some percentage of bullion minted as a charge or tax for doing the minting. In modern times, seigniorage arises when the state prints non-interest-bearing money which the private sector holds. The government earns the interest on the assets bought in the process by which the money was put into circulation, while the public gives up these interest earnings. If paper money bore interest at market rates, there would be no seigniorage, because the interest earned on money holdings would be equivalent in value to the interest earned on the securities given up in exchange for the money.

9 It is well known that this would lead to the socially optimum stock of international reserves because both the private and social costs of creating reserves are zero. The cost to society of creating reserves is zero because the IMF is simply creating a paper asset in return for the receipt of other pieces of paper (bonds) from individual countries, and paper is cheap. Countries will add to their stocks of reserves until the private (and social) benefits at the margin are also zero. The social gain to holding reserves is the benefit on all intramarginal units—i.e. the integral or area under the demand function for reserves. For a discussion of this issue see Mundell, R. A. (1971) *Monetary Theory: Inflation Interest and Growth in the World Economy*, Goodyear, pp. 170–186, and Grubel, Herbert (1971) 'The demand for international reserves: A critical review of the literature', *Journal of Economic Literature*, Vol. 9, No. 4, pp. 1148–66.

10 Except to the extent that actual cash is held the international reserve stock under this system will also be socially optimal. Countries will hold the social wealth maximising stock of reserves by simply adjusting the domestic source components of their money supplies.

11 Each member was assigned a quota when the fund was formed. This was the amount of gold and domestic currency it had to contribute to the fund. Provisions were in place for altering these quotas through time.

12 See Meier, Gerald M. (1982) *Problems of a World Monetary Order*, Oxford University Press, pp. 240 and 247.

8

World Equilibrium under Flexible Exchange Rates

President Nixon's announcement in December 1971 that the USA would no longer buy and sell gold at \$35 per oz marked the end of the Bretton Woods system. After an unsuccessful attempt to salvage fixed exchange rates with the Smithsonian Agreement, the major countries drifted onto a system of managed flexible exchange rates. As a prelude to the analysis in Chapter 10 of the functioning of this system, we now develop the theory of world equilibrium first under a system of freely floating rates and then under managed floating.

The model is fundamentally the same as the one developed in Chapters 4 and 6.[1] The conditions of commodity market equilibrium are identical to those in Chapter 6.

$$Y = C(Y,r) + I(r,Y) + GX + B_T(Y,Y^*,P/\pi P^*) \qquad (8.1)$$

$$Y^* = C^*(Y^*,r^*) + I^*(r^*,Y^*) + GX^* - \frac{P}{\pi P^*} B_T(Y,Y^*,P/\pi P^*) \quad (8.2)$$

where Y is output, r the interest rate, P the price of output, π the exchange rate (price of the asterisked currency in terms of the non-asterisked currency), GX government expenditure, and $C(.)$, $I(.)$, and $B_T(.)$ are the functions determining consumption, investment, and the balance of trade. Consumption and investment are positively related to income and negatively related to the real interest rate. A rise in the non-asterisked country's income deteriorates its balance of trade while a rise in the other country's income improves it. A rise in the relative price of the non-asterisked country's output deteriorates its balance of trade.

Expectations-augmented supply curves can be added to incorporate a more general mechanism of price adjustment but this would add little to our conclusions. Instead we assume either full-employment conditions, with Y and Y^* exogenous, or Keynesian less-than-full-employment conditions, with P and P^* exogenous.

The conditions of asset equilibrium in the two parts of the world are

$$M = P{\cdot}L(r + E_p, Y) \tag{8.3}$$

and

$$M^* = P^*{\cdot}L^*(r^* + E_p{}^*, Y^*) \tag{8.4}$$

where M and $L^*(.)$ are the nominal money stocks, E_p and E_p^* are the expected rates of inflation and $L(.)$ and $L^*(.)$ are the demand functions for real money balances in the two countries.[2] The demand for real balances is positively affected by home income and negatively affected by the cost of holding money. The latter is equal to the real interest rate that could be earned in alternative investments plus the expected deterioration of real money holdings as a result of inflation. When (8.3) and (8.4) hold, each country's residents must have a zero excess demand for non-monetary assets. Whether there is one non-monetary asset in the world or two depends on our assumption about international capital mobility. If there is complete immobility of capital, then there are two assets, one in each country, each owned exclusively by home residents. If there is perfect capital mobility then there is essentially only one world asset, owned by residents of both countries. If capital mobility is imperfect there must be a separate asset in each country, with each country's asset owned by both countries' residents.

Complete Immobility of Capital

When private transactions in capital across international boundaries are prohibited, the model is closed by adding the balance of payments equation

$$B_T(Y, Y^*, P/\pi P^*) - \frac{d\bar{R}}{dt} = 0 \tag{8.5}$$

where $d\bar{R}/dt$ is the level of direct foreign exchange market intervention measured by the change through time in the stock for foreign exchange reserves.

The five equations (8.1) to (8.5) solve for the five variables r, r^*, π, and either Y and Y^* or P and P^*, depending on what we assume about wage and price flexibility. Upon substitution of (8.5), the system reduces to two subsystems consisting of (8.1) and (8.3) for the non-asterisked country and (8.2) and (8.4) for the asterisked one. The former subsystem solves for r and Y or P and the latter for r^* and Y^* or P^*. The solutions then plug into (8.5) to yield the equilibrium level of π.

Substitution of (8.5) into (8.1) and (8.2) yields

$$Y = C(Y,r) + I(r, Y) + GX + \frac{d\bar{R}}{dt} \tag{8.1'}$$

and

$$Y^* = C^*(Y^*,r^*) + I^*(r^*, Y^*) + GX^* - \frac{P}{\pi P^*} \frac{d\bar{R}}{dt} \tag{8.2'}$$

Clearly, if the float is clean $d\bar{R}/dt = 0$, each country's aggregate demand is independent of developments in the other country—the flexible exchange rate is a perfect insulator. Each country can conduct policy as if the other did not exist.

Little can be gained by a detailed analysis of monetary and fiscal policy in the pure flexibility case.[3] The interested reader can apply the standard *IS–LM* tools to demonstrate that an increase in the money supply leads to a fall in the interest rate and an increase in output when there is less than full employment, and no change in the interest rate combined with an increase in the price level proportional to the increase in M when there is classical full employment. The domestic currency devalues in both cases, with the devaluation being proportional to the increase in money and prices in the full-employment case. It can also be shown that an increase in government expenditure increases the country's interest rate and output or prices and causes its currency to devalue.

When the float is dirty, the authorities in the intervening country—in this case the non-asterisked one—can decrease the external value of the domestic currency and increase domestic aggregate demand and output or prices by buying foreign exchange in the market. The aggregate demand effect is obvious from an examination of equation (8.1') and the exchange rate effect is evident from (8.5). In the latter equation, π has to increase to increase $B_T(.)$, and the increase in $B_T(.)$ is in turn necessary in (8.1') to increase aggregate demand. Resulting increases in output or the price level cannot totally eliminate the balance of trade effect because their existence depends on it.[4] As is evident from equation (8.2), any increase in domestic aggregate demand and output or prices comes at the expense of aggregate demand and output or prices abroad. However, if the intervening country is very small the percentage effect on output or prices abroad will also be small.

The important conclusion in the complete capital immobility case is that direct foreign exchange market intervention can affect the exchange rate and aggregate demand without any changes in the money supply or government expenditure. In addition, of course, the authorities in either country can produce any desired level of the exchange rate by appropriate adjustments of the levels of the domestic money stock and government expenditure. Of course, this involves the sacrifice of price level and employment goals.

Perfect Capital Mobility

When capital is perfectly mobile internationally the model is closed by specifying the relationship between the two countries' real interest rates. The interest parity theorem states that

$$i - i^* = \frac{\pi' - \pi}{\pi} \tag{8.6}$$

where i and i^*, are the nominal interest rates and π' is the forward exchange rate.[5] (Recall that π is the non-asterisked currency price of the asterisked currency.) When market participants use all available information, the forward exchange rate will equal the spot rate that the market expects to hold at the expiration of the forward contract. Were this not the case a speculator could make an expected profit by taking an uncovered position. For example, suppose that the domestic currency is expected to devalue by more than indicated by the forward discount on it. One could sell it forward and expect to buy the domestic funds necessary to cover the forward commitment for less than the price agreed to under the contract. When everyone tries to sell forward, the forward price of domestic currency in terms of foreign currency is bid down to equal the expected future spot price. Similarly, if the domestic currency is expected to appreciate by more than the forward rate indicates (that is, if its expected future price in terms of foreign currency is above its forward price) it pays to buy it forward. The foreign currency necessary to honour the commitment to purchase can be obtained when the contract matures for less domestic currency than will be received under the forward agreement. Letting the expected future spot price equal the forward price, we can now define

$$\frac{\pi' - \pi}{\pi} = E_\pi \tag{8.7}$$

where E_π is the expected rate of change of the exchange rate.

The nominal interest rate in each country can be expressed as the sum of the real rate and the expected rate of inflation. Thus

$$i = r + E_p$$

and

$$i^* = r^* + E_{p^*} \tag{8.8}$$

These relationships follow from the fact that the interest rate on an asset of fixed nominal value at maturity, and/or of fixed nominal yield, must be high enough to compensate the holder for the expected decline in the real purchasing power of the asset due to inflation, as well as for the real return that could be earned from alternative investments.

Substituting (8.8) and (8.7) into (8.6) and rearranging, we obtain

$$r = r^* + E_\pi + E_{p^*} - E_p \tag{8.9}$$

If expectations are rational—that is, if expectations about different related variables are internally consistent—the expected rate of change of the relative price variable $P/\pi P^*$ must equal

$$E_q = E_p - E_\pi - E_{p^*} \tag{8.10}$$

where $q = P/\pi P^*$.[6] Equation (8.9) can then be rewritten

$$r = r^* - E_q \tag{8.9'}$$

The parameter E_q is the expected relative change in the real value of domestic goods in terms of foreign goods in the international market, earlier defined as the country's real price ratio.[7]

Substitution of (8.9') into (8.1) to (8.4) to eliminate r^* yields a four-equation system that solves for Y or P, Y^* or P^*, π, and the world interest rate r. Since the world interest rate is determined by world asset and world real goods market equilibrium, it is useful for expositional purposes to aggregate the individual country equilibrium conditions into a world *IS–LM*-type model. To get a world *LM* curve, we must assume that the demand functions for money in the two countries are the same except for scale. This rather drastic restriction has no important effect on our conclusions because our interest is in the structure of the system, in how it works, rather than in detailed policy considerations. As shown in the Mathematical note 2 at the end of the chapter, this aggregation assumption enables us to write

$$M^* + M = P_w L^w(r, Y_w) \tag{8.11}$$

where $P_w = P^{*\theta} P^{1-\theta}$, $Y_w = Y^{*\theta} Y^{1-\theta}$, $\theta = M^*/(M^*+M)$, and the initial level of the exchange rate is unity.[8] P_w and Y_w are thus geometrically

weighted indexes of the individual countries' prices and output, with
the weights being the countries' shares of the world money supply in
the base period. This is the world LM curve which appears as LM_w in
Figure 8.1(a). It is a geometrically weighted horizontal average of the
two individual country LM curves presented in Figure 8.1(b) and (c).
To obtain a world IS curve, we first note, as we did in Chapter 6, that
the income–expenditure equations (8.1) and (8.2) solve
simultaneously to determine outputs in the two countries as functions
of the world interest rate, the relative price variable, q, and the two
countries' levels of government expenditure. Thus

$$Y = Y(r, GX, GX^*, P/\pi P^*) \tag{8.12}$$

and

$$Y^* = Y^*(r, GX^*, GX, P/\pi P^*) \tag{8.13}$$

A fall in r will obviously increase output in both countries because it
increases consumption and investment.[9] The relationship between the
interest rate and incomes in the separate countries is indicated by the
two curves EE and EE^* in Figure 8.1. In Figure 8.1(a) we construct the
world IS curve, denoted IS_w, by combining (8.12) and (8.13) in a
geometrically weighted index of world output, with the weights being
θ and $1 - \theta$ as before. Thus

$$Y_w = [Y^*(r, GX^*, GX, P/\pi P^*)]^\theta [Y(r, GX, GX^*, P/\pi P^*)]^{1-\theta}$$
$$= Y_w(r, GX, GX^*, P/\pi P^*) \tag{8.14}$$

An increase in government expenditure in one of the countries will
shift both EE^* and EE to the right. Since IS_w is a horizontal weighted
average of EE^* and EE, it will also shift to the right. An increase in
$P/\pi P^*$ makes the non-asterisked country's goods more expensive in
world markets and causes world demand to shift away from its goods.
EE thus shifts to the left and EE^* to the right. The effect on IS_w will
depend on the structure of the two economies. It is convenient for us to
assume that the net effect of a shift in relative domestic and foreign
prices on world output is zero. The conditions for this aggregation are
derived in Mathematical note 2 at the end of the chapter. We are thus
able to rewrite (8.14) as

$$Y_w = Y_w(r, GX, GX^*) \tag{8.13'}$$

Comparative Statics Results—Less than Full Employment[10]

(a) Monetary policy Now suppose that there is a monetary
expansion in the asterisked country. The curve LM^* shifts to the right
to $LM^{*\prime}$ in Figure 8.1(c). The effect on LM_w will depend on how large

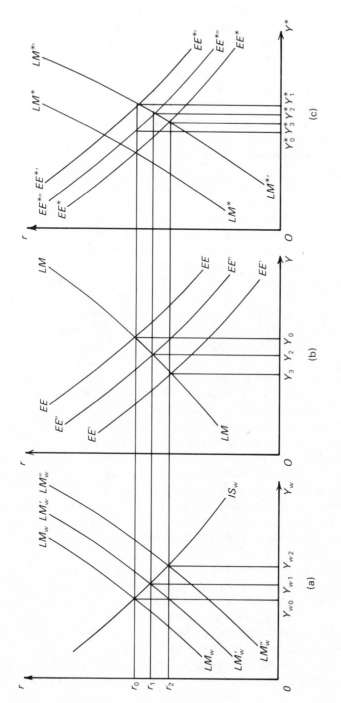

Figure 8.1

the country is in relation to the rest of the world—i.e. on the size of θ. If the country is extremely small, LM_w will be unaffected and the world interest rate will remain unchanged. The excess supply of money in the asterisked country will cause its residents to try to buy assets abroad. This creates an excess supply of the country's currency on the international market and causes it to devalue (π falls). The switch of world demand from the non-asterisked to the asterisked country shifts EE^* to the right and EE to the left, but the leftward shift of EE will be insignificant because of the relative sizes of the countries. The devaluation will continue until EE^* has shifted to $EE^{*\prime}$ and output has risen to Y_1^*.

If we assume that the asterisked country is of significant size relative to the non-asterisked country, the world money supply will be affected. The attempt to dispose of these excess money holdings will shift LM_w to the left and reduce the world interest rate, say to r_1. World output rises as both countries move down along their respective EE curves. But equilibrium cannot occur at the old exchange rate. As the asterisked country's residents try to buy assets abroad with their surplus money holdings they create an incipient balance of payments deficit causing π to fall. This switches world demand from the non-asterisked to the asterisked country, shifting EE^* to the right and EE to the left until world asset equilibrium is re-established. This occurs at $EE^{*\prime\prime}$ and $EE^{\prime\prime}$ with outputs in the two countries settling at Y_2^* and Y_2. Note that the effect of the monetary expansion in the asterisked country is to increase its output and aggregate world output at the expense of output in the non-asterisked country.

Finally consider the extreme case where the non-asterisked country is very small relative to the asterisked country. In this case LM_w shifts to the right to the same degree as LM^* and the new equilibrium occurs at world interest rate r_2 and output levels Y_{w2} and Y_3^*. At this new world interest rate, however, asset equilibrium no longer holds in the non-asterisked country. Its residents want to hold an increased amount of money balances. To acquire them they try to sell non-monetary assets on the world market. This creates an incipient balance of payments surplus causing the local currency to appreciate (π falls and the asterisked country's currency devalues as before). Aggregate demand is switched off the country's goods and EE shifts to the left to $EE^{\prime}$, at which point output has fallen to Y_3 and asset equilibrium has been restored. The accompanying rightward shift of EE^* is trivial because of the relative sizes of the two countries. Again monetary expansion in the asterisked country reduces output in the non-asterisked one.

It is clear that when capital is internationally mobile a flexible exchange rate does not insulate a country from developments in the

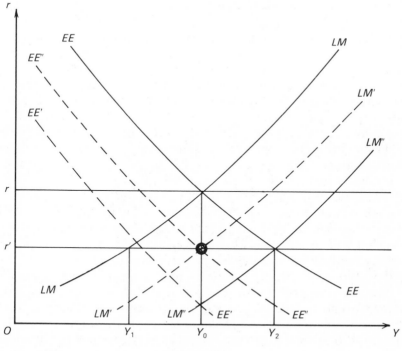

Figure 8.2

rest of the world in the short run when wages and prices are not immediately flexible. Cyclical changes in output abroad lead to counter-cyclical changes in domestic output and employment. To neutralise these imported counter-cyclical influences, a country has to adopt a pro-cyclical monetary policy. Figure 8.2 reproduces Figure 8.1(b) to represent the situation of a country faced with a fall in the world interest rate from r to r'. If the monetary authority does nothing, the incipient sale of assets abroad leads to an appreciation of the domestic currency and a leftward shift of EE to EE', and a fall in output from Y_0 to Y_1. The authorities can offset this decline in output by increasing the domestic money supply sufficiently to shift the LM curve to LM'. Equilibrium is then re-established with a much smaller appreciation of the domestic currency and a leftward shift of EE to only $E''E''$. Alternatively, the authorities could allow domestic output to rise in full response to the fall in the world interest rate by increasing the money supply sufficiently to drive LM to LM''. Output increases to Y_2 and the exchange rate does not change. It is as if the country was on a fixed exchange rate. The analysis of Figure 8.2 assumes that the domestic economy is very small in relation to the rest of the world.

Were it larger, the domestic monetary expansion would shift LM_w and further lower the world interest rate. The monetary expansion required to maintain the output levels Y_0 and Y_2 would then be larger.

It should also be recognised that speculators will not be idle in the face of pro-cyclical variations in the exchange rate. To the extent that these exchange rate movements are anticipated, speculative activity will smooth them out. Take the case where the authorities in Figure 8.2 hold the domestic money supply constant in the face of a fall in the world interest rate. If speculators think that the appreciation of the domestic currency will be reversed as monetary policy in the rest of the world reverses itself, the fall in π will be accompanied by an expectation that it will subsequently rise $(E_\pi > 0)$. This will cause a forward discount on domestic currency and drive the domestic interest rate up relative to the interest rate abroad. Domestic residents will want to hold less money balances at the world interest rate r' and LM will shift to the right. This will moderate the leftward shift of EE and fall in π necessary to maintain domestic asset equilibrium.

It would be too much to assert that speculative activity could eliminate all movement in the exchange rate. For this to happen, asset holders would have to have perfect information about the structure of the world economy and the behaviour pattern of the foreign monetary authority. If this were the case, wages and prices would not be sticky and no variations in output and employment would occur to begin with.

The case where the authorities expand the domestic money supply sufficiently to eliminate all portfolio pressure on the exchange rate and allow domestic output to expand fully in response to the fall in the world interest rate is an interesting and important one. We refer to this monetary rule as an *acquiescent monetary policy*. The domestic authorities acquiesce in producing the same credit conditions in the domestic economy as exist in the rest of the world. The result is that the foreign business cycle is transmitted in full to the domestic economy despite the existence of flexible exchange rates.

One might be tempted to regard an acquiescent monetary policy as indistinguishable from a policy of maintaining the exchange rate at some target level. But this is not in general the case even though the exchange rate remains unchanged in the above example. There is no reason why world relative prices have to remain constant through time in the face of technological change, shifts in demand, etc. If $P/\pi P^*$ changes through time and the same credit conditions are maintained in all countries through acquiescent policies, the nominal price ratio P/P^* will remain unchanged. The exchange rate will therefore have to adjust to bring about the required change in relative prices—or in what we referred to earlier as the real price ratio.[11] If a fixed exchange rate monetary policy were followed, the nominal price ratio would have to change to bring about the required change in the real price ratio and credit conditions would therefore have to be eased at some point in the country whose price level has to rise.

It will be demonstrated in Chapter 9 that acquiescent monetary policies have been important in the era of managed floating that began in 1971, and that one country, Canada, has for the most part followed such a policy since the early 1950s. The question arises as to why central banks act this way. Certainly, one finds nothing in official statements to indicate an attempt to offset portfolio adjustment effects on the exchange rate while allowing relative price effects full rein. There appears to be little evidence of a conscious policy. The most likely reason for the prevalence of acquiescent policies is the orderly markets approach to day-to-day operations in the capital market. Central banks see it as their duty to smooth out market adjustments by resisting market pressures sensed at the trading desk. When the public has excess money holdings and is attempting to purchase assets abroad, there is sudden pressure on interest rates and the exchange rates—markets become 'disorderly'. The trading desk senses this and smooths out the market by selling domestic securities and mopping up the excess cash in the system. And when the public is trying to sell assets abroad to acquire money, the authorities, as if led by an invisible hand, purchase assets and supply the necessary cash to prevent wrenching short-term market adjustments. In contrast, relative price effects on the exchange rate make themselves felt more gradually so the smoothing out process does not tend to eliminate them.

This is not to suggest that acquiescent monetary policies would lead to the same inflation rates in all countries. Political pressures on the monetary authorities to finance public spending by money creation can differ from country to country. Since these institutional circumstances change gradually, securities and foreign exchange markets can adapt slowly and 'disorder' is unlikely to appear. But short-run shifts in the demand or supply of money around these established trends are likely to cause 'disorderly conditions' and the resulting interest rate and exchange rate pressures will tend to be smoothed out.

If the world consisted entirely of small countries, each following an acquiescent monetary policy, world monetary growth would tend to be a random walk. Shifts in the demand for money that occur simultaneously in a large enough group of countries to alter world credit conditions will induce the remaining countries to validate those same credit conditions in their economies. Shocks originating in one part of the world would thus tend to spread to the rest of it. World monetary policy would have no direction in the short run, although long-run money growth would be the average of growth in the individual countries as determined by local institutional circumstances.

It is perhaps fortunate that the world does not consist entirely of small countries. The USA makes up about 50 per cent of the output of the major industrial countries among which capital mobility is high.[12] Shifts in credit conditions in the USA would thus have world-wide effects. The next largest countries, Germany, France, and Japan each produce around 10 per cent of the major industrial countries' output— not enough to give them much influence on world credit conditions. If the major countries other than the USA follow acquiescent monetary policies, the US Federal Reserve System will tend to act as the world monetary authority even under flexible exchange rates. In this sense, the US dollar could be viewed as a key currency even if no other country pegged to it.

(b) Fiscal policy   We now turn briefly to the inter-country effects of fiscal policy and other equivalent real sector shocks. These are analysed on Figure 8.3. Suppose that government expenditure increases in the asterisked country. In general, this shifts both EE^* and EE to the right. However, when the asterisked country is extremely small in relation to the rest of the world the shift in EE will be of trivial magnitude. IS_w will also be unaffected as will the world interest rate. As output increases in the asterisked country an excess demand for money arises. This leads to an incipient sale of assets abroad and balance of payments surplus, resulting in an appreciation of the domestic currency. EE^* shifts back to its original position, neutralising entirely the effects of the policy. Had the authorities in the asterisked country been following an acquiescent monetary policy, they would have resisted the portfolio pressure on the exchange rate by expanding the money supply. This would have shifted LM^* to the right to intersect EE^*. If the initial shift in EE^* was to $EE^{*\prime}$, output would rise to Y_1^* and the world interest rate would stay at r_0.

Now suppose that the asterisked country is of significant size compared to the non-asterisked country. The rightward shift of EE is now substantial, though not as great as the shift of EE^* because it occurs on account of a feed-through effect via a change in the trade balance. The world IS curve IS_w shifts to the right by more than EE but less than EE^* since it is an horizontal average of the latter two curves, so the world interest rate rises to r_1. At that interest rate, there is an excess demand for money in the asterisked country and an excess

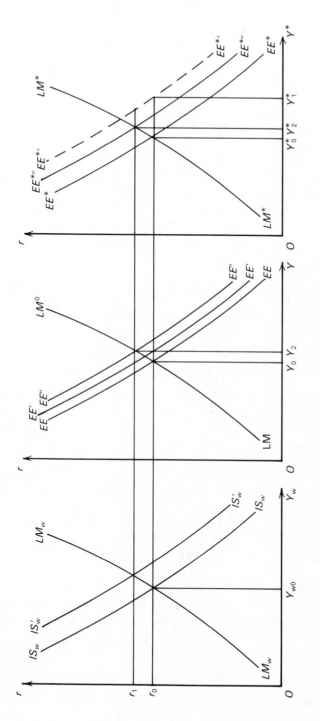

Figure 8.3

supply of money in the non-asterisked one. The residents of the latter country thus try to buy assets from the former country's residents leading to an appreciation of the asterisked country's currency. This shifts EE^* to the left to $EE^{*\prime\prime}$ and EE to the right to $EE^{\prime\prime}$. The resulting output levels are Y_2 and Y_2^*. The fiscal policy in the asterisked country increases world output, including its own, by an amount that depends on its size and hence its influence in determining the world interest rate. If the asterisked country is the smaller of the two and follows an acquiescent monetary policy, then it will expand its and the world's money stock, driving the world interest rate down a bit. This will accentuate the effect of its policy on its own output and moderate the effect on the other country's output. If the non-asterisked country is the smaller of the two, and follows an acquiescent monetary policy, it will reduce M, lowering the world money supply and raising the world interest rate. This will reduce the effect on its own output and increase the effect on the asterisked country's output (compared to what it would have been with constant money supplies in both countries).

Finally, consider the case where the non-asterisked country is extremely small in relation to the asterisked country. The increase in GX^* will shift EE^* and IS_w to the right by almost identical amounts and cause the world interest rate to rise (not shown on Figure 8.3). EE will also shift to the right since the increase in aggregate spending abroad spills over into the domestic economy through the trade balance. However, the horizontal shift of EE will be less, proportional to that of IS_w, and an excess supply of money will arise in the non-asterisked country at the new higher world interest rate. An incipient purchase of assets abroad will thus cause its country's currency to devalue, shifting EE to the right to intersect LM^0 at the new world interest rate. If the non-asterisked country follows an acquiescent monetary policy, its authorities will mop up the excess money holdings and prevent the devaluation. The improvement in income resulting from the fiscal policy abroad will therefore be smaller and may even be reversed.

In conclusion, we can say that a fiscal expansion in a country will lead to an expansion of its output and employment as long as the country is either large or follows an acquiescent monetary policy. It will lead to an increase in output abroad if the expanding country is large *and* the other country does not follow an acquiescent monetary policy.

Comparative Statics Results—Classical Full Employment

The long-run full-employment case is straight forward and requires

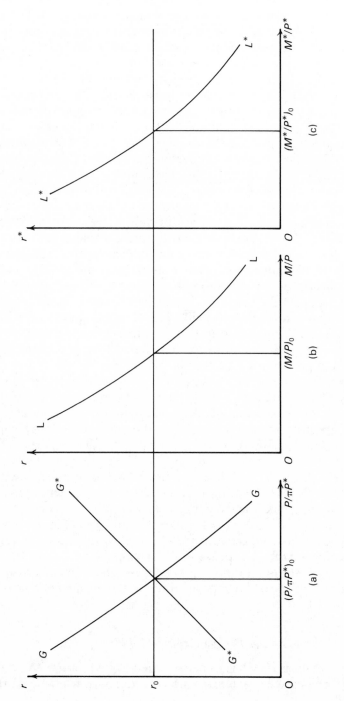

Figure 8.4

only brief discussion. The analysis is facilitated by Figure 8.4. The two equations (8.12) and (8.13) solve simultaneously for the equilibrium world interest rate and relative price variable $P/\pi P^*$. The former equation appears in Figure 8.4(a) as the negatively sloped curve GG— a rise in the world interest rate reduces consumption and investment, creating a deficiency of aggregate demand and requiring a fall in domestic relative to foreign prices to expand the trade balance and make up the deficiency. Equation (8.12) appears as the G^*G^* curve and is positively sloped for the same reason that GG is downward sloping—the slopes are opposite because a fall in P reduces $P/\pi P^*$ while a fall in P^* increases it. The intersection of these curves gives the equilibrium world interest rate and the equilibrium real price ratio $(P/\pi P^*)_0$. Figure 8.4(b) and (c) give the conditions of asset-market equilibrium. The demand functions for money are portrayed by the curves LL and L^*L^*. Given the world interest rate determined in Figure 8.4(a), and the full-employment output levels, these curves determine the equilibrium real money stocks M/P and M^*/P^*.

An expansion of the money stock in the non-asterisked country, leads to a proportional rise in P so that the real money stock remains constant. π must rise proportionally with P to maintain $P/\pi P^*$ at its equilibrium level established in Figure 8.4(a). An expansion of the asterisked country's money stock increases P^* proportionally and lowers π to maintain $P/\pi P^*$ where it was before. An increase in GX shifts both GG and G^*G^* upward since a higher interest rate is necessary at each level of $P/\pi P^*$ to choke off sufficient consumption and investment to 'make room' for the demands of government. GG will shift up more than G^*G^* because the shift in the latter curve depends on a feed-through of aggregate demand via the non-asterisked country's propensity to import. The equilibrium real price ratio $P/\pi P^*$ will thus rise. The rise in the world interest rate will increase both P and P^* to bring about the necessary reductions in real money holdings. And the exchange rate will adjust to produce the required ratio $P/\pi P^*$ given the changes in P and P^* in Figures 8.4(b) and (c). The effect of an increase in GX^* on the world interest rate and the levels of P and P^* is also positive. In this case, however, $P/\pi P^*$ falls because G^*G^* shifts up by more than GG. The movement of the exchange rate will be in the opposite direction to the movement when GX rose.

Managed Floating Under Perfect Capital Mobility

The above analysis now has to be modified to take into account the effects of foreign exchange market intervention. Governments can try to manipulate the exchange rate in two ways—directly, by purchasing or selling the local currency in the foreign exchange market, and indirectly, by adjusting domestic monetary and fiscal policy. The above analysis presented the principles of indirect intervention—the exchange rate inevitably depends on the domestic policy stance. We now consider direct intervention.

The authorities in a non-key-currency country—i.e. one that intervenes in the foreign exchange market to affect the exchange rate—create domestic money by purchasing either domestic bonds from the public or the treasury or foreign assets (foreign exchange reserves).

Thus, the domestic stock of high-powered money can be expressed as the sum of its source components,

$$H = R + D \tag{8.15}$$

where R and D are the foreign and domestic source components respectively.

When the authorities intervene in the foreign exchange market and buy foreign assets (increase R), they increase domestic high-powered money and the money supply. Normally this will drive the external value of the domestic currency downward. Similarly, a sale of reserves will reduce the domestic money supply and cause the domestic currency to appreciate. However, these money supply changes and resulting exchange rate adjustments could just as easily be effected by purchasing or selling domestic bonds. Foreign exchange market intervention thus has no special role that could not have been played by equivalent money supply changes arising from any source.

If the authorities intervene in the foreign exchange market while holding the domestic money supply constant, every increase or decrease in R must be matched by an equivalent decrease or increase in D. When they purchase foreign assets they create an excess supply of domestic currency on the foreign exchange market. But when they sell domestic bonds they reduce the money holdings of domestic residents who replenish them by selling assets to foreigners. This results in an excess supply of domestic currency on the foreign exchange market that exactly offsets the excess demand created by the authorities' intervention. Thus, if the authorities do not allow their foreign exchange market intervention to affect the money supply, they cannot alter the exchange rate by buying or selling domestic currency on the international market.

This conclusion must be qualified by noting that the effect of the change in D on the exchange rate may lag behind the effect of the increase in R. When the authorities buy foreign assets they make an immediate foreign exchange market transaction. When they sell domestic bonds, the public has to come to the realisation that its money holdings are too small before an exchange market transaction will arise. A purchase of foreign assets by the authorities may thus result in a temporary devaluation of the domestic currency in the short run, and a sale of foreign assets may result in a temporary appreciation.

Imperfect Capital Mobility

Imperfect capital mobility arises when the assets of the two countries are not perfect substitutes in portfolios, and r therefore differs from r^* in the absence of expected changes in the exchange rate. This is consistent with but does not require complete freedom of transactions in assets between the two countries' residents. If restrictions are imposed on certain types of transactions—such as, for example, a prohibition of foreign ownership of bank stocks, timber resources, farm land, etc—the basic structure of the model remains unimpaired. However, international interest-rate differentials will be created because the assets of the two countries will become imperfect substitutes in portfolios even when they would not otherwise have been. Only when the restrictions are sufficiently comprehensive to eliminate all conduits through which private capital can move internationally does the model depart in genre from the perfect capital mobility framework.

When each country's residents hold both countries' assets and do not regard them as perfect substitutes, the interest parity equation (8.6) must be rewritten

$$i - i^* = \phi + \frac{\pi' - \pi}{\pi} \tag{8.6'}$$

where ϕ is the risk differential. Substituting the relationship between nominal and real interest rates and making use of the efficient markets hypotheses, we obtain

$$r = r^* + \phi + E_\pi + E_p^* - E_p = r^* + \phi - E_q \tag{8.9'}$$

To complete (8.9') we must investigate the factors determining the interest differential ϕ. At each point in time asset prices and interest rates in the two countries must adjust until world residents are willing to hold the existing stocks of the two countries' assets. If all of a sudden one country's assets are perceived as more risky, the price of its assets will be bid down and the interest rate in the country will rise. The question then is: How is ϕ related to the other variables in our model?

Two factors determining ϕ come immediately to mind. First, when output in a country rises its residents try to switch their portfolio mix away from non-monetary assets and toward money to finance the higher volume of transactions. When they do this they will try to sell a higher ratio of domestic to foreign assets than foreigners will be willing to acquire at the initial domestic/foreign interest rate differential. Domestic asset prices will be bid down relative to foreign asset prices and the domestic interest rate will rise relative to the foreign rate. This suggests that ϕ should be expressed as $\phi(Y, Y^*)$ where $\phi_y > 0$ and $\phi_y^* < 0$. Secondly we must consider the potential role of government in shifting the relative demands for the existing stocks of domestic and foreign assets. When the authorities in the non-asterisked country accumulate foreign exchange reserves by purchasing foreign currency denominated assets in the international market, they will cause an excess supply of domestic assets and excess demand for foreign assets at the old domestic/foreign interest rate differential. This happens because any direct accumulation of assets by domestic residents on public account must be balanced by an equal reduction of assets on private account due to the fact that domestic wealth is given at each point in time. The interest rate differential will be affected because the government buys only foreign assets while the private sector reduces domestic and foreign assets in roughly the proportions they make up of an existing portfolio. The result is an excess supply of domestic assets and excess demand for foreign assets which causes a rise in the domestic interest rate relative to the foreign rate. The function $\phi(.)$ should contain R as an argument, with $\phi_R > 0$. Equation (8.9′) can thus be rewritten

$$r = r^* + \phi(Y, Y^*, R) + E_\pi + E_P^* - E_P \tag{8.9″}$$

When the assets of the two countries are imperfect substitutes in portfolios, modifications must be made to the demand functions for money, (8.3) and (8.4), to recognise the fact that interest rates in both countries now affect the opportunity cost of holding each country's money. Thus

$$M = P \cdot L(r + E_P, r^* + E_P^*, Y) \tag{8.3′}$$

$$M^* = P^* \cdot L^*(r^* + E_P^*, r + E_P, Y^*) \tag{8.4′}$$

Equations (8.3′), (8.4′), (8.9″), (8.1) and (8.2) represent a closed system in the five variables, r, r^*, π, and Y and Y^* or P and P^*, depending upon whether we impose classical or Keynesian labour-market assumptions.

While imperfect capital mobility is the most realistic description of the situation faced by the major industrial countries, little can be gained by pursuing this case further here. Except for the effects of foreign exchange market intervention, all the major conclusions reached in the perfect capital-mobility case also hold when international capital mobility is imperfect. The major difference is that domestic and foreign interest rates are no longer equal—there is no single world interest rate. An individual country's influence on world interest rates in general and on its own interest rate in particular still depends to an important degree on its size in relation to the rest of the world. The largest country will still dominate world capital markets and other countries, in their desire to keep capital markets 'orderly', will be led to maintain in their economies the same credit conditions as exist abroad. Thus, the notion of an acquiescent monetary policy applies to the imperfect capital-mobility case as well as to perfect capital mobility.

With one exception, the perfect capital mobility model can be used as a rough approximation to conditions in the real world. The exception is that foreign exchange market intervention in the face of a fixed money supply may now have an effect on the exchange rate that was not possible when capital mobility was perfect. It is clear from (8.9″) that changes in the stock of official reserves will affect domestic relative to foreign interest rates. The authorities must sell domestic bonds of equivalent value to any purchase of foreign assets if the domestic money supply is to be held constant. When they sell domestic assets they remove money from circulation. This forces the public to sell assets on the international market to replenish its money holdings. The public will tend to sell domestic and foreign assets roughly in the proportions they comprise of domestic portfolios. The authorities, on the other hand, will be purchasing foreign assets exclusively. There will thus be an excess supply of domestic assets in the international market and an excess demand for foreign assets, leading to a rise in the domestic interest rate and fall in the foreign rate. Domestic residents will want to hold a smaller stock of money at these new domestic and foreign interest rates and foreigners will want to hold more money balances. Domestic residents will thus try to buy assets from foreigners. This will create an incipient balance of payments deficit, leading to a devaluation of the domestic currency on the foreign exchange market. An accumulation of foreign exchange reserves by the domestic authorities will thus tend to devalue the domestic currency and a sale of foreign exchange reserves will tend to appreciate it when capital mobility is imperfect.[13]

Mathematical Notes

1 The total differentials of (8.3), (8.4), (8.1') and (8.2') are

$$dM = L_i dr + Ly\, dY + L(.)dP \qquad (M8.1)$$

$$dM^* = L_i^* dr^* + L_y^*\, dY^* + L^*(.)dP^* \qquad (M8.2)$$

$$(1-C_y-I_y)dY = (C_r+I_r)dr + dGX + d\left(\frac{d\bar{R}}{dt}\right) \qquad (M8.3)$$

$$(1-C_y^*-I_y^*)dY^* = (C_r^*+I_r^*)dr^* + dGX^* - d\left(\frac{d\bar{R}}{dt}\right) \qquad (M8.4)$$

where $L_i = [\partial L(.)/\partial(r+E_p)]$ and the other partial derivatives are conventionally notated. The initial level of $d\bar{R}/dt$ is assumed equal to zero and the initial levels of P, P^*, and π are set equal to unity.

Equations (M8.1) and (M8.3) solve for dY

$$dY = \frac{(C_r+I_r)}{\Delta}(dM - L(.)dP) + \frac{L_i}{\Delta}dGX + \frac{L_i}{\Delta}d\left(\frac{d\bar{R}}{dt}\right) \quad (M8.5)$$

where

$$\Delta = L_i - L_i C_y - L_i I_y + L_y C_r + L_y I_r < 0$$

The comparable solution of (M8.2) and (M8.4) for dY^* is

$$dY^* = \frac{(C_r^*+I_r^*)}{\Delta^*}(dM^* - L^*(.)dP^*) + \frac{L_i^*}{\Delta^*}dGX^* - \frac{L_i^*}{\Delta^*}d\left(\frac{d\bar{R}}{dt}\right) (M8.6)$$

where

$$\Delta^* = L_i^* - L_i^* C_y^* - L_i^* I_y^* + L_y^* C_r^* + L_y^* I_r^* < 0$$

It is evident from the signs of the partial derivatives that increases in M and GX, and M^* and GX^* increase Y and Y^* respectively in the less-than-full-employment case where $dP = dP^* = 0$, and that an increase in dR/dt increases Y and reduces Y^*. In the full employment case where $dY = dY^* = 0$, increases in M and GX, and M^* and GX^* increase P and P^* respectively, while an increase in $d\bar{R}/dt$ raises P and reduces P^*.

Substitution of (M8.5) and (M8.6) into (M8.1) and (M8.2) yields the following expressions for the equilibrium changes in dr and dr^*.

$$dr = \left(\frac{1-C_y-I_y}{\Delta}\right)[dM - L(.)dP] - \frac{L_y}{\Delta}dGX - \frac{L_y}{\Delta}d\left(\frac{d\bar{R}}{dt}\right) \quad (M8.7)$$

$$dr^* = \left(\frac{1-C_y^*-I_y^*}{\Delta}\right)[dM^*-L(.)dP^*]-\frac{L_y^*}{\Delta^*}dGX^*+\frac{L_y}{\Delta^*}d\left(\frac{d\bar{R}}{dt}\right) \text{ (M8.8)}$$

In the less-than-full-employment case increases in M and M^* lower r and r^* respectively, while increases in GX and GX^* increase them. An increase in $d\bar{R}/dt$ raises r and lowers r^*. In the full-employment case it is evident from (M8.5) and (M8.6) that when GX, GX^* and $d\bar{R}/dt$ do not change

$$dM - L(.)dP = dM^* - L^*(.)dP^* = 0$$

Increases in M and M^* thus lead to respective proportional changes in P and P^*. This implies that monetary expansion in the respective countries has no effect on real interest rates. An increase in GX raises r while an increase in GX^* raises r^*. A rise in $d\bar{R}/dt$ increases r and lowers r^*. The fact that each country's money supply and government expenditure variables do not enter the equations for the other country indicates that the flexible exchange rate is a perfect insulator.

2   Equations (8.3) and (8.4) can be summed as follows

$$M + \pi M^* = P{\cdot}L(r,Y) + \pi P^*L^*(r^*,Y^*) \tag{M8.9}$$

where the variables are all converted into currency units of the non-asterisked country.

Differentiating this totally and letting the initial values of P, P^*, and π be unity, we obtain

$$dM + dM^* = L_r dr + L_r^* dr^* + L_y dY$$

$$+ L_y^* dY^* + L(.)dP + L^*(.)dP^* \tag{M8.10}$$

Multiplying and dividing individual terms by the appropriate variables to convert the differentials into relative changes and setting

$$\theta = \frac{M}{M+M^*} = \frac{L(.)}{L(.)+L^*(.)},$$

we get

$$(1-\theta)\frac{dM}{M} + \theta\frac{dM^*}{M^*} = (1-\theta)\,\eta\frac{dr}{r} + \theta\eta^*\frac{dr^*}{r^*}$$

$$+ (1-\theta)\,\epsilon\frac{dY}{Y} + \theta\epsilon^*\frac{dY^*}{Y^*} + (1-\theta)\frac{dP}{P} + \theta\frac{dP^*}{P^*}$$

where

$\eta = rL_r/L(.)$, $\eta^* = r^*L_r^*/L^*(.)$, $\epsilon = YL_y/L(.)$ and $\epsilon^* = Y^*L_y^*/L^*(.)$.

Letting the interest and income elasticities of demand for money be the same in the two countries and assuming that $E_q = 0$ so $r = r^*$, we can convert this expression to

$$(1-\theta)\frac{dM}{M} + \theta\frac{dM^*}{M^*} = \eta\frac{dr}{r} + \epsilon\left((1-\theta)\frac{dY}{Y} + \theta\frac{dY^*}{Y^*}\right)$$

$$+ (1-\theta)\frac{dP}{P} + \theta\frac{dP^*}{P^*} \qquad (M8.12)$$

This equation can be interpreted as the total differential of

$$M + M^* = [P^{(1-\theta)}P^\theta]\, r^\eta\, [Y^{(1-\theta)}Y^{*\theta}]^\epsilon = P_w r^\eta Y_w^\epsilon \qquad (M8.13)$$

where $P_w = P^{(1-\theta)}P^{*\theta}$ and $Y_w = Y^{(1-\theta)}Y^{*\theta}$. The world demand function for money in (M8.13) is an approximation to the more general form $P_w L^w(r, Y_w)$.

To obtain the world *IS* curve we first differentiate (8.1) and (8.2) and translate the differentials into relative changes. This yields

$$\frac{dY}{Y} = \frac{\rho}{Z}\frac{dr}{r} + \frac{U_g}{Z}\frac{dGX}{GX} + \frac{\theta}{1-\theta} + \frac{U_m^*\xi^*}{Z}\frac{dY^*}{Y^*} + \frac{U_m B_{Tq}}{Z}\frac{dq}{q} \quad (M8.14)$$

$$\frac{dY^*}{Y} = \frac{\rho^*}{Z^*}\frac{dr}{r} + \frac{U_g^*}{Z^*}\frac{dGX^*}{GX^*} + \frac{1-\theta}{\theta}\frac{U_m\xi}{Z^*}\frac{dY}{Y} - \frac{U^*m\, B_{Tq}}{Z^*}\frac{dq}{q} \quad (M8.15)$$

where $Z = 1 - C_y - I_y + U_m\xi$, $Z^* = 1 - C_y^* - I_y^* + U_m^*\xi^*$, $\rho = [r(C_r+I_r)]/Y$, $\rho^* = [r(C_r^*+I_r^*)]/Y^*$, U_m and U_m^* are the ratios of imports to output in the respective countries, X is the initial level of exports and imports of both countries since trade is initially balanced, ξ and ξ^* are the respective countries' income elasticities of demand for imports, and U_g and U_g^* are the ratios of government expenditure to output in the two countries. As before, the initial levels of P, P^*, π, and q are unity.

Equations (M8.14) and (M8.15) can be further refined by noting that the ratios of imports to income, U_m and U_m^*, will depend on the sizes of the two countries. If one country is extremely large and the other extremely small the large country's ratio of imports to income must be nearly zero—otherwise, a small change in its income would produce an extremely large relative change in the other countries' exports and income swamping all other factors in that country. Let us suppose that each country's ratio of imports to income approaches U as we shrink it to infinitesimal size and zero as we expand it to infinite size relative to the other country. This is equivalent to writing $U_m^* = (1 - \theta)U$ and $U_m = \theta U$. Substituting these expressions into (M8.14) and (M8.15) we obtain

$$\frac{dY}{Y} = \frac{\rho}{Z}\frac{dr}{r} + \frac{U_g}{Z}\frac{dGX}{GX} + \frac{\theta U\xi}{Z}\frac{dY^*}{Y^*} + \frac{\theta U B_{Tq}}{ZX}\frac{dq}{q} \qquad (M8.14')$$

and

$$\frac{dY^*}{Y^*} = \frac{\rho^*}{Z^*}\frac{dr}{r} + \frac{U_g^*}{Z^*}\frac{dGX^*}{GX^*} + \frac{(1-\theta)U\xi}{Z^*}\frac{dY}{Y} - \frac{(1-\theta)UB_{Tq}}{Z^*X}\frac{dq}{q} \quad (\text{M8.15}')$$

It is easy to see that as one country gets very large relative to the other a change in the small country's income has an insignificant feed-through effect on the large country's income. Moreover, while a change in international relative prices will produce equal and opposite effects on the two countries' trade balances, the percentage effect of the change in the trade balance on the large country's income will be insignificant.

Simultaneous solution of (M8.14′) and (M8.15′) for dY/Y and dY^*/Y^* yields

$$\frac{dY}{Y} = \left(\frac{\rho}{ZZ'} + \frac{\theta U\xi^*\rho^*}{ZZ'Z^*}\right)\frac{dr}{r} + \frac{U_g}{ZZ'}\frac{dGX}{GX} + \frac{\theta U\xi^* U_g^*}{Z'ZZ}\frac{dGX^*}{GX^*}$$

$$+ \frac{\theta UB_{Tq}}{ZZ'X}\left(1 - \frac{(1-\theta)U\xi^*}{Z^*}\right)\frac{dq}{q} \quad (\text{M8.16})$$

$$\frac{dY^*}{Y^*} = \left(\frac{\rho^*}{Z^*Z'} + \frac{(1-\theta)U\xi\rho}{ZZ'Z^*}\right)\frac{dr}{r} + \frac{U_g^*}{Z^*Z'}\frac{dGX^*}{GX^*}$$

$$+ \frac{(1-\theta)U\xi U_g dGX}{ZZ'Z^* GX} - \frac{(1-\theta)UB_{Tq}}{Z^*Z'X}\left(1 - \frac{\theta U\xi}{Z}\right)\frac{dq}{q} \quad (\text{M8.17})$$

where

$$Z' = 1 - \frac{(1-\theta)\theta U^2\xi\xi^*}{ZZ^*} > 0$$

The relative change in world income is a weighted average of the relative changes in the two countries' incomes

$$\frac{dY_w}{Y_w} = \theta\frac{dY^*}{Y^*} + (1-\theta)\frac{dY}{Y}$$

Upon substitution of (M8.16) and (M8.17), this becomes

$$\frac{dY_w}{Y_w} = J_r\frac{dr}{r} + J_g\frac{dGX}{GX} + J_g^*\frac{dGX^*}{GX^*} + J_q\frac{dq}{q} \quad (\text{M8.18}')$$

where

$$J_r = \frac{\theta\rho^*}{Z^*Z'} + \frac{(1-\theta)\rho}{ZZ'} + \theta(1-\theta)\frac{U(\xi^*\rho^*+\xi\rho)}{ZZ'Z^*} < 0$$

$$J_g = \frac{(1-\theta)U_g}{ZZ'} + \frac{\theta(1-\theta)U\xi^* U_g^*}{ZZ'Z^*} > 0$$

$$J_g^* = \frac{\theta U_g^*}{Z^* Z'} + \frac{\theta(1-\theta)U\xi^* U_g^*}{Z^* Z' Z} > 0$$

$$J_q = \left(\frac{\theta(1-\theta)UB_{Tq}}{ZZ'X}\right)\left(1 - \frac{(1-\theta)U\xi^*}{Z^*}\right) - \left(\frac{\theta(1-\theta)\,UB_{Tq}}{Z^* Z'X}\right)\left(1 - \frac{\theta U\xi}{Z}\right)$$

It is desirable for expositional purposes to aggregate the two countries' outputs so that changes in q re-allocate world output among the countries but do not change the aggregate. To do this we must be able to assume that $J_q = 0$. It is natural to try to proceed by assuming, as we did on the asset side, that the two economies are identical except for scale. But this is not possible because the marginal propensities to import—$\theta U\xi$ and $(1 - \theta)U\xi^*$—depend on the relative sizes of the two economies. This means that

$$Z = 1 - C_y - I_y + \theta U\xi \neq 1 - C_y^* - I_y^* + (1 - \theta)U\xi^* = Z^*$$

even when $C_y = C_y^*$, $I_y = I_y^*$, and $\xi = \xi^*$, unless it happens that $\theta = \frac{1}{2}$. However, it is apparent that the expression for J_q above equals zero under three conditions—when $\theta = \frac{1}{2}$, when $\theta = 0$, and when $\theta = 1.0$. Under all other circumstances the condition $Jq = 0$ is an approximation. Since our main interest is in situations where the two economies are roughly similar in size or where one of them is extremely small, the bald assumption that $J_q = 0$ will serve us well. Since we have no interest in the quantitative details of policy, the approximate nature of our results when $0 < \theta < \frac{1}{2}$ and $\frac{1}{2} > \theta > 1.0$ presents no difficulty.

Comparative Statics Results: Less than Full Employment

The comparative statics effects of changes in the money supplies and government expenditures in the two countries on world interest rates and output can be obtained by rearranging equation (M8.12) as follows

$$\frac{dr}{r} = \frac{1-\theta}{\eta}\left(\frac{dM}{M} - \frac{dP}{P}\right) + \frac{\theta}{\eta}\left(\frac{dM^*}{M^*} - \frac{dP^*}{P^*}\right) - \frac{\epsilon}{\eta}\frac{dY_w}{Y_w} \quad \text{(M8.12')}$$

and solving it simultaneously with (M8.18') letting $dP/P = dP^*/P^* = 0$. This yields

$$\frac{dY_w}{Y} = \left(\frac{J_r(1-\theta)}{V\eta}\right)\frac{dM}{M} + \left(\frac{J_r^\theta}{V\eta}\right)\frac{dM^*}{M^*} + \frac{J_g}{V}\frac{dGX}{GX} + \frac{J_g^*}{V}\frac{dGX^*}{GX^*} \quad \text{(M8.19)}$$

$$\frac{dr}{r} = \frac{1-\theta}{V\eta}\frac{dM}{M} + \frac{\theta}{V\eta}\frac{dM^*}{M^*} - \frac{J_g\epsilon}{V\eta}\frac{dGX}{GX} - \frac{J_g\epsilon}{V\eta}\frac{dGX^*}{GX^*} \qquad \text{(M8.20)}$$

where

$$V = 1 + \frac{J_r\epsilon}{\eta} > 1$$

It is obvious that increases in M and M^* lower the world interest rate and increase world output while increases in GX and GX^* increase world output and the world interest rate. Moreover, as a country becomes very small the effects of its money supply and government expenditure on the world interest rate and world output become small.

The effects on the income levels in the individual countries can now be obtained by substituting (M8.20) into each country's asset equilibrium condition. We need only work with one of the countries because the results for the other are symmetrical. The asset condition for the non-asterisked country can be rewritten

$$\frac{dY}{Y} = \frac{1}{\epsilon}\frac{dM}{M} - \frac{\eta}{\epsilon}\frac{dr}{r} \qquad \text{(M8.3')}$$

which upon substitution of (M8.20) becomes

$$\frac{dY}{Y} = \frac{1}{\epsilon}\left(1 - \frac{1-\theta}{V}\right)\frac{dM}{M} - \frac{\theta}{\epsilon V}\frac{dM^*}{M^*} + \frac{J_g}{V}\frac{dGX}{GX} + \frac{J_g^*}{V}\frac{dGX^*}{GX^*} \quad \text{(M8.3'')}$$

It is evident that increases in the domestic money supply and domestic and foreign government expenditure, increase domestic output when both countries are of significant size, while an increase in the foreign money supply reduces domestic output. The domestic authorities could eliminate this negative effect of foreign monetary expansion by increasing the domestic money supply by

$$\frac{dM}{M} = \frac{\theta}{V - (1-\theta)}\frac{dM^*}{M^*}$$

As the domestic economy becomes very small relative to the foreign economy, $\theta \to 1$, $J_g \to 0$ and $J_g^* \to (U_g^*/Z^*Z')$. Equation (M8.3'') reduces to

$$\frac{dY}{Y} = \frac{1}{\epsilon}\frac{dM}{M} - \frac{\theta}{\epsilon V}\frac{dM^*}{M^*} + \frac{U_g^*}{VZ^*Z'}\frac{dGX^*}{GX^*}$$

Domestic government expenditure has no effect on domestic output. As the domestic economy becomes very large relative to the foreign economy, $\theta \to 0$, $J_g \to U_g/ZZ'$ and $J_g^* \to 0$. Equation (M8.3″) then reduces to

$$\frac{dY}{Y} = \frac{1}{\epsilon}\left(1 - \frac{1}{V}\right)\frac{dM}{M} + \frac{U_g}{VZZ'}\frac{dGX}{GX}$$

Foreign monetary and fiscal expansion have no effect on the domestic economy.

The comparative statics effects on the exchange rate can be obtained by solving (M8.1″) simultaneously with (M8.16) after substituting (M8.20) into the latter equation. Noting that $d\pi/\pi = dq/q$, we obtain

$$\frac{d\pi}{\pi} = \frac{-1}{NV\eta}\left(\frac{\eta}{\epsilon} + \frac{\rho}{Z^*Z'} + \frac{(1-\theta)U\xi\rho}{ZZ'Z^*}\right)\frac{dM}{M}$$

$$+ \frac{1}{NV\eta}\left(\frac{\eta}{\epsilon} + \frac{\rho}{ZZ'} + \frac{\theta U\xi\rho}{ZZ'Z^*}\right)\frac{dM^*}{M^*}$$

$$+ \frac{1}{NV}\left[\frac{U_g}{ZZ'}\left(1 - \frac{U\xi}{Z}\right) + \frac{U\epsilon\rho}{ZZ'\eta ZZ'} + \frac{(1-\theta)U_g\xi\epsilon U\rho}{ZZ'\eta ZZ'Z^*}\right.$$

$$\left. - \frac{\theta(1-\theta)U_g\epsilon P(U\xi)^2}{ZZZ^*\eta ZZ'Z^*}\right]\frac{dGX^*}{GX}$$

$$+ \frac{1}{NV}\left[\frac{U_g}{Z^*Z'}\left(1 - \frac{U\xi}{Z^*}\right) + \frac{U\epsilon\rho}{Z^*Z'\eta Z^*Z'} + \frac{\theta U_g\xi\epsilon U\rho}{Z^*Z'\eta Z^*Z'Z}\right.$$

$$\left. - \frac{(1-\theta)\theta U_g\epsilon\rho(U\xi)^2}{Z^*Z'Z\eta Z^*Z'Z}\right]\frac{dGX^*}{GX^*} \tag{M8.21}$$

where

$$N = \frac{UB_{Tq}}{ZZ'X}\left(1 - \frac{(1-\theta)U\xi}{Z^*}\right)$$

and we have assumed that $\rho = \rho^*$, $U_g = U_g^*$ and $\xi = \xi^*$. Monetary expansion in either country causes its currency to devalue. The other country can prevent this appreciation of its currency by increasing its money supply in the same proportion.[14] Fiscal policy in a country always causes its currency to appreciate.[15]

Comparative Statics Results: Full Employment

Setting $dY/Y = dY^*/Y^* = 0$ in equations (M8.16) and (M8.17), we obtain

$$\frac{dr}{r} = \frac{-U_g}{\rho+\theta U\xi^*\rho/Z^*}\frac{dGX}{GX} - \frac{U\xi^*U_g/Z^*}{\rho+\theta U\xi\rho^*/Z^*}\frac{dGX^*}{GX^*}$$

$$- \frac{UB_{Tq}}{(\rho+\theta U\xi^*\rho^*/Z^*)X}\left(1 - \frac{(1-\theta)U\xi^*}{Z^*}\right)\frac{dq}{q} \qquad \text{(M8.16')}$$

$$\frac{dr}{r} = \frac{-U_g^*}{\rho^*+\theta U\xi\rho/Z}\frac{dGX^*}{GX^*} - \frac{(1-\theta)U\xi U_g/Z\, dGX}{\rho^*+\theta U\xi\rho/Z\quad GX}$$

$$+ \frac{(1-\theta)UB_{Tq}}{(\rho^*+\theta U\xi\rho/Z)X}\left(1 - \frac{\theta U\xi}{Z}\right)\frac{dq}{q} \qquad \text{(M8.17')}$$

These can be solved simultaneously for dq/q and dr/r as functions of dGX/GX and dGX^*/GX^*.

$$\frac{dq}{q} = -\frac{K_g}{K_q}\frac{dGX}{GX} + \frac{K_g^*}{K_q}\frac{dGX^*}{GX^*} \qquad \text{(M8.22)}$$

$$\frac{dr}{r} = -\left(\frac{U_g Z^*}{Z^*\rho+\theta U\xi\rho^*} - \theta\bar{N}\frac{K_g}{K_q}\right)\frac{dGX}{GX}$$

$$-\left(\frac{\theta U\xi U_g Z^*}{Z^*\rho+\theta U\xi\rho^*} + \theta\bar{N}\,\frac{K_g^*}{K_q}\right)\frac{dGX^*}{GX^*} \qquad \text{(M8.23)}$$

where

$$K_g = \frac{U_g Z^*}{Z^*\rho+\theta U\xi^*\rho^*} - \frac{(1-\theta)U\xi U_g Z}{Z\rho^*+\theta U\xi\rho}$$

$$K_g^* = \frac{U_g^* Z}{Z\rho^*+\theta U\xi\rho} - \frac{\theta U\xi^* U_g}{Z^*\rho+\theta U\xi\rho^*}$$

$$K_q = \theta\bar{N} + (1-\theta)\bar{N}^*$$

$$\bar{N} = \frac{UB_{Tq}}{X(Z^*\rho+\theta U\xi^*\rho^*)}[Z^* - (1-\theta)U\xi^*]$$

$$N^* = \frac{UB_{Tq}}{X(Z\rho^*+\theta U\xi\rho)}(Z - \theta U\xi)$$

In analysing the comparative statics effects we assume that $U_g^* = U_g$, $\rho = \rho^*$ and $\xi^* = \xi$ as before. It can easily be demonstrated that as θ approaches zero, unity, or $\frac{1}{2}$, K_g and K_g^* become negative. Both $\bar{N}$ and $\bar{N}^*$ are always positive. It thus turns out from (M8.22) that a rise in GX raises q while a rise in GX^* lowers it. From (M8.23) it is immediately evident that a rise in GX^* raises r for intermediate values of θ between zero and one. Since the results are necessarily symmetrical it follows (and can be shown) that a rise in GX also increases r. (In the special case where $\theta = \frac{1}{2}$, equal rises in GX and GX^* lead to equal increases in r.) As $\theta \to 0$ and the asterisked country becomes small the effect of an increase in GX^* on r vanishes. And as $\theta \to 1$ and the non-asterisked country becomes small, the effect of GX on r vanishes.

Appendix: Forward and Spot Exchange Rates, Efficient Markets, and the Interest Parity Theorem

Forward exchange arises as a means of shifting or eliminating risk. Suppose, for example, that a British exporter extends 30-day credit to an American customer. If the American importer is required to pay in dollars the British exporter runs the risk that the dollar will depreciate during the 30-day period so that his receipts in pounds will be less. If the importer is required to pay in pounds he then bears the risk of depreciation of the dollar—more dollars than expected will have to be given up to discharge the debt. Of course, if the dollar happens to appreciate there will be an unexpected gain to the British exporter or US importer, depending on whether the future payment has to be made in dollars or pounds.

The risk bearer in this transaction can avoid the risk by selling dollars for pounds forward 30 days. If the payment is to be made in dollars, the British exporter simply undertakes a commitment to purchase pounds with dollars 30 days hence at a price or exchange rate agreed upon now. By doing this he can be certain exactly how many pounds he will receive from his exports. If the account is denominated in pounds, the US importer can purchase pounds with dollars forward 30 days at a forward exchange rate agreed upon now and thus be certain exactly how much in dollars his imports will cost. When the 30 days have passed and the contract matures, the actual purchase or sale takes place at the agreed exchange rate.

Whether the risk associated with the exchange rate adjustments is actually eliminated or simply shifted to some other party depends upon who is on the other side of this forward purchase of pounds and sale of dollars. If the person selling pounds forward happens to be a British importer who is obliged to make a payment in dollars in 30 days, or a US exporter who expects to be paid 30 days hence in pounds, the risk is eliminated. The parties on both sides of the forward transaction achieve certainty about their wealth positions. The amount paid and received is independent of what happens to the exchange rate during the 30-day period. If the person selling pounds forward is not otherwise subject to risk of exchange-rate movements during the 30 days, that person is assuming exchange risk by entering into the forward contract. By selling pounds forward he is taking an uncovered position. If the pounds turn out to be worth more in terms of dollars when the contract matures than the forward price agreed upon 30 days previously, he loses. If the actual or spot price of the pound when the contract matures is less than the forward price, he gains.

A person taking an uncovered position is acting as a speculator—exposing himself to exchange risk in the expectation of gain. A person who is entering into a forward contract to avoid risk—i.e. who is covering himself—is hedging. The British exporter or American importer purchasing pounds forward in the above example are acting as hedgers. If they did not enter into a forward contract, thereby allowing themselves to go uncovered and be exposed to risk, they would be acting as speculators.

If every forward transaction undertaken by a hedger involved a hedger on the opposite side, risk would be eliminated. If a hedger is not forthcoming on the other side of a transaction, the risk is being shifted to a speculator. To get someone to act as a speculator and assume exchange risk a premium may have to be paid. This would take the form of a forward exchange rate more favourable to the speculator agreeing to assume the risk and less favourable to the hedger attempting to avoid it.

Between any two currencies there will normally be a current or spot exchange rate and 30, 60 and 90 days as well as 6 months and 1 year forward rates. Spot rates and each maturity of forward rates must be internally consistent across countries. That is, one should not be able to obtain, net of brokerage fees, more 30-day forward dollars by switching from pounds to francs and then francs to dollars than one could obtain by directly exchanging pounds for dollars forward. Otherwise, profits could be made from arbitrage transactions involving simultaneous conversion of pounds into francs, francs into dollars, and dollars into pounds, all forward 30 days. Such arbitrage would drive the forward rates into internal consistency with each other. Unlike speculative transactions, arbitrage has the property that profits are virtually assured. The only way a loss could result is through a shift in exchange rates while the set of the arbitrage transactions are in the process of being made.

If foreign exchange transactors are not risk averse and use all the information available to them in making their financial decisions, the forward rates on a particular currency will equal the spot rates the market expects to rule at the times the forward contracts mature. Suppose, for example, that the current spot price of the pound in terms of the dollar is $2.50 and that the 30-day forward price is also $2.50. Now suppose that it is widely believed that in 30 days the pound will be selling for $2.25. A speculator with this belief can make an expected profit by selling pounds forward 30 days in return for dollars. He can expect to be able to purchase pounds spot in 30 days for $2.25 and resell them at $2.50 in discharging his forward obligation. When everyone tries to do this an excess supply of 30-day forward pounds is created, driving the forward price down. The forward rate will settle at $2.25, the point at which expected profits are no longer possible. Similarly, if the spot rate expected in 30 days is $2.75, speculators can profit by buying pounds forward at the forward rate of $2.50. They will expect that the pounds delivered at $2.50 in 30 days can be resold spot for $2.75. Speculators attempting to take advantage of this profit opportunity will drive the forward rate up to $2.75.

The notion that forward rates will always equal the appropriate expected future spot rates is termed the efficient markets hypothesis. It requires that transactors act on all available information and that a sufficient number of them are risk neutral. The notion that people do not ignore available information in conducting their business is not hard to accept. But the idea that a sufficient number of speculators are not risk averse is more controversial.

The number of risk-averse transactors required depends on the circumstances. If there is very little hedging pressure on a particular forward rate—that is, if the amount hedgers are trying to sell forward approximately equals the amount other hedgers are trying to buy— little in the way of uncovered commitments is necessary to bring supply into line with demand. And a very slight change in these speculative commitments is all that is necessary to move the forward rate into line with the expected future spot rate. Even if speculators are risk averse, not much of a premium would be required to get them to supply the uncovered positions hedgers on balance demand. But if hedging pressure is great, extensive uncovered obligations are required to keep hedgers from bidding the forward rate out of line with the expected future spot rate. To get these speculative commitments to come forward, a substantial risk premium might have to be paid if most speculators are risk averse. If speculators are required to supply substantial quantities of dollars forward, for example, the forward price of dollars may have to be considerably above what they expect the future spot price to be to get them to commit the necessary funds. The forward rate would therefore not equal the expected future spot rate.

It might seem that an expected profit could be made by buying and holding a particular currency whenever the forward rate differs from the *current* spot rate. Suppose, for example, that the pound is worth $2.50 spot and $2.75 forward 1 year. Could not a US speculator simply convert dollars into pounds and hold them for a year, expecting to make a profit of 25¢ by selling them at the expected future spot rate? Or better still, why not guarantee a profit—through arbitrage rather than speculation—by switching dollars into pounds now at $2.50 and entering into a forward commitment to switch the pounds back into dollars 1 year hence at $2.75? The profit for the year would then be certain, regardless of what happens to the spot rate.

It turns out that the above profit opportunity can arise only if interest rates in the USA and UK are the same. But if they are the same, arbitrage transactions of the sort noted above will swamp the market. Investors will sell US-dollar-denominated securities, switch the funds into pounds and invest them in 1-year, pound-denominated securities, covering themselves with a sale of pounds for dollars 1 year forward. As everyone tries to sell US bonds their prices will be bid down and the interest rate on them up. Similarly, as everyone tries to buy UK bonds, their prices rise and the interest rates on them fall. This process will continue until arbitrage is no longer profitable. Since the gain from buying pound spot at $2.50 and selling the forward at $2.75—known as the forward premium on the pound or discount on the dollar—is 10 per cent, the interest rate on 1-year bonds must be 10 percentage points higher in the USA than in the UK to keep interest arbitrage from occurring. The forward discount on the dollar must equal the excess of US over UK interest rates,

$$i_{us}-i_{uk}= \frac{\pi'-\pi}{\pi} \tag{A8.1}$$

where i_{us} and i_{uk} are the respective interest rates and π and π' are the spot and forward prices of the pound in dollars. This is the *interest parity theorem*. If the efficient markets hypotheses also holds, π' will equal π^*, the expected future spot rate.

The theorem as stated in (A8.1) implies that if the forward and spot rates are equal, interest rates must be the same in the two countries. This would not be true in the real world because British and American securities are not likely to be equally risky. If, say, UK securities are viewed by the market as more risky than their US counterparts, wealth holders will require a higher interest rate in the UK than in the USA, to make the two countries' securities equally attractive. Equation (A8.1) will thus only hold after the interest rate differential has been adjusted for the difference in risk. It must be rewritten

$$i_{us}-i_{uk}-\phi= \frac{\pi'-\pi}{\pi} \tag{A8.1'}$$

where ϕ is the US/UK risk differential.

Equality of the forward rate with the expected future spot rate implies that the forward discount on the US dollar equals

$$\frac{\pi' - \pi}{\pi} = \frac{\pi^* - \pi}{\pi} = E_\pi \tag{A8.2}$$

where E_π is the expected rate of change of the exchange rate.

The real price ratio of the USA *vis-à-vis* the UK is

$$RPR^{us/uk} = \frac{P_{us}}{\pi P_{uk}} \tag{A8.3}$$

where P_{us} and P_{uk} are the price levels in the two countries. The relative change in the *equilibrium* level of this ratio over the course of a year can be expressed

$$\frac{\Delta RPR^{us/uk}}{RPR^{us/uk}} = \frac{\Delta P_{us}}{P_{us}} - \frac{\Delta P_{uk}}{P_{uk}} - \frac{\Delta \pi}{\pi} \tag{A8.4}$$

Such a change can arise as a result of a shift of world demand from American to British goods or vice versa, or from differential rates of productivity change in the two countries. Treating these relative changes as expected relative changes, we can write

$$E_{RPR}^{us/sk} = E_P^{us} - E_P^{uk} - E\pi \tag{A8.5}$$

The expected rate of change in the exchange rate thus becomes

$$E_\pi = E_P^{us} - E_P^{uk} - E_{RPR}^{us/uk} \tag{A8.5'}$$

and (A8.1') can be rewritten

$$i_{us} - i_{uk} = \phi + E_P^{us} - E_P^{uk} - E_{RPR}^{us/uk} \tag{A8.6}$$

A rise in interest rates in the USA relative to the UK can thus occur for three possible reasons:

1 An increase in the market's evaluation of the risk of holding US compared to UK securities, as indicated by a rise in ϕ.
2 An increase (reduction) in the forward discount (premium) on the US dollar as a result of an increase in the expected rate of inflation in the US as compared to the UK—that is, an increase in $E_P^{us} - E_P^{uk}$.
3 An increase (reduction) in the forward discount (premium) on the US dollar due to an expected decline (increase) in the value of US relative to British goods in world markets—that is, a fall in $E_{RPR}^{us/uk}$.

In conclusion it should be emphasised that the forward discount on a country's currency and the levels of domestic and foreign interest rates are determined simultaneously within the framework of overall world monetary equilibrium. Suppose, for example, that the market comes to expect a lower external value of the domestic currency 6 months hence. Speculative activity will drive the forward rate down to equal the new expected future spot rate, and arbitrage will in turn lead to a rise in domestic and fall in foreign interest rates. This will in turn reduce the demand for money in the domestic economy and increase it abroad. The attempts of domestic residents to dispose of excess money balances and foreigners to acquire additional money holdings will cause the spot rate to devalue. This will reduce the forward discount and moderate the shift of domestic and foreign interest rates which will in turn moderate the effects on the demand for money at home and abroad and the movement in the spot rate. In the new equilibrium the forward discount will be greater, the current external value of the domestic currency lower, and domestic interest rates higher relative to foreign rates than before the exogenous change in expectations occurred. In the process there may also be an increase in output, employment and prices in the domestic economy and a decline abroad.

Notes

1 The presentation here is not dependent on the discussion in those earlier chapters. Readers unfamiliar with the basic income–expenditure approach adopted in all three chapters are encouraged to read Chapter 4, Appendix I.

2 Ideally the price indexes in the demand for money functions should be indexes of the prices of goods consumed rather than produced. These indexes would depend on both P and P^*. However, nothing is lost and the results are greatly simplified by ignoring this complication.

3 The interested reader is referred to Mathematical note 1 at the end of the chapter.

4 The domestic interest rate will always rise. (See Mathematical note 1 at the end of the chapter.) This must happen to offset the effect of the increase in income or prices on the demand for nominal money balances in equation (8.3), and maintain domestic-asset equilibrium. Because of the increase in the interest rate, the rise in the domestic price level in the full-employment case can never be sufficient to fully offset the effect of the devaluation on the balance of trade.

5 The forward exchange rate is the rate at which one can make a commitment now to exchange domestic and foreign currency at some future date, usually 30, 60, or 90 days hence. See the Appendix to this chapter for a more detailed discussion.

6 Equation (8.10) follows from the fact that the relative change in the ratio of two variables equals the relative change in the numerator minus the relative change in the denominator.

7 The variable q will equal the terms of trade in a two-good world where each country's good is consumed at home and exported and neither country produces the other's good. These conditions correspond to the formal model that is being used here. Under these circumstances, E_q equals the expected rate of change of the terms of trade.

8 This definition of θ is equivalent to the one in Chapter 6, since $\psi = 0$ and $M = D$ and $M^* = D^*$.

9 It will be recalled that the negative effect of the interest rate on consumption is simply assumed. See Chapter 4, note 4, and Appendix I to that chapter.

10 The results that follow are worked out rigorously in Mathematical Note 2 at the end of the chapter.

11 The real price ratio is discussed in the text of Chapter 5 and in note 19 of that chapter.

12 The bulk of the remaining countries tend to have comprehensive restrictions on capital mobility through foreign exchange controls, etc. Their circumstances are best analysed using the perfect capital-immobility model.

13 If the Ricardian equivalence theorem holds and the private sector holds in its portfolio all assets that the authorities hold, an accumulation of official foreign exchange reserve holdings will not have the effect outlined because the private sector can adjust its foreign holdings to re-establish the same overall public plus private portfolio mix as existed before the official reserve accumulation. See Stockman, Alan C. (1980) 'A theory of exchange rate determination', *Journal of Political Economy*, August, Vol. 88, pp. 673–698, and (1983) 'Real exchange rates under alternative nominal exchange rate systems' *Journal of Money and Finance*, Vol. 2, No. 2, pp. 147–166, and Obstfeld, M. (1982), 'The capitalization of income streams and the effects of open market policy under fixed exchange rates', *Journal of Monetary Economics*, Vol. 9, January, pp. 87–98.

14 The required increase in the money supply will be exactly proportional to the increase in the foreign money supply only when the conditions of aggregation hold—namely θ equals zero, unity, or one-half.

15 This can only be strictly demonstrated under the aggregations assumptions about θ.

16 The real price ratio is discussed on pp. 70–77 and in Chapter 5, note 3. It is further discussed on p. 111.

9

Monetary Policy under a Managed Float

The Bretton Woods system collapsed completely in 1971 when the USA ended its commitment to buy and sell gold at \$35 per oz in dealings with foreign central banks. Exchanges between central banks and private individuals had been suspended in 1968 with the establishment of the two-tier system. Nixon's action by itself would have had little effect on the international monetary system had the governments of other major countries not decided to let their currencies float against the dollar. As suggested in Chapter 5, they did this not because of liquidity problems or differences in monetary policy but because of shifts in international relative prices that were taking place on account of real forces. Had they not let their exchange rates float, they would have had to let their internal price levels adjust to accommodate changes in the relative prices of their goods in world markets.

In December 1971, the major industrial countries held meetings at the Smithsonian Institution in Washington to try to agree on a realignment of, and return to, fixed par values of the respective currencies. New par values were established and it was agreed that exchange rates be allowed to fluctuate to within ±2.25 per cent of these new central rates—a wider band of permissible fluctuations than under the Bretton Woods Agreement.[1] In April 1972, the countries in the European Economic Community agreed to limit fluctuations of intra EEC rates to within half the range allowed by the Smithsonian Agreement—this was popularly referred to as the 'snake' in the 'tunnel'. But these new fixed parities also broke down and by 1973 a large number of the major exchange rates were floating. A new era of managed floating of exchange rates came into being. Although there was no uniformity among countries. Some currencies floated independently, others floated jointly, some were pegged to the dollar, pound, French franc or other currencies, or to the SDR. Some were pegged to baskets of currencies other than the SDR basket. One joint float arrangement is the recently established European Monetary System (EMS). When the original 'snake' established in 1972 ran into difficulties, an inner group of countries—Germany, Denmark, Belgium, Holland and Luxembourg—carried on with a 'snake' arrangement. Then in 1979, a larger group, consisting of the above plus France, Italy, and Ireland, formed the EMS. A European unit of account consisting of a basket of member currencies was adopted, with all members holding their currencies to within ±2.25 per cent of their central rate in terms of this European Currency Unit (ECU). The ECU floats with respect to the US dollar, British pound and other major non-member currencies.

Even though exchange rates were allowed to float they were nevertheless 'managed' in two important ways. First, countries intervened in the foreign exchange market to buy or sell their currency in exchange for other 'key' currencies in an attempt to influence its external value. And second, countries tended to adjust their rates of monetary expansion to offset market pressures on the external values of their currencies. Exchange rates were thus not allowed to float freely within the framework of truly independent internally oriented monetary and fiscal policies.

Rules versus Authority under Managed Floating

The intellectual dominance of Keynesian ideas during the 1950s and 1960s was the basis for an overwhelming acceptance of the notion of discretion in economic policy. Fiscal policies were to be adjusted to promote expansion during hard times and fight inflation in times of excess. Monetary policy, which became increasingly emphasised as an alternative and supplement to fiscal policy, was to be applied through the manipulation of interest rates to fine tune the economy in order that continuous full employment could be maintained. The arguments of the monetarists that monetary policy should not be given subsidiary emphasis and that the money supply rather than interest rates should be looked at in determining whether policy was tight or easy gradually began to get the attention of professional economists and later the policy makers. Along with this growing emphasis on monetary policy and monetary aggregates came the notion that continual fine tuning of the economy by monetary manipulation might be a source of instability rather than stability. The arguments of Milton Friedman that monetary changes affect economic activity with a long and variable lag and that the current and future states of the economy are very difficult to determine and forecast became increasingly persuasive.[2] Friedman argued that the authorities should concentrate on trying to expand the money supply at a constant rate (he suggested 4 per cent per year for the USA) and thereby avoid inadvertently destabilising the economy. In the subsequent debate it became generally established that the crucial issue was whether the demand for money is a predictable function of well-defined and measurable variables. The arguments of Friedman and his followers that it was predictable gradually persuaded the majority of the profession.[3] By the mid-1970s central banks in many countries were espousing monetary rules, and the notion that money is crucial in causing inflation and output variability and that it should be expanded at a stable rate was widely accepted. The loss of monetary control following the Viet Nam war in the late 1960s and the subsequent world-wide inflation was an important factor leading to the acceptance of Friedman's views.

It is interesting that under the Bretton Woods system, given the fixed exchange rates and the key currency role of the US dollar, monetary policy really mattered in only one country—the USA. World inflation and cyclical fluctuations depended only on what the USA did. Other countries were forced to make sympathetic changes in their money supplies in order to maintain the fixed values of their currencies in terms of the US dollar. To the extent that the USA followed a sensible monetary policy, the whole world benefited. In fact, the US authorities, despite the criticisms of the monetarists at the time, did quite a good job of managing the US (and indirectly world) money supply during the 1950s and 1960s, judged by current standards. Those years were a model of stability in comparison with present conditions. United States monetary growth was quite stable, despite the absence of an explicit monetary rule, and it appears that the demand for money was stable as well.

There are two potential forces that could lead to instability of the demand for money. First, domestic residents could be constantly shifting their desired asset holdings between money and non-monetary assets. Secondly, international residents could be constantly shifting their international liquid reserve holdings—their working balances—from one 'key' currency to another. These latter shifts in the demand for money have been termed 'currency substitutions'. Thus while the demand function for the combined stocks of money of all countries might be stable, the demand for the individual money stocks composing the aggregate might not.

Instability of the demand for 'key' currency country's money is of considerable consequence for world economic stability. Instability of the demand for a peripheral country's money is not of much consequence as long as exchange rates are fixed and capital is internationally mobile. Such instability results simply in a high degree of variability of the country's official foreign exchange reserve holdings—this can be costlessly counteracted by adjusting the domestic source component.

Up until the late 1960s, neither potential source of instability of the demand for the US dollar seems to have been a problem. People and institutions do not seem to have been prone to shift back and forth between money and other assets. And since only the odd isolated currency was ever in danger of being devalued or appreciated in terms of the dollar at any point in time there was little reason for world asset holders and traders to alter US dollar holdings in a way that would significantly affect the demand for US money. In the early 1970s, however, there was an increasing tendency for world relative prices to change and in a fixed exchange rate world this meant adjustments in countries' internal price levels. As monetary authorities tried to tighten up aggregate demand to prevent inflationary effects in Japan, Germany, and elsewhere, they began to acquire increasing quantities of US dollar reserves, which led to the speculation that their currencies would have to be appreciated (and, hence, that the dollar would have to devalue). The result was a shift out of the dollar that further increased the reserve accumulations of the foreign authorities and at the same time shifted the demand for US money to the left. And once managed floating was firmly established after 1973, expectations that the dollar would devalue or appreciate were not implausible at any point in time. Expectations that the dollar will devalue lead to a reduction in the demand for US money and expectations that it will appreciate lead to an increase. Obviously a constant money growth rule in the USA would not lead to stable world output and employment under these conditions. When the demand for US money declines the constant growth in the US is inflationary. Output and prices rise in the USA, putting pressure on output and prices abroad. Moreover if foreign monetary authorities do not expand the domestic source components of their money supplies in keeping with US monetary conditions, they will experience portfolio adjustments leading to upward pressure on their currencies. The tendency to keep capital markets orderly and maintain domestic financial stability thus leads the foreign authorities to produce the same monetary conditions in their countries as in the USA. This we have termed an *acquiescent monetary policy*. As a result foreign money supplies will tend to expand when the demand for US money declines and contract when the demand for US money increases. This sympathetic variation in foreign monetary conditions could be avoided only if the foreign authorities are prepared to permit significant short-run overshooting adjustments in their exchange rates as their residents respond to expectations about the direction dollar exchange rates will go. The USA can forestall these speculative problems by following a stable rate of monetary growth only if stable monetary growth will lead to a stable external value of the dollar and this will only happen if the relative prices of US as compared to foreign goods—i.e. the real price ratios—do not change significantly through time.

Acquiescent Monetary Policy—Some Evidence

Though the presence of acquiescent monetary policies cannot be conclusively established here, there is considerable circumstantial but persuasive evidence. The classic case is Canada during its flexible exchange rate periods between 1951 and 1962 and after 1971. The top half of Figure 9.1 plots, for the period 1951 to 1981, Canada's real and nominal price ratios together with an index of the implicit external value of the Canadian dollar.[4] The real price ratio is the Canadian consumer price index (CPI) divided by a weighted average of the CPIs of fifteen other major industrial countries,[5] where all the CPIs are multiplied by indexes of the US dollar prices of the respective currencies. The real price ratio thus gives the relative price of Canadian goods in world (including Canadian) markets. The nominal price ratio is the Canadian CPI divided by a weighted average of the CPIs of the other fifteen countries with no adjustments for exchange-rate changes. It measures the ratio of the nominal price level in Canada to the nominal price level in the rest of the world. The implicit value of the Canadian dollar in the international market is an index obtained by dividing the real price ratio by the nominal price ratio. The bottom half of Figure 9.1 gives Canada's real and nominal price ratios *vis-à-vis* the USA together with the US dollar price of the Canadian dollar. The nominal price ratio is the Canadian CPI divided by the US CPI, and the real price ratio is the nominal price ratio multiplied by the US dollar price of the Canadian dollar.

It is clear from the top half of Figure 9.1 that Canada's nominal price ratio declined rather smoothly over the whole period while her real price ratio varied substantially around essentially the same trend. The external value of the Canadian dollar tended to fluctuate in step with the real price ratio and shows little correlation with the nominal price

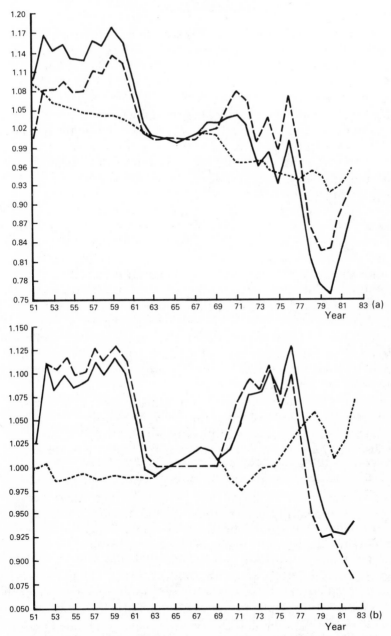

(a) Canada-Rest of World; ——, Real Price Ratio; – – –, External Value of
Domestic Currency; ...., Nominal Price Ratio (b) Canada-USA; ——, Real
Price Ratio; – – –, US Dollar Price of Canadian Dollar; ...., Nominal Price
Ratio.

*Figure 9.1   Nominal and Real Relative Prices and the External
Value of the Canadian Dollar: 1951–1982*

ratio. In the Canada–USA comparison on the bottom half of the chart the results are essentially the same. The nominal price ratio varied between 0.97 and 1.05 along a horizontal trend, while the real price ratio and exchange rate varied between 0.92 and 1.12 along the same trend. Moreover, the real price ratio and the exchange rate vary closely together and quite independently of the nominal price ratio. It is also important to notice that the major movements in the real price ratio and value of the Canadian dollar were enduring—the rise in the early 1950s was maintained until the early 1960s, and the movements in the middle and late 1970s were major adjustments rather than temporary fluctuations.

These data suggest that the Canadian authorities allowed the exchange rate to adjust to take care of changes in the real value of domestic goods in world markets while keeping monetary policy in Canada similar to that abroad. Essential to this conclusion is the view that movements in the real price ratio caused the exchange rate to move and not the other way around. Short-term variations in credit conditions in Canada relative to those in the rest of the world could cause variations in the exchange rate which would not be immediately reflected in movements in nominal prices, and would therefore cause corresponding movements in the real price ratio. But it is reasonable to believe that the major exchange rate and real price ratio adjustments observed were not temporary enough to have arisen from this source. Had the real price ratio adjustments been caused by monetary changes and exchange rate movements, the effects would have shown up in nominal price ratio adjustments within a year or two. The observed movements in the nominal price ratio indicate that this did not happen. One can conclude that the real price ratio adjustments were the driving force and the authorities produced similar credit conditions in Canada as abroad, letting the exchange rate rather than nominal prices bear the brunt of these real relative price changes.

Some evidence of acquiescent monetary policies in other countries can be obtained from movements in the real and nominal price ratios of the USA and movements in the external value of the US dollar. These are shown in the top half of Figure 9.2. The US nominal price ratio declined steadily, except for a few smooth reversals, over the whole period 1951 to 1982. Prior to 1971 the real price ratio declined a bit more slowly than the nominal price ratio, accompanied by some appreciation of the US dollar on account of various devaluations by foreign countries. After 1971 the real price ratio declined very substantially relative to the nominal price ratio until 1973, rose relative to it between 1973 and 1977, declined substantially in relation to it between 1977 and 1979, and then rose sharply relative to it in 1981

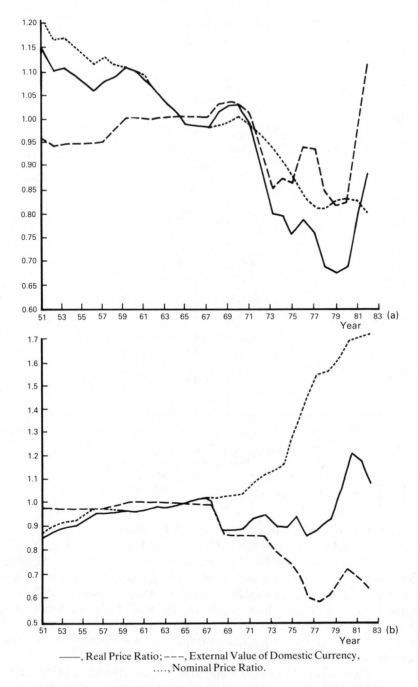

Figure 9.2   Nominal and Real Relative Prices and the External
Value of the Domestic Currency: 1951–1982 (a) United States.
(b) United Kingdom.

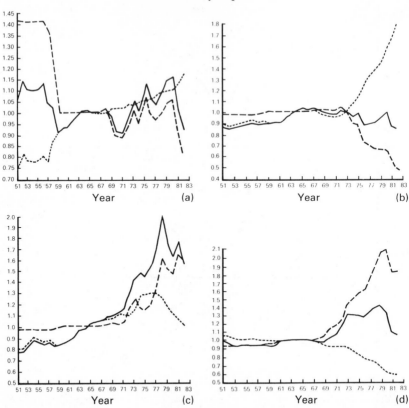

—, Real Price Ratio; – – –, External Value of Domestic Currency;
...., Nominal Price Ratio.

*Figure 9.3   Nominal and Real Relative Prices and the External
Value of the Domestic Currency: 1951–1982 (a) France.
(b) Italy. (c) Japan. (d) Germany.*

and 1982. These differences between the real and nominal price ratios
were reflected in a marked devaluation of the US dollar between 1971
and 1973, an appreciation between 1973 and 1977, a further
devaluation between 1977 and 1979, and a sharp appreciation in 1981
and 1982. This evidence suggests, as the Canadian evidence did, that
during the era of managed floating the non-dollar countries on
average tended to let their exchange rates adjust to take account of
real relative price changes and maintained local monetary conditions
very similar to those in the USA.

The bottom half of Figure 9.2 gives the real and nominal price ratios
of the UK and the external value of the pound between 1951 and 1982.
The real price ratio rose rather steadily between 1951 and 1967 and
then entered a period of variability and decline to 1977. It then rose

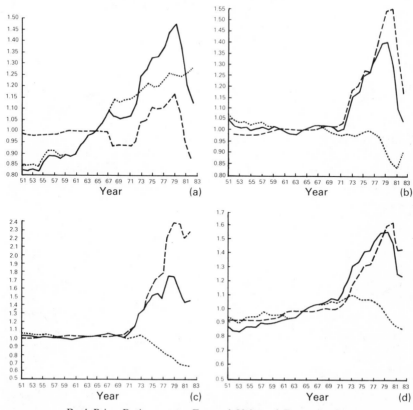

———, Real Price Ratio; – – –, External Value of Domestic Currency;
...., Nominal Price Ratio.

*Figure 9.4   Nominal and Real Relative Prices and the External
Value of the Domestic Currency: 1951–1982 (a) Denmark.
(b) Belgium. (c) Switzerland. (d) Netherlands.*

sharply between 1977 and 1980 and then declined. The exchange rate
tended to follow the same pattern as the real price ratio. The nominal
price ratio reflects smoothly and increasingly expansionary monetary
policy in the UK relative to the rest of the world between 1971 and
1977, with gradual tightening of the rate of growth thereafter. Britain
obviously lost control over her money supply once the pound was
allowed to float. However, the monetary expansion appears to have
been smooth and does not seem to be responsible for the movements
in the real price ratio and external value of the pound.

The situations with respect to France, Italy, Japan and Germany are
given on Figure 9.3. The movements in all these countries are
consistent with acquiescent monetary policies although the Italian
situation is obscured by the fact that, like Britain, the authorities lost

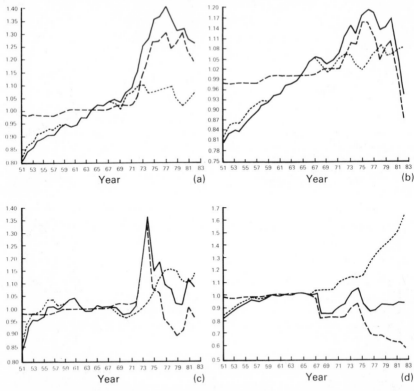

——, Real Price Ratio; – – –, External Value of Domestic Currency;
...., Nominal Price Ratio.

*Figure 9.5   Nominal and Real Relative Prices and the External
Value of the Domestic Currency: 1951–1982 (a) Norway.
(b) Sweden. (c) Australia. (d) New Zealand.*

control over monetary growth once the discipline of fixed exchange
rates was removed. Also the variations in the real price ratio in Japan
and the corresponding adjustments in the external value of the yen
were quite sharp with new levels being maintained no longer than a
year in many cases. This does not enable us to rule out the possibility
that variability of monetary conditions in Japan as compared to the
rest of the world could have been responsible for the observed real
price ratio and exchange rate variations.

  Figure 9.4 presents the data for Denmark, Belgium, Switzerland
and the Netherlands. These strongly suggest that monetary policies in
the four countries were acquiescent. The same is true of the Austrian
data, which is not shown. The data for Norway, Sweden, Australia and
New Zealand, shown in Figure 9.5, suggests the same conclusion.

It would be quite inappropriate to view the above evidence as conclusive confirmation that monetary policies in the non-dollar countries were acquiescent. But the evidence is highly suggestive and should be a focal point for further work.

Finally, it should be noted in passing that the movements in the real price ratios of all countries after 1970 were quite dramatic and involved major swings rather than simple year-over-year variability. This is consistent with the hypothesis suggested earlier that the Bretton Woods System broke down not because of liquidity problems but because of real structural shifts in the world economy. Countries let their exchange rates float rather than absorb substantial adjustments in their internal price levels.

Currency Substitution—Some Recent Evidence

In a recent study, R. I. McKinnon presents evidence that the demand for US money has shifted significantly on account of currency substitutions on two occasions in the 1970s.[6] Tables 9.1 and 9.2 are updated versions of his Tables 1 and 2. Table 9.1 gives the percentage rates of monetary growth for the ten major industrial countries together with a weighted average of these, which can be regarded as the rate of 'world' monetary growth. Table 9.2 presents the individual countries' and world average rates of inflation.

It is clear from Table 9.1 that unusually high rates of world monetary expansion occurred in 1971 to 1972 and 1977 to 1978. These were associated, not with exceptionally high monetary growth in the USA, but with rapid expansion in the rest of the world. These exceptional rates of growth of the world money supply were followed by bursts of world inflation in 1973 to 1974 and 1979 to 1980 respectively. To interpret this as the result of a shift in desired reserve holdings from US dollars to foreign currency it is necessary to explain why the US dollar was expected to devalue during these two periods. The upper half of Figure 9.2 suggests an explanation. It is quite evident from the graph that the real price ratio fell sharply in 1971 to 1973 and again in 1976 to 1978, and that these adjustments were allowed to fall on exchange rates rather than price levels by the monetary authorities of most of the countries concerned. It is not unreasonable to suppose that these exchange rate movements were anticipated by asset holders as they were occurring. This would account for the hypothesised shift of reserve holdings out of US dollars.

McKinnon's interpretation differs from the one here in two respects. First, he attributes the expansion in the rest of the world's

TABLE 9.1   *World Money Supply Increases: Ten Industrial Countries*
(Percentage changes between year-end stocks)

	USA	Canada	Japan	UK	Germany	France	Italy	Netherlands	Belgium	Switzerland	Weighted world average
(GNP weights 1970)	(0.5174)	(0.0432)	(0.1042)	(0.0648)	(0.0989)	(0.0804)	(0.0491)	(0.0167)	(0.0137)	(0.0115)	
1960	0.6	4.0	36.6	0.4	7.2	14.1	13.6	6.7	1.9	5.0*	7.03
1961	3.3	12.7	18.4	2.0	14.5	15.5	16.0	7.7	7.7	15.3	8.18
1962	2.5	4.3	16.6	-5.0	6.8	18.1	17.6	7.5	7.2	11.3	6.23
1963	3.2	7.3	34.6	14.5	7.2	14.5	13.6	9.3	9.6	7.3	9.43
1964	4.7	9.4	13.0	3.2	8.5	8.3	7.5	8.0	6.6	6.5	6.57
1965	4.8	14.3	18.2	3.9	7.7	9.4	16.4	10.0	7.1	3.8	7.88
1966	2.4	7.3	13.9	0.0	1.9	7.8	13.3	6.8	6.6	3.8	4.72
1967	7.5	4.0*	14.1	7.6	10.0	4.8	15.7	6.2	3.2	6.7	8.38
1968	8.1	0.6	13.3	3.9	7.6*	8.0	11.9	11.4	7.2	11.9	8.26
1969	3.3	-4.2	20.6	0.0	5.3	-2.5	15.9	8.1	-6.0	11.0*	4.96
1970	4.3	1.8	16.8	9.3	8.6	11.4	27.4	11.8	7.0	11.0	8.19
1971	6.5	13.1	29.7	15.2	12.8	11.8	19.0	15.0	11.1	18.4	11.77
1972	9.1	12.2	24.7	14.0	14.1	14.9	17.3	17.6	15.2	5.7	12.73
1973	5.7	8.8	16.8	5.1	1.7	9.8	24.3	0.0	7.5	0.0	7.65
1974	3.0	1.5	11.5	10.8	10.7	15.2	9.4	12.2	6.2	-3.3	6.51
1975	5.5	19.0	11.1	11.0*	14.3	12.6	13.4	19.7	15.7	4.4	9.22
1976	5.9	1.5	12.5	11.3	3.3	7.5	18.8	8.2	7.0	10.5	7.36
1977	8.2	10.4	8.2	21.5	12.0	9.3*	21.4	13.2	8.3	0.6	10.27
1978	8.2	7.0	13.4	16.4	14.2	11.1	26.6	4.1	5.9	19.7	10.98
1979	8.0	1.4	3.0	9.1	3.2	11.9	23.7	2.8	2.5	-1.3	7.60
1980	5.5	10.1	-2.0	3.9	4.0	6.3	12.9	6.0	0.2	-0.1	4.96
1981	5.4	6.3	10.0	16.5	9.8	15.9	9.8	-2.4	2.2	-5.2	7.96
1982	5.5	5.8	5.7	10.9	7.1	10.8	16.8	10.1	3.9	7.0	7.09

Source: All data are non-interest bearing. They are taken from line 34 of the *International Financial Statistics*: 1975–1980 data from the February 1982 issue, and 1960–1974 data from the 1981 yearbook.

* Implies a discontinuous series where arbitrary averaging was used.

TABLE 9.2 *World Price Inflation: Ten Industrial Countries*
(Percentage changes from past year's period average)

	USA	Canada	Japan	UK	Germany	France	Italy	Netherlands	Belgium	Switzerland	Weighted world average
(GNP weights 1970)	(0.5174)	(0.0432)	(0.1042)	(0.0648)	(0.0980)	(0.0804)	(0.0491)	(0.0167)	(0.0137)	(0.0115)	
1960	0.1	0.1	0.1	1.3*	1.1	3.6‡	0.9	-2.5§	1.1	0.6§	0.6
1961	-0.4	1.1	0.1	3.8	1.5	3.0	-0.1	-1.2	0.1	0.2	0.5
1962	0.2	2.8	-1.6	2.1	3.5	0.5	3.1	1.2	0.7	3.5	0.7
1963	-0.4	1.9	1.7	1.2	0.4	2.8	5.3	2.5	2.5	3.8	0.8
1964	0.2	0.4	0.2	2.9	1.1	3.6	3.2	6.2	4.7	1.3	1.1
1965	1.3	2.1	0.7	3.7	2.4	0.7	1.6	3.5	1.0	0.5	1.5
1966	3.3	3.5	2.4	2.8	1.8	2.7	1.6	4.5	0.6	1.9	2.9
1967	0.2	1.8	1.8	-1.2	-1.0	-0.9	-0.1	0.0	0.0	0.3	0.3
1968	2.4	2.2	0.9	3.9	-0.7	1.7	0.3	1.1	1.2	0.1	1.5
1969	4.0	4.7	2.1	3.4	1.8	10.7	3.9	0.0	3.4	2.9	4.0
1970	3.6	1.4	3.6	7.1	4.9	7.5	7.3	6.4	6.0	4.1	4.4
1971	3.3	1.2	-0.8	9.0	4.3	2.1	3.4	1.0	1.9	2.2	3.1
1972	4.5	7.0	0.8	5.3	2.6	4.6	4.1	4.0	4.1	3.6	4.1
1973	13.1	21.5	15.9	7.3	6.6	14.7	17.0	12.4	7.4	10.7	12.9
1974	18.9	22.1	31.3	23.4	13.4	29.2	40.7	13.6	20.1	16.2	21.9
1975	9.2	6.7	3.0	24.1	4.7	-6.1	8.5	7.5‡	4.5	-2.3	7.5
1976	4.6	5.1*	5.0	17.3	3.7†	7.4	23.8	7.8	7.1	-0.7	6.6
1977	6.1	7.9	1.9	19.8	2.7	5.6	16.6	5.8	2.4	0.3	6.6
1978	7.8	9.3	-2.5	9.1	1.2	4.3	8.4	1.3	-2.0	-3.4	5.6
1979	12.5	14.4	7.3	12.2	4.8	13.3	15.5	2.7	6.3	3.8	11.1
1980	14.0	13.5	17.8	16.3	7.5	8.8	20.0	8.2	5.8	5.1	13.9
1981	9.1	10.2	1.4	10.6	7.8	11.0	16.6	9.2	8.2	5.8	8.8
1982	2.1	6.0	1.8	8.7	5.8	11.1	13.9	6.6	7.7	2.6	4.5

Source: All data are wholesale price indices from *International Financial Statistics* (various issues), line 63.
* Series based on industrial output prices.
§ Series based on home and import goods prices.
† New Series based on industrial product prices.
‡ Series based on industrial goods prices (tax included).

money supply to the result of attempts by countries to keep their currencies from appreciating by purchasing dollars. This put foreign high-powered money into circulation but did not take the dollars acquired out of circulation because these foreign exchange reserves were invested in US-dollar-denominated assets. We have no quarrel with this explanation except to argue that because of interconnections between the capital markets in the various countries, and acquiescent monetary policies, these countries would have expanded their money supplies even if they had not tried to prevent their currencies from appreciating by purchasing dollars. Second, McKinnon ascribes the devaluation of the US dollar in 1977 to 1978 to the fact that US officials created uncertainty by trying to 'talk' the rate down. We ascribe it to real relative price adjustments on the grounds that had the devaluation been speculative it would have resulted in a subsequent appreciation. It was not until 1981 that the dollar again began to appreciate.

Though McKinnon's analysis ended with the 1980 figures, it is useful to extend it to see if currency substitution might have had a role in the world-wide recession of 1981 and 1982. The rate of world monetary growth fell drastically in 1979 and again in 1980, recovering to the 1979 level in 1981 and 1982. The world inflation rate fell in 1981 and 1982, 2 years after the decline in the rate of monetary growth. World monetary changes thus explain the recession of 1981 and 1982 as well as they explain the inflations of 1973 to 1974 and 1979 to 1980. Notice that the rate of US money growth also fell but the fall lagged 1 year behind the fall in world monetary growth. World monetary growth fell in 1979 but US monetary growth did not. It is possible that an upturn of the dollar was anticipated prior to its occurrence in 1980, but there is no way of knowing. We therefore cannot conclude that currency substitution took place in 1979. Moreover, world monetary growth recovered in 1981 and 1982 while US monetary growth did not. Had the appreciation of the dollar that occurred after 1980 been anticipated, it would have caused a substitution toward the dollar and a reduction in world relative to US monetary growth. Currency substitution does not contribute to an explanation of the recent world recession. The decline in world monetary growth can, of course, explain it without currency substitution.

International Policy Implications of Currency Substitution

The important policy implication is that a constant money growth rule as advocated by Friedman may no longer be appropriate for the USA in isolation. That country's influence on world capital markets and interest rates is sufficiently strong that other countries are driven by conventional central-banking practice to produce the same monetary conditions at home as in the USA. If real forces lead to adjustments of real relative prices through time, a stable rate of US money growth together with sympathetic monetary policies abroad will lead to frequent adjustments in the external value of the dollar. Expectations regarding these exchange rate movements may lead to shifts in the demand for US money and resulting changes in world monetary conditions. The empirical importance of these effects will depend on the magnitude of currency holdings likely to be shifted into and out of US dollars as a proportion of the US money stock. Data on this are not readily available. Estimates of US dollar deposit holdings held outside the USA are easy to obtain, but these figures are not what we need. We need to know the proportion of these holdings, as well as dollar holdings inside the USA, representing working balances of individuals doing business and holding funds in more than one currency. Until evidence is presented to show that these holdings are small, the currency substitution hypothesis must be taken seriously.

One way of avoiding the destabilising effects of currency substitutions is to have all major countries simultaneously follow constant money growth rules. Actual rates of monetary growth can differ between countries, with the result that their equilibrium inflation rates will differ, but world stability requires that these individual rates be constant. Shifts in desired reserve holdings on account of expected real relative price and exchange rate movements will not affect the world money supply although they will affect the demand for money in the individual countries. Relative shifts in countries' demands for money will be reflected in exchange rate movements brought on by incipient portfolio adjustments—countries whose demand for money declines will experience devaluations in terms of the currencies of countries whose demand for money increases. These exchange rate adjustments will be accompanied by adjustments in the relative employment levels in different countries, with world employment levels remaining rather stable. These employment adjustments will be the result of exchange rate induced aggregate demand shifts, not world-wide variations in monetary conditions and interest rates. They will be minimised to the extent that the actions of speculators smooth out exchange rate variations.

A second remedy is for the US Federal Reserve to stabilise the growth rate of some aggregate world money supply by adjusting the US component of that aggregate. To the extent that asset holders expect the dollar to devalue and switch reserve holdings from dollars to foreign currency, and the consequent monetary ease in the US leads foreign authorities to engage in monetary expansion, the Federal Reserve reduces the rate of US monetary growth to keep world monetary growth constant. This has the advantage that the switch in desired reserve holdings is allowed to occur through a reduction in the US money supply and an increase in the foreign money supply. No additional movement of the exchange rate and consequent adjustment of domestic and foreign output and employment need occur. This contrasts with the previous approach which held the rates of growth of money constant in all countries and forced the shift in the demands for the different national monies to result in adjustments in output and employment to equate the demand for each money with its supply. The second approach would appear to be superior on two grounds—first it minimises exchange rate movements and their consequent effects on the individual economies, and second, it requires no formal international co-operation, only the willingness of the US authorities to act.

McKinnon suggests a third remedy—an international agreement to allow official reserve changes to affect the supplies of all national monies involved. When the demand for the dollar declines and that for foreign currencies increases, and downward pressure on the dollar results, the accumulation of dollar reserves by the foreign authorities as they attempt to prevent their currencies from appreciating should be allowed to reduce the US money supply and increase the foreign money supplies, keeping the world money supply constant. The difficulty with this approach is it assumes that the foreign authorities intervene in the foreign exchange market, which they may or may not do. The foreign money supplies can expand to maintain orderly capital markets and prevent portfolio pressure on the exchange rate by adjustments in individual countries' domestic source components, with no change in official reserves necessarily occurring. A second difficulty is possible differences in the money multipliers in the US and abroad. Official reserve adjustments affect the domestic and foreign stocks of base money equally. If the money multiplier is bigger in the USA than in other countries, the contraction of US money would exceed the expansion of foreign money and the world money supply would fall. The opposite would occur if the money multipliers are bigger abroad than in the USA. This approach also has the disadvantage that it requires international co-operation.

The important conclusion that follows from all this is that individual countries' monetary policies should not be viewed in isolation even under flexible exchange rates. The interconnectedness of the capital markets in the major countries combined with the tendency of central banks to avoid portfolio pressure on their domestic exchange rates leads each country's authority to produce the same credit conditions at home as exist in the rest of the world. As a result the normal insulating properties of flexible exchange rates are not utilised. An approach to monetary policy that recognises these facts must be devised before stable world monetary conditions can be continuously created when variations in real relative prices and exchange rates occur.

The Case for Flexible Exchange Rates Revisited

The case for flexible exchange rates made by Milton Friedman in the early 1950s was persuasive.[7] In the decades that followed the preponderance of academic opinion shifted to his view, although government policy makers remained unconvinced. As noted, however, the conversion of many countries to flexible rates in the early 1970s had less to do with the diffusion of ideas than the march of events. The case for flexible exchange rates was that they allow individual countries to follow independent monetary policies and maintain full employment regardless of what happens in the rest of the world. Moreover, since balance of payments problems are eliminated, countries are not forced to engage in trade and capital restrictions in order to deal with them in a politically acceptable manner.

The case for flexible exchange rates can now be re-examined in the light of the preceding analysis. Of special interest are the implications of international capital mobility. Friedman's argument was in the context of the international monetary theory of the time which relegated capital movements to the background and viewed balance of payments adjustments strictly in terms of the balance of trade. The argument thus applies without modification or comment to the zero capital-mobility case. Exchange rate adjustments cure balance of payments problems as well as bringing about necessary changes in the relative prices of domestic and foreign traded and non-traded goods. A fixed exchange rate provides some discipline for the country's authorities in the long run but not in the short run. Substantial short-run increases in individual countries' price and employment levels can be created with the accompanying flow of balance of payments disequilibria financed by reductions in the accumulated stocks of foreign exchange reserves.

In a world of capital mobility, the case for flexible exchange rates takes on a somewhat different perspective. When a country's real price ratio *vis-à-vis* the rest of the world changes substantially through time, a flexible exchange rate enables exchange rate adjustments to take the place of adjustments in the nominal prices. However, flexible rates are unnecessary to deal with balance of payments problems—these can be handled simply by adjusting the domestic source component of the country's money supply. Flexible exchange rates still have the advantage that individual countries can follow independent monetary policies. However, monetary independence is a much more difficult matter than it at first appears. For the most part, central banks in the major industrial countries tend to reproduce within their borders the monetary conditions created by the US Federal Reserve System. Easy money in the USA, unmatched by similar conditions in other countries, tends to put downward portfolio adjustment pressure on the US dollar and corresponding upward pressure on the currencies of other countries. Central banks seem to perceive this portfolio pressure through their trading desks and tend to relieve it by creating monetary ease in their own economies. Similarly, monetary tightness in the US spreads like wildfire throughout the entire world (that part of it connected to the US by open capital markets) without adjustments in trade, relative domestic and foreign interest rates, or even actual movements of capital. Countries thus tend to mimic US monetary policy even when exchange rates are flexible.

Monetary policy is a quite different process in a small open economy than in a closed or major key currency economy like the USA. Its impact on economic activity does not occur through the standard textbook channel of interest rates and investment spending. Rather, it operates through an incipient international portfolio adjustment which leads to a change in the exchange rate which in turn changes income and employment via the resulting effect on the balance of trade. It is also very likely that any independent monetary expansion or contraction in a small open economy will lead to an overshooting adjustment of the exchange rate. An excess supply of money, for example, leads to an attempt by domestic residents to purchase assets abroad, which leads in turn to a devaluation. The devaluation must be sufficient to bring the quantity of money demanded into line with the quantity in circulation. The only way it can do this in the very short run is by raising the prices of traded goods and hence the price level. In the longer run, output and employment and ultimately the prices of non-traded goods can rise, reducing the required adjustment of the exchange rate. The initial devaluation will thus be larger than the comparative static equilibrium adjustment of the rate. To the extent that the market anticipates this overshooting, a forward premium on the domestic currency will temporarily arise. This will lower the domestic interest rate, increasing the demand for domestic money and smoothing out the time path of the exchange rate.

Shifts in the demand for money may also lead to overshooting exchange rate adjustments. To the extent that a country's real price ratio changes and the market anticipates a consequent adjustment of the exchange rate there may be a currency substitution toward or away from domestic currency. This could lead to overshooting but one must be cautions about any predictions because informed speculation will tend to smooth out movements in the rate rather than destabilise it.

It would appear that constant money growth in the smaller industrial economies in the face of variable monetary expansion in the US could lead to considerable variability of the exchange rate and have destabilising effects on output and employment. The model developed in the previous chapter, for example, produced output and employment variations in the small economy that were the inverse of those in the rest of the world. Yet following an acquiescent monetary policy in the face of variable US monetary growth will result in changes in domestic output and employment of the same sort as those in the USA. When there is a world capital market, domestic real interest rates rise and fall with world real rates regardless of local monetary policy—these interest rate changes result from the dominance of US monetary policy. With acquiescent monetary policy, world employment and output vary cyclically in response to and along with the variations in world interest rates. When an individual peripheral country follows a constant money growth rule its currency devalues in those periods when US money growth is low in relation to the constant domestic money growth and appreciates when it is high. The required exchange rate variations are accentuated by the effect of low interest rates in increasing the domestic demand for money during US monetary expansion and of high interest rates in reducing the demand for money when monetary policy is contractionary in the USA. On top of this is the likelihood of overshooting combined as well with the possible stabilising or destabilising effects of speculation. It should be noted that these demand-for-money and money-supply effects may operate with different lags.

Although stable monetary growth will permit a country to choose its own long-run inflation rate, it is not clear that short-run stability would be greater than under an acquiescent policy when US monetary growth is unstable. To unravel this issue one would need a dynamic model of the world economy that contains both real and monetary sectors and incorporates the timing of adjustments as well as long-run comparative statics. Unfortunately, the results of such experiments depend critically on the precise structure and coefficients of adjustment chosen. Current knowledge does not permit us to choose these parameters in a non-arbitrary fashion, so little insight into the functioning of an actual economy can be obtained. The question of whether a constant money growth rule is preferable to an acquiescent policy cannot be answered at this time—the best a country could hope for is to free ride off a stable monetary policy in the USA, letting exchange rate adjustments take care of shifts in its real price ratio.

It would appear that flexible exchange rates combined with acquiescent monetary policy offer everything to smaller industrial countries that fixed exchange rates do, and more. If a country's real price ratio is constant, flexible and fixed exchange rates will lead to the same result. If the real price ratio varies a flexible exchange rate will absorb the adjustment instead of the internal price level. If US policy is relatively stable, acquiescent monetary policies in the smaller countries will give them the same stability.

But all this assumes that the authorities in the smaller countries have the competence and political independence to follow an acquiescent monetary policy. Local political pressures may be such that the authorities are driven on occasion to monetary excess and then to tightness. In this event variable domestic monetary growth in the face of stable monetary expansion in the USA could create exchange rate, output, and employment instability as well as unwanted inflation where these would not otherwise have occurred. This in turn could result in pressures to restrict capital movements to prevent incipient portfolio adjustments from creating exchange rate variability. The fluctuations in output and employment, unnecessary domestic inflation, and the restrictions on the allocation of resources and international movements of capital that countries impose in order to deal with these problems may be more damaging than the nominal price level adjustments that would result from constraining the authorities and domestic policy by a fixed exchange rate. This is especially true for periods in which the country's real price ratio does not vary much.

Notes

1 The agreement also raised the official price of gold to $38 per oz from $35.
2 Friedman, Milton (1959) *A Program for Monetary Stability*, Fordham University Press.
3 Friedman, Milton (1956) *Studies in the Quantity Theory of Money*, University of Chicago Press.
4 The real and nominal price ratios and the implicit external value of a country's currency are defined in the text of Chapter 5 and in note 19 of that chapter.

5 The other countries are Austria, Belgium, Denmark, France, Germany, Italy, Netherlands, Norway, Sweden, Switzerland, Japan, Australia, New Zealand, the UK, and the USA. The weights are the shares of the individual countries in world output in 1966 to 1970. The source is *International Financial Statistics*.

6 McKinnon, R. I. (1982) 'Currency substitution and instability in the world dollar standard', *American Economic Review*, Vol. 73, no. 3, June, pp. 320–333. See also his paper (1981) 'The exchange rate and macroeconomic policy: changing postwar perceptions', *Journal of Economic Literature*, Vol. 19, No. 2, June, pp. 537–557.

7 Friedman, Milton (1953) 'The case for flexible exchange rates', in *Essays in Positive Economics*, University of Chicago Press.

10

Conclusions

Our purpose has been to analyse alternative international financial arrangements within the context of a simple and coherent theoretical framework. While the resulting contribution is to a large extent expositional, there are a number of original findings. It is worthwhile at this point to draw together and briefly review them.

An important departure of this work from most conventional treatments is the handling of capital mobility. The standard price–specie–flow mechanism and its counterpart in key currency systems assumes either that international capital movements do not respond to market forces at all, or that they respond in a crude way to intercountry differences in market interest rates. In both cases, balance of payments adjustments emerge as real phenomena in which international relative price adjustments are the major factor bringing about equilibrium. Once capital movements are properly incorporated in a full model of world portfolio equilibrium the nature of balance of payments disequilibria changes dramatically. Balance of payments adjustments become monetary phenomena through which the demands and supplies of money in individual countries are brought into equality. Excess money holdings on the part of a country's residents lead them simply to purchase assets abroad, creating a balance of payments deficit that must be financed by an outflow of gold or a loss of official reserves. Once sufficient gold or reserve flows have occurred to re-establish portfolio equilibrium, the deficit disappears. This balance of payments adjustment will occur very quickly and does not require any change in exports relative to imports to re-establish equilibrium.

Two important implications deserve special note. First, under a gold standard system the price–specie–flow mechanism does not work as the conventional wisdom would have us believe. If the residents of a particular country have excess holdings of gold, they do not bid up the domestic price level and cause a balance of trade (and hence payments) deficit which leads to gold flows abroad. They simply sell gold for non-monetary assets in the international capital market. No change in the balance of trade need occur. Second, under key currency systems, like the one established at Bretton Woods, balance of payments problems should not be a major concern. The authorities can eliminate a deficit, or accumulate any desired stock of reserves, by simply tightening domestic credit. A withdrawal of cash from the system by open-market sales of bonds reduces the supply of money in private hands relative to the demand. The private sector re-establishes portfolio equilibrium by selling assets abroad in return for money. The authorities can then mop up the excess supply of foreign exchange in order to prevent the domestic currency from appreciating. In the process they create an equivalent amount of domestic money. This balance of payments adjustment has little if any effect on output, prices, or the balance of trade, so it is essentially costless.

A related conclusion is that the price level in an individual country, under either a gold standard or a key currency system is determined by the general level of prices in the world as a whole (which depends on the world money or gold stock) together with the *relative* prices of domestically produced goods in world markets. The domestic money supply is endogenously determined. Balance of payments adjustments occur to bring it into line with the quantity of money demanded, which depends on world (including domestic) interest rates and the levels of domestic output and prices determined by the real market forces just noted. A country cannot stop domestic inflation by tightening up the domestic money supply under a fixed exchange rate because it has no control over that money supply.

It follows in turn that sterilisation of the effects of changes in official foreign exchange reserves on the money supply is not possible in a world of international capital mobility. The German Government, for example, could not have sterilised the effects of reserve inflows in the 1960s no matter how hard it tried. And in any event, it was not the inflow of reserves that was causing inflation. The latter can only arise under fixed exchange rates when the rest of the world inflates or when domestic goods become relatively more valuable in terms of foreign goods. The only way such inflation can be prevented is by letting the domestic currency appreciate. Any unwanted official reserve accumulations are merely a signal that the monetary authority is expanding domestic credit too slowly. They can be prevented at no cost in terms of output, employment, and prices by increasing the rate of growth of the domestic source component of the money supply. Similarly, persistent balance of payments deficits under conditions of international capital mobility are a signal that the authorities are trying to pump money into the domestic economy at a faster rate than the public is willing to absorb it. They can be eliminated by moderating domestic credit expansion, and have nothing to do with the surplus or deficit in the balance of trade.

It is commonly thought that the international gold standard broke down because countries sterilised the monetary effects of gold flows in an unwillingness to play the gold standard game. This could not have been true since sterilisation is, for practical purposes, impossible when capital is internationally mobile. We advance the hypothesis, and present some supporting evidence, that the gold standard broke down not because of sterilisation but because of changes in the international relative price structure. When a country's goods become significantly more (less) valuable in world markets it faces a rise (fall) in its general price level as long as a fixed exchange rate is maintained. We suggest that countries abandoned gold in order to let exchange rate adjustments absorb these relative price effects and take the pressure off domestic prices and employment. It appears that the breakdown of the Bretton Woods system in the early 1970s occurred for the same reason and not because of liquidity problems as many suggest.

International liquidity should not be a problem in a properly functioning key currency system. Any non-key-currency country lacking international reserves can accumulate them costlessly by simply reducing the rate of domestic credit expansion, thereby forcing the public to sell an increased flow of assets abroad to maintain portfolio equilibrium and acquire the desired flow of increments to money holdings. As long as official reserve accumulations are in the form of key currency denominated, interest-bearing assets, they have no effect on the key currency country's money supply and hence on world prices and employment. World monetary policy is determined by the monetary authorities in the key-currency country. Other countries have no choice but to produce the same monetary conditions at home either by appropriate expansions of domestic credit or by accumulating foreign exchange reserves.

One implication of this is that the US balance of payments deficits of the 1960s were not the problem they were thought by many to be at the time. Indeed, it is questionable whether the surpluses of the non-key-currency countries (and hence deficit of the key-currency country) should be viewed as balance of payments disequilibria at all. To a large extent reserves were being accumulated because the authorities needed larger reserves in keeping with the increased volume of trade. After the breakdown of the Bretton Woods system these reserve accumulations continued.

It appears that the liquidity problems of the 1960s arose because of the special role of gold. The system was a key-currency dollar standard in which the dollar was pegged to gold and hence gold and dollars were substitute forms of reserves. The fact that central banks chose to hold part of their reserves in gold combined with the failure of the world gold stock to expand significantly meant that there was a danger that the USA would run out of gold and not be able to indefinitely maintain the price at $35 per oz. This led to speculation against gold. The actual breakdown of the system in the early 1970s, however, appears to be due not to speculation against gold but to shifts in the relative price structure. Otherwise abolition of the support on gold would have left the system functioning as before, but without the speculative pressure on gold.

It appears that the era of managed floating which began after the fixed exchange rate system broke down in the early 1970s has presented some new problems of monetary management. The monetary authorities in each country have a tendency to prevent portfolio adjustment effects on their exchange rate by creating the same credit conditions in the domestic economy as exist in the rest of the world. We call this acquiescent monetary policy. Since the USA makes up about 50 per cent of the output of the sixteen major industrial countries, this means that the Federal Reserve runs world monetary policy even under a system of flexible exchange rates. It also means that shifts in the US demand for money have important implications for world financial stability. There are two kinds of factors leading the demand for money to shift. The first is the tendency of asset holders to shift back and forth between money and other assets—the problem Friedman and his critics were worried about. The second is the tendency of the traders and investors to switch their reserve holdings between US dollars and other currencies—the problem of currency substitution. This will lead to variations in the demand for money in the US even though the world demand for money does not change—it is merely a shift in the composition of world money holdings. Shifts between money and other assets do not seem to have been a problem. On the other hand, recent important work by R. I. McKinnon suggests strongly that currency substitutions into and out of US dollars have been taking place, and that these have been responsible for the bursts of world-wide inflation in 1973 to 1974 and 1979 to 1980. It appears that the substantial declines in the relative prices of US goods in world markets in 1971 to 1972 and 1977 to 1978, which were effected through exchange-rate changes rather than relative nominal price-level changes, led the market to anticipate these exchange-rate movements as they were occurring. The result was a shift out of US dollars into foreign currency holdings which reduced the demand for money in the USA and eased credit conditions there. Other countries, in order to prevent upward portfolio pressure on their exchange rates resulting from these currency substitutions, expanded their money supplies to maintain equivalently easy credit conditions. The result was the two bursts of inflation noted.

This analysis suggests that the implementation of monetary policy in the USA must be rethought. The most promising approach seems to be to have the Federal Reserve maintain a constant rate of growth of the aggregate money supply of the several most important countries by varying the US component of that aggregate. Currency substitution can then take place without affecting world monetary conditions. However, much more work needs to be done in this area before conclusive policy recommendations can be made.

It is perhaps appropriate to end with some thoughts about whether and how the international monetary system should be restructured. One cannot read and analyse international monetary history without being impressed by the futility of attempts at grand design. The world drifted onto a gold standard in the march of events, and then drifted off it when circumstances changed. The only successful experience with international co-operation was the Bretton Woods system, which was more of a compromise than a grand design. This worked well for a while until the international price structure began to shift and the world drifted into a loose system of managed floating. This system appears to be presenting some problems of international monetary management that have not yet been fully understood. Past experience suggests that these problems are not likely to be solved by international negotiations. The most reasonable hope is that the USA's approach to its monetary policy can be changed in such a way that a stable rate of world monetary expansion will automatically arise. The USA has an incentive to do this because it too suffers from world inflation and recession.

Index